Leadership
GLOSSARY

Leadership
GLOSSARY

Essential Terms for the 21st Century

Jeni McRay, Editor

MISSION BELL MEDIA

FIRST EDITION

Library of Congress Cataloging-in-Publication Data

A catalog record of this book is available from the Library of Congress.

ISBN 978-0-9907300-2

MISSION BELL MEDIA

Rolf A. Janke, CEO
Leah Watson, Director of Marketing
Sara Tauber, Editorial Manager

Produced by Golson Media
Bill Kte'pi, Writer and Researcher

Contents

Contents | **xv**

Introduction

Leadership is one of the earliest subjects of study in the social sciences, with ancients such as Plato and Confucius devoting much of their work to studying the question of how to lead, and the earliest historians focused largely on accounts of kings' reigns or the mythological origins of the state. Long before there was a formal science of psychology, the question of what separated a leader from others was one that fascinated many writers and thinkers. In the Middle Ages, a self-help genre with roots in antiquity reached full flower with "Mirrors for Princes," guides written not for the self-improvement of the everyman but to improve the governance and conduct of the leader. Fields such as management, political science, and education all originated with a top-down view that principally considered the role of the leader, and even the field of biography originated as the life accounts of "Great Men."

We can formally date the birth of contemporary leadership studies to some point in between the Ohio State Leadership Studies of the 1940s, which focused on identifying behaviors associated with successful leadership, and the establishment of the first leadership studies doctoral program in 1979 (at the University of San Diego). The field has especially seen growth since the establishment in 1992 of the first undergraduate leadership studies school, the University of Richmond's Jepson School of Leadership Studies. But these developments had several important antecedents.

After the Industrial Revolution and urbanization changed American work life, 20th century business culture became engrossed in the study of management. The spread of compulsory public schooling led to the professionalization of teachers and the formal study of teaching methods, while the Progressive movement simultaneously began a similar study of parenting, leading to a flood of "how-to" parenting books that has not yet abated. As the size, scope, and responsibility of the federal government expanded during the New Deal era and World War II, the academic disciplines of public policy and public administration began to form.

Early theories of leadership focused on behavior, much as the Great Men biographies had focused on personality traits. As leadership studies matured, contingency theories were developed, like Robert Blake and Jane Mouton's managerial grid model, Robert House's path-goal theory, Paul Hersey and Ken Blanchard's situational leadership theory, and Fred Fiedler's contingency model, later reconceptualized as cognitive resource theory. More recent work has focused on transformational leadership, charisma, authenticity, servant leadership, adaptive leadership, and leadership's complement, followership.

Leadership studies is a still-developing field, one applicable to and drawing from numerous disciplines. Our glossary includes not only the terminology native to the field but also terms from the related areas of political science, education and pedagogy, organizational psychology, management, and the social sciences. The Asch conformity experiments, for instance, which measured the frequency with which test subjects offer an incorrect answer in order to conform with the majority opinion, were not conducted with leadership in mind, but they nevertheless have informed our understanding of individual and group behavior in leadership situations. In the most basic terms, understanding leadership entails understanding individual minds and group behaviors.

The headwords for this glossary were generated as an intriguing series of trees: an initial list was created by reading through various papers in the field and highlighting those terms a layman would need explained. Major studies and concepts from the history of leadership studies are included, from the Michigan Studies of Leadership to Patrick J. Montana and Bruce H. Charnov's varieties of power. Each of those terms then led to other terms for context or explication, a process that continued until we felt that we had carved the thing down to the bone. Fundamental ideas from psychology, sociology, and political science are thus included in order to provide proper context for the leadership theories that depend on them. In covering the history of leadership studies, we include not only the path that led directly to today's interdisciplinary field but also intertwined paths, such as the study of management, where we find Frederick Winslow Taylor and Peter Drucker.

Ideas and terminology are drawn not only from areas like governance and management but also from less obvious types of leadership, such as parenting, activism, diplomacy, and education, and from informal leader types, such

as "early adopters." These areas often include leadership scenarios similar in broad strokes to those of the worlds of business or politics but with important differences. Classroom management, for instance, offers specific leadership challenges given the student-to-teacher ratio (usually much higher than the employee-to-supervisor ratio in a workplace) and the different power dynamics in the teacher–student relationship compared to the supervisor–worker relationship.

Other terms, such as "critical thinking," "decision making," and "self-awareness," are included because of their relationship to certain leadership skills or practices or to the many aspects of communication. Because leadership often entails a degree of persuasion, terms germane to persuasion, influence, and argumentation are examined, from "bullying" to the "cognitive biases" that impair our perceptions. Likewise, because leaders so often preside over change, we include various concepts related to perceptions or experiences of change and transition, such as creeping normality.

In discussing real-world leadership practices, we have included terms related to different organizational structures, government institutions, and political ideologies. A small number of historical leaders are included as illustrative examples, from Alexander the Great to Charles Coughlin, as are the recent events of the Arab Spring and the Occupy movement. We also include a few examples of leadership actions (successful and otherwise) from modern history, such as Roosevelt's court-packing plan, the Cold War–era deterrence theory, and Lyndon Johnson's "Daisy" campaign ad.

It is our hope that this volume will not only help newcomers to leadership studies navigate the field but also suggest further areas of study.

About the Editor

Dr. Jeni McRay, commonly known to her students as "Dr. J," is an assistant professor of leadership studies at Fort Hays State University (FHSU) in Kansas. Her current responsibilities include developing and teaching undergraduate courses as part of unique cross-border partnerships with SIAS University and Shenyang Normal University in China. In this program, Chinese students earn dual degrees, one from their home institution and one from FHSU. This requires a unique blend of curriculum development, distance delivery, and intercultural knowledge and communication. Dr. McRay oversees all instructional materials and lectures/presentations and works closely with cooperating instructors who are employed by the Chinese institutions. In addition, she develops and teaches in the virtual online graduate program at FHSU and consults with a

variety of organizations. Prior to this, Dr. McRay served in faculty and administrative roles at Southwestern College in Winfield, Kansas, including as a chief academic officer of its Professional Studies programs, and she was the recipient of the Affiliate Faculty Member of the Year award in 2004.

Dr. McRay earned her master's degree through Newman University in Wichita, Kansas, and her Ph.D. through the College of Educational Leadership at Kansas State University, with an emphasis in Adult and Continuing Education. Her primary areas of expertise and research include leadership development training, faculty development, higher education administration, online instructional design and delivery, adult and professional programs, learning/teaching styles, communication skills, and emotional intelligence.

Leadership
GLOSSARY

16PF Questionnaire

The 16PF or Sixteen Personality Factor Questionnaire was developed by Raymond Cattell in the 1940s and measures 16 primary personality traits: warmth, reasoning, emotional stability, dominance, liveliness, rule-consciousness, social boldness, sensitivity, vigilance, abstractedness, privateness, apprehension, openness to change, self-reliance, perfectionism, and tension. Later versions of the questionnaire were adapted to measure the Big Five (cf.).

The 48 Laws of Power

Robert Greene's *The 48 Laws of Power* was published in 1998 and details similarities Greene perceived between historical leaders and the powerful figures of the contemporary world, and 48 rules of behavior he distilled from his observations. Law 18, for instance, is "Do not build fortresses to defend yourself—isolation is dangerous." The law is illustrated with a story about a Chinese emperor who

Robert Greene, the author of The 48 Laws of Power. (Flickr/Robert Greene)

was so focused on hiding from his enemies that he lost touch with his subjects. Critics have pointed out that Greene's historical research was superficial and scattershot, and that he subjected none of his laws to experimental testing. But it was a runaway hit nonetheless, not only in the business world (American Apparel founder Dov Charney was a fan and appointed Greene to the board of directors), but the most-requested book in prison libraries. Greene co-wrote a follow-up, *The 50th Law*, with rapper Curtis "50 Cent" Jackson.

Abilene paradox

The Abilene paradox is a phenomenon in group decision making, wherein the group selects an option that is no one person's first choice, and often contrary to the desire of most members of the group. Jerry Harvey coined the term in his 1974 article of the same name, drawn from an anecdote about a family that takes a hot summer drive to Abilene, each dreading the trip but thinking the rest want to take it. Unlike groupthink, in which a poor decision is made that group members are at least initially (before the consequences are reaped) happy with, members party to an Abilene paradox are aware of their discomfort, unaware only that the other members share it. Harvey theorized that the Watergate scandal could have originated similarly. Like groupthink, the Abilene paradox can be prevented by effective leadership.

Absenteeism
Absenteeism is the level or pattern of absence from work, school, or some other obligation, and is used as a measure of performance, and in some cases as a predictor of performance quality or indicator of wellness in the relationship between the absentee and his obligation.

Absorption
In psychology, absorption is a personality trait measuring the tendency of an individual to become absorbed by his/her fantasies, dreams, and other mental imagery. It is measured by asking the subject questions about several sub-areas, including vivid memories, imagistic thought, altered states of consciousness, and responsiveness to engaging or inductive stimuli. Absorption is strongly correlated to openness to experience and impacts the strength of both positive experiences (such as daydreaming and the enjoyment of stimuli like music or art) and negative experiences. When absorption amplifies the strength of negative experiences, it can lead to a hypersensitivity that develops into a panic disorder or somatoform disorder.

Abusive supervision
Behavior from a leader or manager toward followers and subordinates that goes beyond using criticism or punishment as an incentive into belittling, verbal attacks, or other mistreatment may be considered abusive supervision. Abusive supervision has a tendency to create an atmosphere among employees in which social undermining is common and attention may be diverted away from achieving organizational goals and toward surviving or succeeding in a socially competitive atmosphere.

Academic freedom
Academic freedom is an ideological tenet that says that the teachers and scholars who make up "the academy" should be granted full freedom of inquiry and expression, without being subject to censorship or being threatened with loss of employment, imprisonment, or other repercussions. Academic tenure is widely adopted as a means of preserving academic freedom by protecting teachers from being fired without sufficient provable cause. Most Americans espouse a commitment to academic freedom in the abstract, but in practice it is considerably limited. The famous Scopes "monkey trial," for instance, debated the merits of evolution more than the merits of academic freedom, even though it is the most famous academic freedom case in American history. In the 21st century, "academic freedom" has become a euphemism for anti-evolution bills introduced in state legislatures to allow, or even require, the teaching of intelligent design or creationism.

Accommodating style
One of the leadership styles plotted on the managerial grid model, the accommodating style was originally called the country club style. Accommodating managers have a high concern for people and low concern for production, and so tend to the comfort and security of workers in the hope that a friendly and safe atmosphere will lead to better performance.

Adaptive expectations
In economics, adaptive expectations is the process by which consumers' experience in or

knowledge of the past impacts their model of future events. Adaptive expectations are especially discussed in reference to price expectations and consumers' expectations of future trends like inflation, the value of their home, their wages, or the cost of various goods as a percentage of their income.

Adaptive leadership

Adaptive leadership is a leadership framework developed in the 1990s by Ronald Heifetz, one of the cofounders of the Center for Public Leadership. Adaptive leadership teaches individuals and organizations to deal with changing conditions through specific processes. This approach focuses not on traits or other characteristics of a leader but on actions of leading. For instance, in an organization, the core practices of the organization are identified, while well-designed experiments test new practices, which are then integrated into the organization.

Adaptive performance

Adaptive performance is an employee's capacity to adjust to changes in the work environment. In a 2000 journal article, E. D. Pulakos et al. presented a taxonomy of eight dimensions of adaptive performance: handling emergencies and crises; handling stress in the workforce; creative problem solving; dealing with uncertainty and unpredictability; learning new technology and procedures; demonstrating interpersonal adaptability; demonstrating cultural adaptability; and demonstrating physically oriented adaptability.

Adhocracy culture

One of four organizational cultures identified by Robert Quinn's Competing Values Framework, adhocracy culture is externally focused on the well-being of the organization as a whole and favors a flexible organization structure. Adhocracies value innovation in the workplace.

Adultism

Adultism is a system of beliefs resulting from the power adults inevitably have over children and the abuse of that power. The need for children to have less autonomy than adults does not automatically justify the belief that children have less worth than adults nor that every adult has authority or moral superiority over every child. Adultism can influence the approaches taken by parents, teachers, and other authority figures over children; it can lead to the problems and abuses of children being taken less seriously than those of adults; and it can be extended into ageism against young adults, by linking worth to age. Further, the inconsistent definition of de facto adulthood—with the voting age, drinking age, age of consent, working age, and age of candidacy being set to different ages in most American jurisdictions—creates an underclass of young adults with only a partial set of adult rights. The term in this sense was coined in a 1978 journal article in *Adolescence* by J. Flasher.

Adversarial process

An adversarial process is one that pits (usually) two sides against each other in order to resolve a situation. The legal system, for instance, determines an accused party's guilt or innocence (or the winning side in a civil suit) through an adversarial process in which each side is represented by an attorney who presents their case to a judge and sometimes a jury. Decision makers like presidents (like Lincoln, as portrayed in Doris Kearns Goodwin's *Team of Rivals*) and business leaders sometimes surround themselves with adversarial advisers, both to ensure that they hear all sides of an issue passionately presented and to make sure no one adviser's voice goes unchallenged.

Advice

In the social sciences, the study of advice is a subset of the study of decision making. Advice is a recommendation made to the decision maker. R. S. Dalal and S. Bonaccio's 2010 article "What Types of Advice Do Decision-Makers Prefer?" lists four kinds of advice: recommendation supporting an action; recommendation against an action; the provision of relevant information without advocating an action; and recommendation of a decision-making process. While the first type has been the subject of most advice research, Dalal and Bonaccio's finding was that the third type is the best-received by decision-makers. Advice may be professional or come from personal acquaintances.

Advice utilization

Advice utilization is the degree to which a decision-maker (or "judge," as the role is often called in social psychological experiments) takes an adviser's recommendation into account in making a decision. Zero or negative advice utilization is often called advice discounting.

Affect

In psychology, affect (as a noun) is the experience of emotion, though the term often refers to affect display, the external indicators of that experience, such as facial expression, tone of voice, and body language. Flat or blunted affect—limited experience or display of emotion—may be a sign of post-traumatic stress disorder, a personality or mood disorder, or brain damage, and in some cases is a symptom of shock. Flat affect is distinguishable in brain scans, with neural activity varying from that of healthy subjects. Affect is sometimes described as positive or negative, indicating the general type of emotion being experienced.

Affective forecasting

Affective forecasting is an individual's prediction of his future emotional state. Beliefs about one's future emotional state have an impact on decision making for obvious reasons—people are reluctant to make decisions whose outcomes will cause them negative emotions—and yet research since the 1990s has found that people are very poor at predicting these future states. Certain cognitive biases like the hot-cold empathy gap play a part in reducing their accuracy, but given the impact affective forecasting has on decision making, it is maybe as important that people are not aware of what poor predictors they are. Duration and intensity of emotion are the areas most likely to be erroneously predicted, usually in the direction of overestimation—people expect that hurts will last longer and positive events will buoy them longer than actually occurs.

Agency

Agency is individual action, along with its motivations and results. When an individual is said to "have agency," the term is being used more or less as a synonym for autonomy, meaning that the individual is able to act on his/her motivations and beliefs. Many social conflicts, explicit and unconscious, develop over disagreements as to the extent of agency. It can be difficult to explicitly establish the extent of an employee's agency in his work, for instance, and a worker often faces the possibility either for being criticized for not taking initiative and acting on his/her own to resolve a situation, or for overstepping and not consulting with a superior. The interplay between structure and agency is what shapes human behavior. In the example of the aforementioned worker, the social structure of his workplace and past work experiences impact whether he is more likely to err on the side of lacking initiative or of overstepping.

Agent of influence

In psychology, an agent of influence is a person who exerts power on another in order to change their behavior, attitudes, or beliefs. Either the agent or the target may be unaware of the influence.

Agentic leadership

An agentic leader is one who is assertive, competitive, and independent.

Agreeableness

Agreeableness is one of the "Big Five" dimensions of personality, reflecting the individual's investment in social harmony. Individuals with high scores of agreeableness are usually described as kind, generous, or helpful by others, and agreeableness correlates with the health of an individual's relationships with his team members in a workplace context. Among leaders, high agreeableness scores correlate with transformational leadership scores, but in a military environment are negatively correlated with transactional leadership.

Akrasia

An ancient Greek term meaning "lacking command," akrasia is the state of acting against one's best judgment. The question of how it is possible to act against one's best judgment is an old one and is important in forming expectations of how people will behave—a person cannot always be expected to do the thing he or she knows is the best choice. One explanation blames weakness of will, pointing out smokers who choose not to quit, but this does not satisfy scenarios that lack an analogue to nicotine addiction.

Alexander the Great

Alexander III or Alexander the Great was a 4th-century king of Maceon who came to the throne at age 20, and in the next 10 years expanded his empire to include much of the known world of his era, encompassing a stretch from Egypt in the west to the western edge of the Indian subcontinent in the east. It was one of the largest empires of the ancient world and perhaps more importantly, the fastest expansion of such scope. He was not only among the best military leaders in history—albeit benefiting from an experienced and skilled army—he was the student of the philosopher Aristotle and has long served as a symbol of a certain

Alexander the Great, a student of Greek philosopher Aristotle, became known for his unconventional method of cutting the Gordian knot with his sword rather than join the ranks who unsuccessfully tried unknotting it. (Public Domain)

kind of wisdom, demonstrated in his "solution" to the Gordian knot. The knot was a complex tangle that had foiled many attempts to unknot it; Alexander cut through it with his sword. When he died at age 33, he had not yet executed his plan to invade Arabia. Civil wars among his generals and heirs fractured his empire after his death, but his legacy was considerable, resulting in the spread of Greek culture throughout his conquered territory and beyond.

Alpha

The first letter of the Greek alphabet, alpha also refers to an individual with the first (that is, dominant) social position in a group. The term originated in studies of animals, where the alpha is (for example) a pack leader, shown deference by other members of the group, with preferential access to food and other resources, and sometimes first choice of mates. Superior physical abilities are usually the prerequisite for being the alpha, though duties toward the group must be fulfilled in order to retain one's status and the health of the group. Alpha-led groups are distinct from family groups; though gray wolf packs were originally considered alpha-led groups, the terminology was disavowed by its coiner Rudolph Schenkel when he realized that most packs consisted of a pair of parents and their offspring, which provided a different explanation for the pack leader's exclusive sexual access to the elder female. Alpha leadership seems most common among primates, and "alpha male" is used figuratively in human society to refer to swaggering aggressive behavior aimed at dominance.

Ambassador

An ambassador is an officially recognized envoy from one sovereign state or international organization to another, to whom special diplomatic powers are granted. An ambassador is the highest ranked diplomat of his delegation and oversees his country's diplomatic business in the country to which he has been appointed.

Ambiguity effect

The ambiguity effect is a cognitive bias at play in decision-making scenarios in which some of the information relevant to the decision is unknown—and the decision maker is aware of the gap in his/her knowledge. As a result, the decision maker is more likely to select the option with known odds rather than gamble on one with unknown odds. There are many results of the ambiguity effect, many of which might be grouped under the rubric "better the devil you know," including the tendency to reelect incumbents and the resistance people show in altering work practices.

Ambiguity tolerance

In psychology, ambiguity tolerance is the capacity of an individual to deal with ambiguity without responding to it as a threat, and even to perceive ambiguity as desirable. Intolerance of ambiguity manifests in a need for categorization and certainty, a black-and-white view of the world, a preference for the familiar and rejection of the unusual, and difficulty in perceiving that one person can have both positive and negative traits or behaviors. Ambiguity-intolerant people may be authoritarian, closed-minded, prejudiced, anxious, or aggressive.

"The American Dream and the Popular Novel"

"The American Dream and the Popular Novel" is a 1985 study by sociologist Elizabeth Long. Examining American best sellers from 1945 to 1975, Long argued that these books collectively reflected the middle-class construction of the American Dream during that period.

American system of manufacturing

The American system of manufacturing was a distinct set of manufacturing practices that developed in the United States in the 19th century and by the end of that century had spread throughout the industrialized world. Key elements of the system included the use of interchangeable parts, division of labor along an assembly line, and semi-skilled labor that allowed for mass production on a previously unheard of scale. The American system provided the context in which scientific management developed toward the end of the century, dominating American industry by the time the Great Depression began.

Anarchism

Anarchism is a political ideology advocating anti-statism and self-governance, with significant variation beyond the disdain for the state. Anarchism may be individualist, referring to the anarchist ideologies that prize the individual and his autonomy, or social, which includes the many anarchist ideologies motivated by social equality and committed to stateless community.

Anchoring

Anchoring is a cognitive bias impacting decision making, in which the first piece of information introduced is consequently given too high a priority in the decision-making process. Even before the bias was formally studied, the effect had been observed in various circumstances. For instance, during negotiations, from salary negotiations with a potential new hire to the sale of a car, the initial figure that is named impacts the negotiations, regardless of how it was derived or how close it is to the preferred and acceptable figures of either party. Anchoring is a subset of a broader cognitive bias called focusing, in which an individual's ability to make a decision or prediction is negatively affected because he assigns too much importance to a single factor or aspect of the scenario. Moving from the coastal south to New England to reduce one's exposure to hurricane risk, for instance, overlooks the aggregate inconvenience and cost of other inclement weather such as blizzards and ice storms.

Andorra

The small country of Andorra, landlocked between Spain and France, is the only country in the world with two ruling monarchs. A co-principality, Andorra is jointly ruled by the president of France and the bishop of Urgell (in the Spanish autonomous community of Catalonia). Andorra is a constitutional monarchy, in which these two monarchs exercise little practical power; political power is instead vested in the head of government, who is chosen from among the members of the General Council (the parliament) who are elected by the people. Andorra's monarchy has been shared since 1278, initially between the bishop of Urgell and the count of Foix, a county of southern France; the count's title was passed to the French king in 1607 when the last count of Foix, Henry of Navarre, became King Henry IV.

Anti-authoritarianism

Anti-authoritarianism is the ideological opposition to authoritarianism. While many ideologies advocate a limit to the power of the ruling authority—and a strong belief in civil liberties, popular sovereignty, and freethought is sufficient to characterize an ideology as anti-authoritarian, the term is especially associated with various schools of anarchist thought and the opposition to any institution of authority. Anti-authoritarian movements, anarchist and otherwise, arose after World War II in both Europe and North America in response to the fascist regimes that had been defeated in the war and the fascist regime that continued to rule in Spain. In the United States and United Kingdom, such movements have been associated with radical politics and the counterculture—the Beats, hippies, and punks, chronologically—but this has much to do with the concurrent rise in those countries of institutions of authority and conformity.

Anti-intellectualism

Anti-intellectualism is distrust of, hostility toward, or dislike of intellectuals and intellectual pursuits, including the liberal arts, the arts, and social sciences, especially coupled with a characterization of such pursuits as impractical, abstracted, elitist, or out of touch. There are strains of anti-intellectualism aimed at narrower targets, even within these fields and pursuits, such as a prejudice against performance art, postmodernism, or political theory. Though often used as a pejorative characterization, populists sometimes proudly present themselves as anti-intellectual.

Appeasement

Appeasement is the diplomatic policy of making concessions to an enemy nation as a means of avoiding or forestalling conflict. The term is sometimes avoided today because of its association with British Prime Minister Neville Chamberlain's handling of Nazi Germany in the late 1930s and Winston Churchill's subsequent blaming appeasement for necessitating World War II.

Applied psychology

Applied psychology is the application of psychological theories and thinking to real-life problems, not only in mental health counseling and therapy, but in management, education, sports coaching, the law, and other areas.

Appreciative inquiry

Appreciative inquiry (AI) is a decision-making approach that, instead of focusing on solving "problems," encourages the collective envisioning of possibilities followed by a dialogue aimed at identifying the best of those possibilities and the implementation of a design that realizes that best possibility. The developers of AI at Case Western in the 1980s and 1990s believed that problem-solving methodologies were flawed because they focused on the idea of a problem and the solution to that problem rather than on realizing an ideal model.

Arab Spring

The Arab Spring is one of the most significant leadership crises of the 21st century, consisting of a series of demonstrations, protests, and civil wars in the Arab world from 2010 to 2012. It began with the self-immolation of Mohamed Bouazizi in Tunisia in December 2010 as a protest against economic and political conditions. Bouazizi inspired a widespread protest

Thousands of demonstrators gather in Bayda, Libya, for support of Tripoli and Az Zawiyah. The Arab Spring protests continued from 2010 to 2012. (Wikimedia Commons)

movement in Tunisia that led to President Ben Ali's removal from power the following month, days after Bouazizi's death. Similar demonstrations followed in Egypt, Libya, Yemen, Syria, and Bahrain, as well as much of the Middle East and North Africa, resulting in widespread regime changes. Numerous long-time rulers were removed from power, while in Syria a civil war began that continues to the present. Complaints were numerous and varied, but economic policies and political freedoms were high among them.

Architectures of control

Architectures of control are approaches to architecture aimed at influencing behavior in a given space, either through physical barriers (fences, gates, and other movement restrictions) or psychological effects. The most obvious or overt examples are the designs of prisons and other facilities where criminals are held, but in some cities, public spaces may be designed to discourage use by the homeless (card-access ATM vestibules, anti-homeless spikes to prevent sleeping on benches), skateboarders, or graffiti artists. Workplaces are also designed to influence employee behavior, with the open-plan office a recently popular example.

Archontology

Archontology is the study of the chronologies of various political and religious leaders, such as kings or other heads of state, popes and other religious leaders, and the heads of government offices, agencies, and ministries. Archontology was among the earliest forms of history; texts listing the chronology of Sumerian kings, for instance, date to the 3rd millennium B.C.E.

Argument from authority

The argument from authority is a typical approach to arguments that often constitutes a logical fallacy. The basic form of the argument says that because X is an authority on a topic and X says Y about that topic, Y must be true. While this may seem reasonable, the problem is that no authority is infallible, and further, simply citing X's position on a topic does not, for instance, refute evidence that has been provided against Y.

Argumentation theory

Argumentation theory is the study of how arguments are constructed and how logical reasoning is used to support a conclusion. The interdisciplinary field includes studies of persuasion, rules of logic and inference, social linguistics, and formal argument contexts like debate and government body proceedings.

Aristotle

The ancient Greek philosopher Aristotle was a student of Plato's, and educated at his Academy, which historians believe served as a sort of leadership training center. Aristotle studied with Plato for 20 years, leaving to found his own school, the Lyceum, when Plato died. One of the earliest writers on psychology, Aristotle was also a serious political philosopher who wrote of the city (the political unit of his world) as a community partnership in which the potential for greater happiness is the main motive for membership. Aristotle was also the teacher of Alexander the Great, who governed more of the known world of his time than any head of state since.

The Art of War

The Art of War is an ancient Chinese military manual, one of China's Seven Military Classics, and has been an influence on both Eastern and Western strategic thinking, having first been translated into English in 1905. Attributed to

6th century B.C.E. general Sun Tzu, the text was probably revised and redacted several times in later centuries. It may have originated as several different texts later edited into a whole. In any event, the book approaches war as a necessary evil, with the goal of a fast victory in order to avoid significant economic losses. Strategy is treated as a combination of careful positioning of forces based on the physical environment of the battleground, and fast responses to changing conditions. Today, the book is commonly assigned in officer and military intelligence training, and numerous books have adapted its points to management, legal trials, and professional sports.

Arthashastra

The *Arthashastra* is an ancient Indian book on leadership, in the form of economic policy, statecraft, and military strategy. Dating to about the 4th century B.C.E. and ascribed to the scholar Chanayaka, the *Arthashastra* is realist in its ideology and exceptionally detailed in its prescriptions, which range from a complete outline of a bureaucratic government and legal system to a system of collectivist ethics that call for a redistribution of food and wealth during a famine to a list of the qualities required for a virtuous leader. A Rajarshi, or virtuous king, is characterized by his self-control, intellect (cultivated by learning from his elders), use of spies, promotion of public security, setting a good example, self-discipline, benevolence, groundedness, and nonviolence toward all living things. The *Arthashastra* even provides a schedule of how the leader's day should progress, broken into 16 periods of 90 minutes each (the leader is expected to wake up at 3 a.m. and meditate on the coming day before meeting with counselors at 4:30 a.m. and starting his work day). In training a future leader,

self-discipline is important, the prerequisite for everything else.

Asch conformity experiments

In the 1950s, psychologist Solomon Asch conducted a series of experiments on the impact of the majority opinion on the individual opinion. Participants were shown a card with a line on it, and a second card with three lines of different length, labeled A, B, and C. Participants were asked to identify which labeled line was the same length as the line on the first card. Unbeknownst to them, the other participants in the room were confederates, instructed to give the correct answer in six out of 18 rounds, including the first two, and the same incorrect answer in the remaining 12. The goal was to see in how many of those 12 "critical trials" did the participant give the incorrect answer, matching the majority opinion. Seventy-five percent of participants conformed in a critical trial at least once (compared to a less than 1 percent error rate in the control group).

Asociality

In psychology, asociality, nonsociality, unsociality, or social disinterest all refer to a lack of interest in social interaction, as distinct from anti-social behavior, which is active hostility toward social interaction or other people. Introverts are considered mildly to moderately asocial, which may impact their work life and the management strategies that are the most effective in overseeing them, while extremes of asociality are usually the result of a clinical condition or disorder.

Assertiveness orientation

One of the global leadership cultural competencies identified by the GLOBE Project, assertiveness orientation is the extent to which individuals in an organization or a culture exhibit assertiveness or aggression in their interpersonal relationships or become confrontational.

Aston Group

The Aston Group were a group of organizational researchers working at England's Aston University from 1961 to 1970 who were instrumental in furthering the statistical analysis of organizations. Among the work done by the group is Diane Pheysey, Kerr Inkson, and Roy Payne's work on organizational climate; Derek Pugh, David Hickson, and Bob Hinings' work on the influence of technology, size, and environment on organizational structures; and an analysis of bureaucratization in organizations that found larger organizations are more likely to be standardized, formalized, and specialized, and that decision making decentralizes as organizations increase in size.

Atlas Shrugged

Atlas Shrugged is a 1957 dystopian novel by Ayn Rand, dramatizing her philosophy of objectivism. While socialism and communism, which Rand reviled, are political systems based on the importance of the worker, Rand's sympathies were with wealthy capitalist industrialists, who in this novel react to stricter regulations by abandoning their industries, leaving them to collapse. It has remained popular among American libertarians.

Attachment theory

Attachment theory is a psychological theory dealing with a specific area of human relationships: the response to threats, hurt, or separation from loved ones. Attachment theory explores how attachment to other people forms a fundamental human motivation, and in some areas of psychology and psychiatry, has displaced A.

Maslow's hierarchy of needs in explaining the source of human motivations. By the end of the 1970s, attachment theory had become the dominant psychological theory of the motivation of children; in the 1980s it was extended with application to adults' romantic relationships.

Attitude

An attitude is a measurable, mutable positive or negative feeling toward an attitude object (a person or group, thing, event, experience, or idea). Carl Jung referred to attitude as the psyche's "readiness . . . to act or react in a certain way."

Attitude change

Attitude change is the process or phenomenon of an individual's attitude toward an object changing. Attitudes are one of the most mutable aspects of personality, subject to change by social influence, new experience or new knowledge, and changes in emotion. Persuasion aimed at changing attitudes will often appeal to emotions: political campaign ads and public health ads often seek to use emotion to affect attitude, such as by associating a political viewpoint with a response of fear (the threat of war or terrorism) or disapproval (allegations of corruption or misconduct), or associating tobacco smoking with the ugliness of its health effects to counter the romanticized image of smoking in movies.

Attributional bias

An attributional bias is a cognitive bias consisting of the errors made when people attempt to assign reasons—make attributions—to behaviors, whether their own or others.

Authentic leadership

Authentic leaders are those who are self-aware enough to be true to themselves in their roles as leaders. Authentic leadership, especially as has been discussed in recent scholarship (a resurgence of which began with Bill George's 2003 *Authentic Leadership*), is a leadership style that emphasizes sincerity and genuineness. Rather than treating leadership as playing a role, as some schools of thought suggest, authentic leaders are open with their followers and do not fear seeming imperfect.

Authentic Leadership Inventory

The Authentic Leadership Inventory (ALI) was developed by L. L. Neider and C. A. Schriesheim and published in *Leadership Quarterly* in 2011. Building on an earlier effort to measure authentic leadership based on followers' survey answers, the Authentic Leadership Questionnaire, the ALI consists of a 16-item inventory.

Authenticity

In psychology and philosophy, authenticity is the state of the conscious self staying true to one's own character and personality in the face of external pressures. It is by extension of this meaning that one might, more familiarly, refer to one's grandmother's cooking as "authentic," implying it is closer to the cuisine of her ancestral homeland and has not been Americanized. Authenticity is usually referred to only in the positive, as distinct from mere stubborn resistance to change.

Authoritarianism

Authoritarianism is a form of leadership or governance that expects absolute obedience from followers. Spanish political scientist Juan Linz, writing during the Francisco Franco regime, defined four traits of authoritarian governments: restrictions on political institutions (such as political parties, lobbying groups, and even legislatures); an emotional appeal used as the regime's claim to legitimacy, such as claiming that the government is the only thing keeping the people safe from some threat; restrictions on political mobilization, often including the repression of opposition; and vague definitions of the powers bestowed on the executive branch, which avoids well-defined limits on those powers.

Authority

The English word *authority* is derived from the Latin *auctoritas*, which in ancient Rome was the prestige and influence an individual enjoyed, which extended to political power and the ability to command. In English, authority has two distinct but related usages: it can refer both to the power of the state, as exercised by the government or those to whom it delegates power (police officers, for instance) and to the possession of significant knowledge on a subject, in the sense that a history professor may be an authority on ancient Roman politics. In the first usage, authority differs from mere power in that it implies legitimacy and sanction; an insurgent may challenge the authority of a totalitarian regime without questioning its power to enforce its will. The social sciences have extended this type of authority to refer to nonpolitical groups, including business leadership or the authority of parents over their children. "Authority figure" is commonly used to refer to individuals with authority over others, outside government contexts.

Authority problem

An authority problem is a conflict experienced by an individual who has difficulty coping with authority figures such as parents and teachers as an adolescent, or supervisors at work, police officers, and government figures as an adult. This can result in acting out, underperforming, or sabotaging efforts, even when the authority figure's goals align with the individual's.

Autocracy

An autocracy is a form of government in which a single person holds control, without legal restraints. The term *autocrat* was often used in Europe, for instance, to differentiate some rulers from constitutional monarchs, whose political powers were restricted. In practice, the line between an autocracy and an oligarchy—rule by the few—is blurry, since the practical mechanisms of governance require assistance from others and de facto power is necessarily delegated to them.

Autonomy

Autonomy, from the ancient Greek for "self-law," is the ability of a rational individual to make an informed decision, free from coercive external pressures. Employees tend to be more engaged when they are allowed to be autonomous, provided they also have access to the correct resources to do their work, but autonomy must be balanced against the need to meet organizational goals and retain well-defined roles. In social psychology, autonomy is a personal characteristic, the capacity to benefit and derive pleasure from independence, as opposed to sociotropy, which prizes interpersonal relationships. Each responds to a different style of leadership and a different type of workplace.

Autonomous work group

An autonomous work group is self-managed and is left to manage its own projects and develop its own practices and norms, including the distribution of labor and responsibilities among members.

Avolio, Bruce

Bruce Avolio is a leadership scholar, influenced by James MacGregor Burns and particularly active in work on transformational leadership and authentic leadership. Along with Bernard Bass, he has been one of the most prominent transformational leadership scholars, and together in the late 1990s they developed the full range leadership model, measured by the Multifactor Leadership Questionnaire. He is the executive director of the Center for Leadership and Strategic Thinking at the University of Washington's Michael G. Foster School of Business.

Bakunin, Mikhail

19th-century Russian anarchist Mikhail Bakunin is one of the leading figures in the history of anarchism, and founded collectivist anarchism, which advocates eliminating both the state and private ownership of the means of production, with production being controlled collectively by workers. "Does it follow that I reject all authority?" he wrote. "In the matter of boots, I refer to the authority of the bootmaker; concerning houses, canals, or railroads, I consult that of the architect or the engineer. . . . But I allow neither the bootmaker nor the architect nor savant to impose his authority upon me. I listen to them freely and with all the respect merited by their intelligence, their character, their knowledge, reserving always my incontestable right of criticism and censure. . . . I recognize no infallible authority, even in special questions . . . I have no absolute faith in any person."

Balanced processing

Balanced processing is one of the qualities of authentic leadership, and refers to the leader's request to hear opposing viewpoints during the decision-making process, and his even-handed response to opposition and disagreement.

Basking in reflected glory

Basking in reflected glory is a common psychological phenomenon in which an individual celebrates the success of another as though they are a part of it. There is an often-observed fine line between a parent's pride in their child's performance and their basking in the child's reflected glory, for instance, and in the workplace, it is not uncommon to find supervisors or team members celebrating the success of a worker's idea that they not only did not contribute to but actively opposed until it proved successful. Other examples of basking in reflected glory are found in sports fandom and Olympic Games watching, bragging about famous ancestors, and displays of school affiliation. In recent years, research has focused on the role of brand loyalty in basking in reflected glory, particularly with the capacity social media has provided to associate oneself with certain brands via likes, hashtags, and other means.

Bass, Bernard

Bernard Bass was a leadership studies scholar known for his work on transformational leadership, sometimes working with Bruce Avolio and building on the work of James MacGregor Burns. Bass coined the term *transformational leadership*, in 1985, for what Burns had called transforming leadership, and articulated the psychological underpinnings of the theory and transformational leadership's impact on follower motivation. Bass authored the *Bass Handbook of Leadership*, the fourth edition of which was being completed when he died in 2007, which was translated into numerous languages.

Batten School of Leadership and Public Policy

The Frank Batten School of Leadership and Public Policy was established at the University of Virginia in 2007 with a gift from Weather Channel co-founder Frank Batten Sr. The school teaches leadership studies with an emphasis on public policy and political science, offering both undergraduate and graduate degrees, including a number of dual-degree options.

"Bear in the woods"

The "bear in the woods" campaign advertisement for Ronald Reagan's 1984 reelection as president is one of the most famous campaign ads. It depicts a grizzly bear in a forest, who stops his advance when a man appears in the final scene. "There is a bear in the woods," the narrator intones over the footage. ". . . Some say the bear is tame. Others say it's vicious and dangerous. Since no one can really be sure who's right, isn't it smart to be as strong as the bear?" Neither Reagan's opponent Walter Mondale nor the Soviet Union, represented by the bear, was explicitly mentioned, but Reagan's leadership appeal was aptly summed up: while no one could know if the Cold War would ever heat up into direct armed conflict, Reagan was the president who, more than any other, had directed defense spending to prepare for the possibility. It was the sort of fear-mongering that had not been seen in a presidential campaign since "Daisy" (cf.) and was deliberately echoed in the less graceful "Wolves," a George W. Bush reelection campaign ad that specifically called out opponent John Kerry as less able to cope with the wolves of international terrorism.

Behavioral complexity

Behavioral complexity is the capacity of a leader to credibly engage in a wide variety of behaviors. A leader with high behavioral complexity can engage in contrary or opposing behaviors as the situation warrants, without compromising his integrity, making him more flexible in his choices. Much of the work on behavior complexity focuses on paradox, and the competing and sometimes opposing needs of organizational life, and by extension the capacity of skilled leaders to transcend that paradox.

Behavioral script

In behaviorist psychology, a behavioral script is not a literal deliberately composed script, but a description of the behaviors implicitly expected of participants in a given situation. Empirical studies have found that these standardized routines—like the sequence of events when one goes to the doctor for a checkup, or is interviewed for a job—are easily recognized, and that, for instance, when test subjects are read narratives presenting these scenarios, they are better able to recall "on-script" information directly related to the behavioral script than unrelated information, and may even fill in aspects of the script that were not provided. A scenario may describe a patient being weighed and measured by a nurse at his physical, for instance, and the test subject may add the detail of the patient removing shoes before his height measurement is taken, without realizing that detail was not included in the scenario.

Behavioral theories of leadership

Unlike trait-based theories of leadership, which presuppose that leaders come from the ranks of those who possess specific traits, behavioral theories of leadership see leadership as a system of behaviors—and as with other behaviors, leadership thus becomes something anyone can learn, whether through training or their own trial and error. The Ohio State University and University of Michigan leadership studies of the 1940s and 1950s, respectively, were the first major behavioral studies of leadership.

A Behavioral Theory of the Firm

Written by Richard M. Cyert and James G. March of Carnegie Mellon, *A Behavioral Theory of the Firm* was published in 1963, and challenged the mainstream theory of the firm that assumed perfect knowledge and profit maximization. Large corporations were portrayed as coalitions of individuals or groups, who set goals and make decisions both formally and informally, with different and potentially conflicting goals and information resources. The work popularized the idea of satisficing: achieving goals that are "good enough" rather than ideal.

Bell Telephone Company

The Bell Telephone Company was the telephone provider that originally formed as a holder of Alexander Graham Bell's telephone patents, and which is the predecessor of AT&T. Bell was long a center of innovation and ingenuity. In the post-World War II years, Bell's top executives became concerned with developing leadership among its management. Many of the junior executives came from technical backgrounds, either as technical school graduates or having learned on the job; few had four-year degrees from liberal arts institutions. The Institute of Humanistic Studies for Executives was formed in collaboration with the University of Pennsylvania, with a 10-month immersive liberal arts program for executives, constituting 550 hours of classroom work and an intensive reading load emphasizing literature and the humanities. Bell sunk considerable resources into the program: David Riesman discussed his groundbreaking sociological study *The Lonely Crowd* with the class, while a visiting Harvard lecturer addressed the poetry of Ezra Pound. Twenty-four hours of seminar time were devoted to James Joyce's controversial *Ulysses*, still considered obscene by many Americans. Follow-up surveys found that executives graduating from the course read more, were more engaged with current events, and were better able to see multiple sides of a conflict.

A small infant, mother, grandmother, and great-grandmother represent a group that satisfies the emotional need to belong. Belongingness is a powerful human need, such that Abraham Maslow listed the need to belong on his hierarchy of needs. (Flickr)

Belongingness

Belongingness is the human need to belong to a group, and is considered one of the most fundamental human motivations. Belonging to a group is more than just having a friendly relationship with group members; acceptance as a member impacts self-image and identity, and lack of belonging has significant emotional consequences. Belongingness is one of the motivations behind not only family unity and the formation of social groups of friends, but also involved participation in fandom of sports teams, comic books, and science fiction movies, to name a few. It impacts self-presentation by motivating individuals to highlight or conceal different aspects of their selves according to how they believe group members will receive them. Abraham Maslow listed the need to belong on his famous hierarchy of needs, and some psychologists argue that belongingness is one of the major motivations behind the formation of human culture, in contrast with Freud's view that the major psychological forces driving human behavior are aggression and sexuality.

Benchmarking

Benchmarking is a business practice of comparing performance metrics or business processes to extrinsic standards, such as the performance of competitors, or industry-set or regulatory standards. Typically, benchmark comparisons encompass comparisons of performance/quality, cost, and time. Best practice or process benchmarking has become more common in management practices, comparing not simply the final product but each process involved in bringing it to market.

Benevolent authoritative

One of Rensis Likert's management systems, in the benevolent authoritative system, most decision making is conducted at the top of the hierarchy by upper-level management, with little communication from the lower levels to the uppers. Employees at lower levels feel little responsibility for the organization's goals, and motivation is provided by both rewards and punishments.

Bennis, Warren

Warren Bennis was an organizational consultant and author whose work helped to shape the leadership studies field, especially with his 1961 *Harvard Business Review* article "The Revisionist Theory of Leadership." In the 1980s and 1990s he was one of the most sought public speakers on leadership and management.

Best practice

In business and management, a "best practice" is a method for performing a task or organizing a set of information that has been developed for use by multiple unrelated organizations, and is believed to produce the best results. Best practice templates are a product developed and sold by consulting firms.

Bet-the-company culture

One of four corporate cultures identified by T. E. Deal and A. A. Kennedy, characterized by slow reward and high risk. Stress in jobs in these cultures comes mainly from the risks associated with the business, such as in industries with a tremendous cost of entry, like the oil industry or automobile manufacturers.

Big Brothers Big Sisters of America

Founded in 1904, Big Brothers Big Sisters of America is one of the oldest mentorship programs in the country. Volunteer-run, BBBSA pairs children ("Little Brothers" and "Little Sisters") with mentors who spend time with them on a one-on-one basis. One of the most highly rated charities by institutes like Charity Navigator (which rates the organizational efficiency of charities), Forbes, the Better Business Bureau, and the American Institute of Philanthropy, BBBSA has had a profound effect on at-risk children. Children in the program are only half as likely to skip school or use illegal drugs, and report fewer conflicts in school and at home.

Big Five

The "Big Five" personality traits are traits that describe adult personality, sometimes abbreviated as OCEAN: Openness, Conscientiousness, Extraversion, Agreeableness, and Neuroticism. Each of the Big Five includes a number of smaller traits that may or may not be displayed; Extraversion includes both assertiveness and warmth, but not every extrovert exhibits both traits. Several independent teams constructed the Big Five model, the initial work having been done in 1961 by Ernest Tupes and Raymond Christal. The traits are assessed through lexical measures or self-assessing sentences, common measures for many personality tests. Some researchers have suggested that leaders demonstrate high levels of openness, low levels of neuroticism, and balanced levels of extraversion and conscientiousness, and administer personality tests as part of the interview process or when considering a promotion to a leadership position. One of the primary criticisms of the Big Five model is the number of traits it does not account for: conservativeness, gender identity (especially in the sense of the display of stereotypically masculine or feminine traits and behaviors), egotism, honesty, sense of humor, religiosity, and attitude toward risk, among others. Proponents argue that these traits can be correlated to the Big Five: for instance, research indicates that low levels of openness correlate to political conservatism.

Big Man

As used in anthropology with specific reference to the tribes of Melanesia and Polynesia, the Big Man is an individual who exerts influence on the tribe as a result of the respect they command or their persuasive skills, without possessing a formal source of authority. More than just a respected opinion-holder, the Big Man actively supports his followers through economic or physical assistance, in order to maintain his status. This role may be more figuratively perceived in other social groupings, and the presence of a leader without formal authority to lead is an important consideration for formal leaders.

Big Stick

President Theodore Roosevelt famously described his foreign policy in 1901 as "Speak softly and carry a big stick," the combination of negotiations with the implicit threat of military action.

Bobo Doll experiment

In 1961 and 1963, psychologist Albert Bandura conducted experiments in which children watched an adult hitting and verbally assaulting a Bobo doll, a person-sized inflatable toy with a weighted bottom giving it a low center of mass so that it bobs back up to an upright position after being struck. Children who had seen the adult acting aggressively with the doll were more likely to do so themselves; boys were more likely to be aggressive than girls, and those who had seen the adult scolded for being aggressive were less likely. The experiment was designed to demonstrate social cognition theory and the importance of replicating behavior in knowledge acquisition.

Bonaparte, Napoleon

Napoleon Bonaparte was a French military leader who took control of France in a coup d'etat in 1799, overthrowing the Directory that had taken control through the French Revolution, and soon establishing the First French Empire. Napoleon spent most of his time as emperor at war against a series of European coalitions, as he attempted to expand France's borders. He defeated five out of seven of the coalitions, repeatedly defeating opponents by manipulating them into positions of tactical disadvantage, often followed by a surprise attack by reserve troops. The French army was often smaller, but proved almost impossible to defeat, especially after the 1807 introduction of artillery units. Napoleon was eventually defeated at Waterloo in 1815, and spent the remainder of his life in exile on the island of St. Helena, despite numerous plans (many farfetched) to rescue him and restore his rule.

Boreout

Swiss business consultants Peter Werder and Philippe Rothlin introduced the idea of boreout in their 2007 book *Diagnose Boreout*. Boreout is an idea in management theory that proposes that the combination of boredom, lack of work, and lack of engagement—boreout—are a common problem in modern white-collar work, and that consequently, a manager's job is to prevent this from happening.

Boundary spanning

The term *boundary spanning* was coined by Michael Tushman in 1977 to refer to a concept that had been examined in the social sciences since the 1950s—the activity of individuals in an organization who connect that organization's inner workings with external information sources. In the technological ramp-up after World War II, many organizations operated large research and development labs. The manner in which these labs acquired and integrated information from the wider world of research outside the company was of considerable interest, in helping to make commercial research more effective and efficient.

Bradley effect

The Bradley effect is a phenomenon in which an individual's statement of future behavior differs from his actual behavior because of his self-consciousness in reporting his preference to a pollster: specifically, the phenomenon whereby a non-white candidate performs better in polls against a white candidate than in the actual election, due to the number of individuals unwilling to tell a pollster they prefer the white candidate. There is no consensus as to whether the Bradley effect remains a persistent phenomenon in the aftermath of President Barack Obama's reelection, but in either case it is an example of a broader effect in which individuals select a performance prediction to present that represents them in what they feel is a better light than their actual performance.

Brainstorming

Brainstorming is the process of generating spontaneous ideas by an individual or a group, especially the process of doing so without evaluating their value (which is reserved for a separate process later). The term originally referred to temporary insanity as used in legal defenses, but was (perhaps unknowingly) repurposed in the 1960s by advertising executive Alex Faickney Osborn, whose 1963 book *Applied Imagination* claimed that groups were better at generating ideas than individuals.

Bread and Circuses

"Bread and circuses," from the Latin *panem et circenses*, is a metaphor used to describe leaders who appease their followers or the public by superficial means, such as with pleasant distractions or the satisfaction of short-term and superficial requests. These actions are intended to draw attention away from more serious causes of concern. In the workplace, for instance, adding new vending machines or renovating the break area while continuing to ignore employee complaints about workplace safety or the bonus structure would be a bread and circuses maneuver.

Broaden and build theory of positive emotions

The broaden and build theory of positive emotions was first articulated by positive psychologist Barbara Fredrickson in 1998. According to the theory, positive emotions like joy, happiness, and interest or "engagedness" increase one's awareness and allow for a broader range of thinking and more innovative, creative, exploratory mental activity. Negative emotions, by driving the mind toward fight or flight responses, constrict possibilities and lead to narrow manners of thinking.

Brute fact

In philosophy, a brute fact is one that cannot be explained. Some schools of contemporary philosophy argue that at the most fundamental level, behind many or most phenomena are brute facts: the question of why someone likes their coffee with lots of sugar may be explained initially with reference to the individual's tastes and past experiences with coffee, which may then be explained further with a discussion of the neurobiology of taste and the cognitive science of food preferences, and an evolutionary biology discussion of the sweet tooth, just as a chemical explanation for the effect of sugar on the taste profile of coffee can be offered, with discussion of roasting and the evolution of the coffee plant, but either exploration will eventually land on brute facts, if only "why is there something instead of nothing," or why did the coffee plant evolve in the first place, or why did the practice of grinding a plant to make a beverage develop? Some things "just are." Not every school of thought accepts this.

Bullying

Bullying is the use of abuse—physical, emotional, or social—or the threat thereof to intimidate and cause harm to others, especially in such a way as to assert dominance or superiority over the target. Bullying is often characterized by behavior that skirts a perceived line. For instance, a bully may not punch his target, instead repeatedly lightly tapping him in a way that cannot do

A Bully-Free Zone sign hangs in a school in Berea, Ohio. In the United States, new attention has been brought to the issue of bullying as a culture-wide issue. (Flickr)

damage, implicitly or explicitly suggesting that complaining about a touch that is not painful makes the target weak. Classical bullying behaviors are those that are hard for authorities to punish because they seem, on the surface, less serious than an outright assault, or do no obvious "damage." We now know that the psychological effect can be severe even when the physical is not, and online bullying—which lacks a physical element—particularly of students and young people, and in some cases by parents or other authorities, has brought new attention to bullying as a culture-wide problem in the United States.

Bureaucracy

Bureaucracy consists of the non-elected government officials, especially those organized into various agencies and other groups, that oversee much of the policy-making, policy implementation, policy advising, and policy enforcement activity of a government. The word is sometimes used in a more figurative sense to refer to the administrative groups of a large nongovernment institution, and sometimes has a negative connotation, associated with the generation of red tape, unnecessary paperwork and micromanagement policies, and rules-bound stubbornness. Max Weber, though, believed bureaucracy, which delegates policy tasks to different groups of individuals with specialized skills and narrow areas of focus, was the most efficient method of administration, approaching the division of administrative labor in much the same way as the division of manufacturing labor.

Burnout

In social psychology, burnout refers to a state of exhaustion and disinterest in work that persists in the long term. The term was coined from Graham Greene's novel *A Burnt-Out Case*, about an architect who has ceased to enjoy either his work or his life. Burnout has pronounced negative effects both on an employee's work (productivity, quality, focus, engagement) and health (contributing to depression, stress, and the likelihood of coronary heart disease). Theories differ about the causes and remedies of burnout, but strategies for avoiding or coping with it are common products of social and occupational psychology.

Burns, James MacGregor

A Pulitzer Prize winner for his biography of Franklin Delano Roosevelt, James MacGregor Burns is one of the parents of modern leadership studies, thanks to his 1978 book *Leadership*. Later in his career he assembled a group of scholars to attempt a Grand Theory of Leadership, but in this early volume he offered one of the most succinct models of leadership: leadership as "the governance of change." Burns considered leadership not simply in terms of heads of governments and businesses, but as a process by which social change is enacted at many scales.

Business continuity planning

Business continuity planning is planning for the continuation of business operations after an interruption as a result of unpredictable extrinsic factors, such as a natural disaster, burglary, or accident. For instance, if a data center is destroyed, a business continuity plan includes information for restoring data from backups, ideally including designating which workers are responsible for responding to the event. If an office building is made unavailable for a period of time while spraying for bedbugs or recovering from storm damage, arrangements can be made for certain workers to work from home, others to take days off, and still others to work from an alternate temporary site. Business continuity planning is important to how a leader is perceived by others, as his response to change and his ability to manage the business through the change will be seen to reflect on his overall abilities and suitability. Plans can be tested in advance through drills, tabletop exercises, computer simulations, and other means.

Business decision mapping

Business decision mapping is an organizational decision-making tool in which diagrams illustrate the problem in a structured framework with visual language, overlapping in approach with techniques like mind mapping and dialogue mapping. Design theorist Horst Rittel developed IBIS (Issue-Based Information System) in 1968, as a visual language framework that has been adapted to business decision mapping and used in decision-mapping software packages.

Business education

Business education includes high school level business courses as well as college programs, and covers the theory and practice of business, including areas like accounting, marketing, management, and business administration. Common degrees include the Bachelor of Business Administration, the Bachelor of Business Management, the Bachelor of Accountancy, and the Master of Business Administration, but numerous schools have idiosyncratic programs reflecting a special emphasis or commitment to a particular approach or sector. Doctoral degrees are research-focused and less common. At the college level (and sometimes in high school), business education usually relies on the case method.

Business fable

A business fable is a fable or parable that is written to illustrate, sometimes allegorically, lessons about management, salesmanship, or other business practices. *The Greatest Salesman in the World* and *Who Moved My Cheese* are perhaps the best-known examples.

Business game

A business game is a simulation game used to teach business and management skills, ranging from finance and accounting to supply chain management and organizational behavior. Business games developed out of the war games used to teach strategy and tactics in the military, and thus developed alongside an increasing interest in game theory coming out of World War II. Business and war games are a subset of what is now called "serious games," though the term was applied retroactively. Some business games were developed not specifically for education, but as recreation, including the "Tycoon" line of games like Railroad and Roller Coaster Tycoon, or Sim Tower, from the makers of Civilization and the Sims. These games tend to emphasize micromanagement, however, often putting the player in a role that does not have an exact analogue outside of the game situation.

Business magnate

A business magnate, tycoon, or industrialist is a wealthy innovator in a particular industry, who has risen to a dominant position, often by pioneering a young technology or practice. The word *magnate* is derived from the Latin for "great man," reflecting the "great man leadership" model underlying the rhetoric that has historically surrounded discussion of these businesses. The 19th century saw a rise of magnates in the United States, including Andrew Carnegie and John D. Rockefeller, who pioneered the steel and oil industries. Often the best-known magnates are those presiding over the industries that seem to define their eras: Cornelius Vanderbilt in the age of the great railroads, William

Randolph Hearst as nationwide newspaper distribution became a serious cultural and political force, Bill Gates and Ted Turner in the age of the personal computing boom and the spread of cable television. Another term common in the 19th century was "captain of industry," a laudatory term used to refer to those whose businesses had contributed to the well-being of the country, in contrast with the "robber baron" derogatory label that referenced the tactics by which they sometimes built those businesses. Thomas Carlyle, a Great Man historian and early proponent of trait-based leadership theory, coined the "captain of industry" term in 1843.

Business process

A business process is a collection or series of tasks related to the production of a specific product or other aspect of the business's operations.

Business process outsourcing

Business process outsourcing is the contracting of specific business processes to third-party providers; the term is especially associated with the outsourcing of processes to overseas firms, as with the outsourcing of customer or technical support hotlines to India. The Philippines and India are the two largest hosts of outsourced business processes. In addition to customer service outsourcing, many back office functions like finance, human resources, and accounting are outsourced.

Business process reengineering

Dating from the 1990s, business process reengineering is a process of streamlining the processes of an organization in order to improve competitiveness, through better-designed workflow that, ideally, better serves customers while improving efficiency and reducing operational costs. Two reasons business process reengineering emerged when it did were the increased reliance on and availability of information technology, as many businesses began to alter their processes anyway in order to keep up with or make use of the Internet and related technologies, and the rise of outsourcing. Though new ideas initially propelled BPR, the term was also used by some companies to relabel downsizing and other restructurings that had little to do with new methods of streamlining.

Business school

A business school is an institute of higher education that offers business-related degrees, such as in management, accounting, or business administration. Most business schools are programs within a larger university and the students typically take some required and elective courses from programs outside the business school. Other business schools are privately operated.

Business speak

Business speak, usually used pejoratively, is the unwieldy English associated with the business world, bureaucracies, and the business/management consulting industry. Features include argot specific to the work at hand, terms borrowed from other fields and repurposed, a heavy and often unnecessary use of portmanteaus and neologisms, and often confusing syntax.

Buzzword driven development

A management or project development method that focuses on novel, popular, or trendy practices or technologies, with little consideration for their appropriateness either for the work at hand or with one another.

Bystander apathy

In social psychology, bystander apathy refers to a tendency of individuals to fail to offer to help a victim when other people are present, with the probability of any one individual offering help inversely proportional to the number of bystanders present. Interest in bystander apathy began after the murder of Kitty Genovese in 1964, though it was later discovered that media reports of neighbors witnessing her attack without reporting it were inaccurate.

Cadillac management

A management or development approach that treats the most expensive resources—including infrastructure and staff—as the safest route to successful completion.

Caesaropapism

A term popularized by Max Weber, caesaropapism is a form of political leadership in which the secular leader of a government is also the supreme religious leader, or in which the government otherwise has direct control over the relevant spiritual authority. It is not the opposite of theocracy, in that like theocracy there is no separation of church and state, and religious institutions have more political power than in other systems; however, in caesaropapism, it is the state that drives the church, rather than the other way around. The term combines "Caesar" or "emperor" and "pope." Historically, at various periods the Byzantine emperors held caesaropapist power over the Church of Constantinople, while King Henry VIII and Elizabeth I held power of the Church of England which Henry VIII created. (Today, the British monarch's leadership of the Church of England is purely ceremonial, practical power having been ceded to a legislative body.)

Roman Emperor Constantine, center, with bishops of the Roman Church. In caesaropapism, it is the state that drives the church. The Church of Constantine was ruled by the Byzantine emperors during various time periods. (Public Domain)

Carlyle, Thomas

A 19th century Scottish philosopher and historian, Thomas Carlyle is perhaps best remembered for his history of the French Revolution (Dickens's source for *A Tale of Two Cities*) and his description of economics as "the dismal science." He was also an early adherent of trait-based theories of leadership, cataloguing in his 1841 *Heroes and Hero Worship* the physical and mental characteristics of leaders from history.

Cascading failure

In a sufficiently interconnected system, a failure of one part can trigger the failure of successive parts or processes dependent on it, resulting in a cascading failure. Because the initial failure is not necessarily the first failure to be noticed, cascading failures can make problem solving difficult. Vulnerability to, and safeguards against, cascading failure is an important consideration in the design of any system, including organizations.

Case method

The case method is an approach to education in which students and an instructor discuss decisions to be made in a case that has been presented to the students, consisting of background material on a company, its industry, its competitors, and a key decision it needs to make. These case studies are prepared by various publishers, and some of the top business schools (including Harvard) have become known for their output in writing cases. The case method is one that relies on narrative to discuss and explore decision-making processes. The case method began in part because of a lack of existing textbooks when some of the earliest American business schools began operations.

Case study

A case study is a descriptive text of a specific case selected to illustrate a principle, event, phenomenon, or process. The most familiar form is the retrospective case study, which selects a real event in history and describes it in terms used to explore the underlying factors behind what happened, for the purposes of study in the social sciences, business school, or some other discipline. A prospective case study, on the other hand, describes the criteria of a case that's sought. The concepts of case study and the case method are related, but the case study is more than a teaching method, and is a key component of professional-level social sciences research, while the needs of the teaching cases used in the case method are not met by all case studies.

Catholic Church, leadership in

The Catholic Church is among the oldest institutions in the world, and has developed a hierarchy of leadership to oversee its activities. Authority stems from God, in the form of revealed scripture, the body of Catholic canon law, and the leadership of the pope, the Bishop of Rome who has for most of the Church's history held authority over other bishops. Bishops oversee the Church's nearly three thousand dioceses, which represent geographic territories, and within those dioceses priests oversee individual communities (parishes), assisted by deacons. Most duties can be performed by any of those clergy, with the sacrament of Holy Orders reserved for bishops alone, and those of the Eucharist, penance, confirmation, and annointing of the sick reserved for bishops and priests. Additionally, cardinals are priests or bishops who have special responsibilities, among them the election of a new pope when the office is vacated.

CAVE dwellers, CAVE people

CAVE (Citizens Against Virtually Everything) dwellers are neighborhood activists who oppose any change to the community, especially those who do not stand to benefit from such changes (such as two-car households who oppose public transportation expansion, empty nest homes who oppose building a new school). The term dates to at least the 1980s and is typically used in reference to activists who are regular fixtures at town meetings, zoning board hearings, and other municipal government sessions.

Center for Congressional and Presidential Studies

The Center for Congressional and Presidential Studies (CCPS) is operated by the American University School of Public Affairs and conducts both research and study programs on the U.S. Congress, the office of the president, and the relationship between them. The Public Affairs and Advocacy Institute offers an intensive course on lobbying, while the Campaign Management Institute is one of the few nationally recognized programs training students to work on political campaigns.

Center for Creative Leadership

The Center for Creative Leadership (CCL) is a non-profit organization founded in 1970 in Greensboro, North Carolina, to provide executive education and leadership training. Today it publishes a variety of leadership books, including the *CCL Handbook of Leadership Development*, which entered its third edition in 2010. Its offices include training facilities in Greensboro, Colorado Springs, and San Diego, and foreign offices in Brussels, Moscow, and Singapore.

Center for Ethical Leadership

The Center for Ethical Leadership was founded in 1991 by leadership studies professor Bill Grace, in order to offer ethical leadership development programs for neighborhood, business, government, religious, and youth leaders. In the 2000s, the Center evaluated its efforts and determined that training individuals had not been sufficient to meet its goals, and so has shifted focus toward team and community development. The Gracious Space program, for instance, teaches groups to work better together, through training, books, and customized consultations.

Center for Public Leadership

The Center for Public Leadership was established in 2000 at the John F. Kennedy School of Government at Harvard. An academic research center, it focuses on practical leadership skills for business, non-profit, and government leadership roles. Every year it publishes the *National Leadership Index*, quantifying American confidence in key leaders of various sectors.

David Gergen, *director of the Center for Public Leadership, speaks at the World Economic Forum annual meeting in Davos, Switzerland, in 2013.* (Flickr/World Economic Forum)

Chakravartin

An ancient Indian word, a Chakravartin is an ideal leader who is qualified to rule over the entire world. Similar concepts are found throughout the dharmic religions, sometimes representing rulers who practice asceticism.

Change management

Change management is the oversight of transitions in or throughout an organization, and may be either one element of a manager's duties, or the specialization of a particular type of manager. For example, large retail chains like Dollar General treat store-opening as a specialized skill, employing a number of itinerant team leaders whose job it is to oversee the opening of a new location, but who have no involvement in the normal day-to-day operations of a retail location after that initial transition. In other organizations, consultants may be hired to oversee changes in the work environment and corporate hierarchy that result from a merger, significant downsizing, expansion, or other reorganization.

Chargé d'affaires

In diplomacy, the leader of a diplomatic mission not led by an ambassador is called a charge d'affaires.

Charisma

Charisma is the vital and compelling personal charm possessed by some people. The modern conception of charisma is deeply influenced by American ideals of individualism, having developed in the 1950s across numerous spheres—the social sciences, the Christian community, entertainment media—whereas earlier usages reflected not a personal quality of character but the state of having been gifted with the grace of God, or favored by fate. Even in this earlier meaning, however, charisma did not mean quite the same thing as luck, and both usages reflected a quality that in some way set the individual apart from his peers in a manner that inspired people to be more likely to follow him. Charisma is related to many other concepts of markedness: photographers may consider one subject more photogenic than another, independent from their relative attractiveness; an actor may have screen presence, while two actors together may have chemistry.

Charismatic leadership or charismatic domination

One of Weber's ideal types of political leadership, charismatic leadership (sometimes translated as charismatic domination) is a form of leadership that commands obedience on the basis of the exemplary character of the leader. In some cases, that charismatic authority can be passed on from the original leader to a chosen successor, as in the case of Joseph Stalin's succession of Vladimir Lenin. Barring this, it is difficult for an organization's leadership style to survive beyond the original charismatic leader.

Len Oakes and other psychologists have argued that charismatic leaders are more likely to suffer from narcisissim.

Chauvinism

Chauvinism originally referred to a belligerent form of patriotism and partisanship, supposedly coined for a French soldier who remained loyal to Napoleon after his abdication. "Male chauvinism" was coined by the feminist movement to refer to men who were similarly unreasonably convinced of the superiority of men—or of the appropriateness of the status quo in which women occupied an inferior position—and in time, this became the most common usage of the word in English, especially in the United States. Today, chauvinism nearly always refers to male chauvinism. Chauvinism is a problem in the workplace for both men and women; many men, even avowed feminists, have unexamined chauvinistic beliefs or have developed a habit of learned helplessness. Psychoanalytic studies have found that challenging chauvinist beliefs can induce anxiety, and have implied that there are different psychological explanations for sexism than for racism and other forms of intolerance.

Checkbook diplomacy

Checkbook diplomacy is the use of economic aid or investments as a diplomatic tool.

Cherry picking

The act of selecting for presentation or consideration only the data that supports one's argument or a particular conclusion, especially if done deliberately.

Churchill, Winston

Winston Churchill was the prime minister of the United Kingdom for two noncoterminal

Winston Churchill, prime minister of the United Kingdom from 1940 to 1945 and 1951 to 1955, flashing his famous "V" for victory sign while appearing on Downing Street in London. (British Government Photo)

terms, from 1940 to 1945 and from 1951 to 1955. For his part in World War II, he became the first person made an honorary citizen of the United States—and remains the only person other than Mother Teresa to receive that honor while still living. As a young man, he rose to fame as a war correspondent, after which he held a number of political positions. In the 1930s, as a writer estranged from his Conservative party, he spoke out about Nazi Germany, and his criticism of Prime Minister Neville Chamberlain's appeasement toward Hitler was instrumental in his rise to succeed Chamberlain after World War II broke out. (To be fair, Chamberlain himself, upon resigning, recommended Churchill as his successor, in an

unusual move.) He is today remembered for his oratory, including his promise before the Battle of Britain that "we shall fight on the beaches, we shall fight on the landing grounds, we shall fight in the fields and in the streets, we shall fight in the hills; we shall never surrender." After the war, Churchill was the Leader of the Opposition and a prominent figure in world affairs—coining the term *Iron Curtain* in reference to the creation of the communist Eastern Bloc—before returning to government in the 1950s as Britain dealt with its postwar economic crisis.

Civic engagement

Civic engagement is individual or collective participation in the community, especially at the local level and especially where government engagement is somehow involved. Civic engagement might include mobilizing members of the community to oppose the building of a gas pipeline through a conservation area, for instance; volunteering to help remove underwater hazards from a local swimming hole; conducting a voter registration drive; or participating in a town meeting.

Civic intelligence

Civic intelligence, which John Dewey called cooperative intelligence, is the intelligence of individuals, groups, and institutions with regard to civil society and citizenship.

Civic leadership

Civic leadership is leadership by local citizens, or in municipal matters, not necessarily through or as part of the local government. "Civic" means "relating to a town or city," and is synonymous with municipal. Civic leadership studies and training programs are predicated on the belief that every person is a potential leader. The University of South Dakota is one school that offers a civic leadership studies minor, while Fort Hays State University is home to the Center for Civic Leadership, which offers programs in citizen leadership development.

Clan culture

One of four organizational cultures identified by Robert Quinn's Competing Values Framework, clan culture is internally focused on the well-being of the people in the organization and favors a flexible organization structure. Leaders in these organizations act like parental figures. Communication throughout the organization is open and encouraged.

Classics

Classics or classical studies is the study of the culture of Greece and Rome, especially during the era of Classical Antiquity, and of their languages and literature. Interest in classics was revived during the Renaissance, when classical literature was rediscovered and a new appreciation developed for Greek and Latin, ancestors of most of the languages of western Europe. The classics provided the foundation of western culture and civilization, and as such offer a wealth of material for leadership studies, from the antecedents of Western political philosophy to histories of wise and foolish leaders.

Classroom management

Classroom management is the process of overseeing the activity and environment of a classroom, and the challenges it presents are heavily implicated in teacher job dissatisfaction. Classroom management differs from workplace management in several critical ways: most students are minors, which affects a teacher's disciplinary options, as well as impacting the students' emotional and social skills; the student to teacher ratio is often higher than the employee to supervisor ratio; students have few options for dealing with dissatisfaction, compared with employees who are present by choice; the overall goals of a classroom differ from those of other workplaces.

Coaching

A form of teaching, mentoring, or leadership, coaching is a guided development process led by a coach. Though associated today principally with sports and life coaches, the mentorship meaning of "coach" developed in the mid-19th century as slang for a tutor, though the usage of the word in the sports world began only a few years later.

Coercion

Coercion is the use of threats, force, or other pressure to make a party act against their will. While used by bullies and criminals, coercion is also the means by which some government regimes and other leaders have accomplished their ends, and can be found in the workplace, usually in more subtle forms than the threat of physical violence.

Coercive diplomacy

Coercive diplomacy is diplomacy conducted in conjunction with the threat of military force, in order to motivate the other party to acquiesce to a proposal.

Coercive power

Coercive power is one of John R. P. French and Bertram Raven's bases of power, and one of Patrick J. Montana and Bruce H. Charnov's varieties of organizational power. Coercion is the use of force to make the target comply against their wishes, though the target may not realize they are being coerced, and the force may not be physical; an employee who performs a task under threat of their job being at risk is an example of coercion, for instance, and personal coercion uses the threat of disapproval, which is dependent on the coercive party's approval being highly valued by the target.

Co-evolution of genes and culture

One of the hypotheses explaining cultural differences in decision making, as supported for instance by Lesley Newson, is the idea that biological and cultural differences evolved together. As behaviors were passed down from one generation to the next within a culture group, cultural variants developed, shaped by forces similar to those that shape the evolution of genes.

Cognitive ancestral leader prototypes

One theory in evolutionary leadership theory proposes the cognitive ancestral leader prototypes: specific types of leaders whom humans are inclined to choose (when choice is possible) in specific situations. Strong, physically vigorous, risk-taking leaders, especially young and male, are common in times of war, and by extension in times of crisis; older leaders, especially those perceived as nurturing or socially savvy, are preferred in times of peace.

Cognitive bias

A cognitive bias is a pattern in perception, interpretation, or judgment that consistently leads to the individual misunderstanding something about himself or his social environment, making a poor choice, or otherwise acting irrationally. Several hundred cognitive biases affecting judgment, perception, self-evaluation, and memory have been identified by researchers since the middle of the 20th century, and an awareness of cognitive biases is important not only in psychology and management, but in behavioral economics. While cognitive biases show that people cannot be expected to behave rationally at all times, their irrationality can nevertheless be predictable and follow specific patterns.

Cognitive bias mitigation

A number of tools and frameworks have been developed to try to reduce the effects of cognitive biases. Just as the human hand is shaky and may be guided in its drawing efforts by a ruler and compass, so too do such tools as reference class forecasting attempt to guide and render methodical human thinking. In already-methodical contexts, such as formal decision-making processes, this is more easily done. The real problem facing cognitive bias mitigation is the impact of cognitive biases on short-term decision making, from the behavior of people in social situations to the responses of victims, bystanders, and responders in emergencies. One of the best ways to mitigate the harm of cognitive biases on an individual level may simply be to be aware of and on guard against them.

Cognitive complexity

Cognitive complexity is a measure of the complexity of a person's perceptual skills and related faculties. High cognitive complexity allows a person to see nuances, shadings, and subtleties that escape the attention of others. In interpersonal relationships, high cognitive complexity allows one to better perceive the subtle differences between people, their attitudes, wants, and needs, rather than dealing with them with a one-size-fits-all approach.

Cognitive development

Cognitive development is the study of the cognitive skills—including language learning, perceptual skills, and information processing—of children, and the development of these skills into those of adults. The modern field encompasses neuroscience as well as psychology, and grows out of Jean Piaget's work on the developmental psychology of children.

Cognitive resource theory

A reconceptualization of the Fiedler contingency model, developed in 1987 by Fred Fiedler and Joe Garcia. Rather than focusing on the three dimensions of the Fiedler contingency model, cognitive resource theory focuses on the leader's response to stress, on the belief that poor handling of stress impairs the leader's ability to make full use of his reason and the facts available to him when making decisions. Both intelligence and relevant experience assist in handling stress.

U.S. Air Force aircraft unloading in Berlin during the Berlin Blockade, one of the first major crises of the Cold War. From June 1948 to May 1949, the Soviet Union blocked access to Berlin, even though it was under Allied control. (U.S. Air Force)

The Cold War

The Cold War lasted, in most historians' approximations, from 1945 to 1991, and consisted of a period of formal hostility, strategic alliances, and proxy wars, without direct military conflict, between the United States and the Soviet Union. Further, during this period most international affairs, at least in the West, were tinged by this conflict, which served to elevate each country, as well as secure for the United States its preeminent position as the capitalist superpower. Proxy wars had the unintended consequences of setting up future conflicts, as the American and Soviet involvement in the Middle East helped inspire the rise of politicized Islamic fundamentalism, and provided weapons and training for future American enemies, including Saddam Hussein and the Afghani mujahideen who formed al-Qaeda. The necessity of this conflict was never universally accepted, especially once Eastern European communism ceased spreading and the boundaries between capitalist and communist spheres of control became essentially fixed. But it was a conflict that fueled the

United States' military buildup in the 1950s, as well as the space race, and thus proved critical, at least for a time, to the country's manufacturing base, technological competence, and economy. It also proved an ongoing leadership challenge for American presidents, from Dwight Eisenhower warning about the power of the military-industrial complex to George H. W. Bush being condemned as a "wimp."

Collaborative governance

Collaborative governance is a form of governance in which representatives of various interests collaborate in the decision-making process, though typically one group has the official final authority to make the decision. Government groups and agencies may invite representatives from industry and advocacy groups to offer their input in a problem-solving discussion, for instance.

Collaborative leadership

Collaborative leadership is an approach to leadership that is most common in public–private partnerships, online projects such as Wikipedia and other open-source works, and that is often advocated as a solution to complex global issues like climate change. Collaborative leadership involves inputs from multiple sources, with the titular leader or leaders acting as facilitators as well as managers, and often involves cooperation between different groups.

Collective identity

Collective identity is the sense of belonging to a group, and the traits, behaviors, and other elements that members associate with that group, as opposed to their perception of themselves in relation to the group. Social psychologist George Mead noted that while social conditions and structures shape the identity of members, collective identity in turn shapes those structures. The idea of collective identity is at the heart of identity politics, an approach to political activity informed and motivated by one's group associations.

Collective intelligence

Collective intelligence is intelligence that results from the collective and collaborative efforts of many individuals, such as through voting, crowdsourcing, or consensus decision making, as well as less formal means.

Collective responsibility

Collective responsibility is the responsibility borne by individuals for other peoples' actions and behaviors, as a result of tolerating or ignoring them. In the workplace, this extends to employees being held responsible for the overall performance of the organization.

Collectivism

Collectivism puts a priority on the interdependence of people, in contrast with individualism's concern for each individual's independence. Neither is an ideology as such, but rather describes an element an ideology may possess. Most cultures include both collectivist and individualist elements but may incorporate one over the other into its collective self-image. The United States, even more than other Western countries, is a deeply individualist culture, for instance, but within the narrative of American identity are many stories evincing collectivist ideals, like the many stories of communities banding together to aid one of its members (or an outsider), from Amish barn raisings to crowdsourced good deeds or fund-raising by members of Reddit. Collectivism is widely associated with the Soviet Union, but some socialists argue that Western capitalism is actually a collectivist system, in which the freedom of the individual is constrained by economic choices he is forced to make and the social forces that result from capitalist structures.

Command responsibility

The doctrine of command responsibility was first applied in 1921 during the war crimes trials that followed World War I, and states that superior officers are responsible for the war crimes (or crimes against humanity or peace) of their subordinates. The exact interpretation of this doctrine has varied over time and circumstance. Notably, Lieutenant Ehren Watada refused in 2006 to be deployed to Iraq on the basis of the doctrine, claiming that the war was illegal.

Communal reinforcement

In psychology, communal reinforcement refers to the strengthening of peoples' belief in a concept as a result of it being repeatedly asserted in their community, regardless of the evidence or lack thereof. This is one of the mechanisms by which both urban legends and political propaganda propagate.

Communicative rationality

A set of theories, especially espoused by Jurgen Habermas and Karl-Otto Apel, proposing that rationality results from successful communication. Leadership scholars are interested in communicative rationality because of the way it describes the processes by which people reach agreement and make decisions in a group.

Comparative leadership studies

Comparative leadership studies approach leadership studies from a perspective informed by anthropology and the other social sciences, in examining leadership and leadership behaviors across different cultures.

Competence, four stages of

The four stages of competence is a model of learning that developed out of the work of psychologist Abraham Maslow in the 1970s, and describes the stages of learning a skill. The first stage is unconscious incompetence, the state of lacking a skill but not necessarily recognizing the importance of the skill—or believing that one possesses it, despite a lack of training or other means of acquisition. People in this stage may have difficulty recognizing competence in other people. The second stage is conscious incompetence, in which the individual still does not possess competence, but recognizes that fact, enabling them to learn from their mistakes. In the third stage, conscious competence, performance of the skill is possible but requires concentration, like when children use a mnemonic to help them tie their shoes. In the fourth and final stage, unconscious competence, skill has been attained and can be accessed automatically.

Competency

In leadership studies, competencies are the skills and behaviors that determine performance. Different models of leadership propose different lists and groups of competencies, though with significant overlap. For instance, many agencies of the U.S. federal government look for 28 leadership competencies in their leadership development. The Coast Guard groups these into Leading Self, Leading Others, Leading Performance and Change, and Leading the Coast Guard, while the Farm Service Agency (FSA) groups them as Managing Self, Managing Projects, Managing People, Managing Programs, and Leading Organizations. Both list largely similar competencies, though they may call them different things or list them in different groups. The Coast Guard's Leading Self group, for example, consists of competencies in Accountability and Responsibility, Followership, Self-Awareness and Learning, Aligning Values, Health and Well-Being, Personal Conduct, and Technical Proficiency. The FSAs Managing Self group includes Integrity/Honesty, Interpersonal Skills, Continual Learning, Resilience, Oral Communication, Written Communication, Flexibility, and Problem Solving—almost a completely different list. Many of the FSA's Managing Self competencies, however, are grouped by the Coast Guard under Leading Others, which combines Oral and Written Communication into Effective Communications, while dividing Interpersonal Skills into Influencing Others, Respect for Others and Diversity Management, Mentoring, Taking Care of People, and Team Building.

Competing Values Framework

Robert Quinn's Competing Values Framework (CVF) developed out of his studies of organizational effectiveness with John Rohrbaugh in

1983. The name represents the apparent conflict between the traits valued in organizations and leaders—flexibility and stability, for instance. Earlier models of leadership had tended to sort these traits or behaviors into dichotomies, as with Theory X versus Theory Y, or transformational versus transactional leadership. Quinn instead looked at the possibility and benefits of balancing different, even seemingly conflicting, styles of leadership. The CVF is a spatial model created by juxtaposing two value dimensions— internal versus external organizational focus, and stable controlled organizational structure versus flexibility—resulting in four quadrants representing four types of organizational culture. The Organizational Culture Assessment Instrument developed by Quinn and Kim Cameron in 1999 distinguishes these four types as clan culture (internal/flexible), adhocracy (external/flexible), market (external/controlled), and hierarchy (internal/controlled).

Complaint system

A complaint system in an organization is the set of procedures and mechanisms by which workers can report complaints and expect to have them addressed. Originally instituted by or at the request of labor unions, complaint systems underwent an evolution in the late 20th century as the study of conflict management became more sophisticated. Most large organizations now have integrated conflict management systems, with the goal of the organization learning from the conflicts that arise.

Complexity leadership theory

Complexity leadership theory draws on complexity science and complex adaptive systems theory in its investigation of polyarchic leadership (leadership by the many of the many, rather than by the few as in oligarchies). Leadership under this theory is not a skill that can be learned or engineered through training, but a phenomenon that arises through the interaction of individuals in an organization. One of the newer areas of inquiry in leadership studies, complexity leadership theory comes primarily out of studies of medical leadership in the 2000s, and Nick Obolensky's 2010 book *Complex Adaptive Leadership*.

Complexity theory

Complexity theory is a body of theory surrounding complex systems, which are organized but unpredictable. Examples of complex systems are easily observed in nature: the movement of leaves on a tree in response to the breeze, or the motion of ocean waves against the beach, either of which may be an easily explained phenomenon in broad terms, but so complex as to defy making predictions about exactly what shape the water will take as it reaches the shore, or exactly which direction any given leaf will twist or turn. Complex systems involve many interconnected components resulting in these phenomena, and like the leaves or the waves, they may not appear complex at first glance. There is considerable interest in adapting complexity theory to the leadership and management of organizations, and to organizational studies. Organizations are systems made up of numerous components, business processes, and interpersonal interactions, and can be studied like complex adaptive systems that self-organize and evince emergent properties.

Compliance

Compliance is acquiescence to a request. The reasons why people comply are a major area of study in social psychology, and the attempt to gain compliance is called persuasion.

Confidence-building measures

In international relations, confidence-building measures (CBMs) are actions taken to reduce tensions between states and specifically the suspicion or fear of attack between two or more states. Such measures usually involve exchanges and disclosures of information. During the Cold War, for instance, it was common for the United States and the Soviet Union to each inform the other party when war games or alert exercises were being held, or when aircraft or naval operations would be held outside of the usual locations. The importance of these information exchanges cannot be overstated: during NATO's Able Archer 83 exercise in November 1983, members of the Soviet leadership were convinced the exercise was a genuine preparation for war, leading to the Soviet nuclear forces being put on alert. As a feedback model, CBMs have relevance beyond international relations, and are a significant strategy in communication, in which two sides in a potential conflict or tense situation share information in order to prevent anyone acting aggressively.

Confirmation bias

Confirmation bias is a cognitive bias describing the tendency to weight more heavily information that confirms beliefs one already holds or a hypothesis one is testing. As long ago as the 5th century B.C.E., Thucydides wrote of humanity's tendency "to entrust to careless hope what they long for, and to use sovereign reason to thrust aside what they do not fancy." The fact that the bias is measurably more pronounced when in emotionally intense contexts and when the beliefs in question are an important part of one's self-concept is one that has received considerable attention by researchers. It also indicates something about the difficulty of finding consensus in disagreements where both sides are deeply entrenched and emotionally invested, insofar as each side literally perceives the corpus of evidence differently.

Conflict resolution

The facilitation of a fair and agreeable ending to a conflict. Conflict resolution is a process that can transpire on a scale ranging from an interpersonal conflict between two people to international diplomacy and peacemaking, and there are relevant methodological similarities at all scales in between. In academic study, conflict resolution focuses especially on regional and national conflicts and on peacebuilding work in conflict-impacted communities. Prominent schools in the field include Cornell University, home to the Scheinman Institute on Conflict Resolution; George Mason University, the first school to offer a Ph.D. program in conflict resolution; and Tel Aviv University, which offers an International Program in Conflict Resolution and Mediation, in English.

Conformity

Conformity is the action of an individual matching his beliefs, actions, or attitudes to match those of his group, whether voluntarily or under coercion. The desire to conform has been well demonstrated in experiments, notably those of Solomon Asch. Psychologist Herbert Kelman differentiated in a 1958 article between three kinds of conformity: compliance, which is a public face of conformity while maintaining one's own conflicting position internally; identification is conforming not to a group position (or at least not because it is a group position) but to a position held by a specific individual because of specific attitudes the individual holds toward that individual, and a desire to be more like them, such as a beloved celebrity; and internalization, in which the group position is adopted by the individual to a great enough degree that he accepts it as his own and will be loathe to abandon it.

Confucius

A 6th-century B.C.E. Chinese philosopher, Confucius established the school (Confucianism) responsible for the Five Classics of Chinese literature and taught a code of ethics and conduct grounded in traditional Chinese beliefs. His system of ethics was based on the cultivation of good judgment rather than an explicit code of behavior; virtuous actions are made by virtuous thinkers. His political philosophy developed out of this, and he emphasized that a virtuous leader is one that rules not through either coercion or bribery but through morality, such that his followers will feel a deep sense of duty to be led by him. Much of what he prescribed for kings and other rulers would be compatible today with authentic leadership.

Conscientiousness

Conscientiousness is one of the "Big Five" personality traits, characterized by thoroughness, efficiency, and systematic organization. High levels of conscientiousness characterize workplace perfectionists and "workaholics," who may become compulsive enough in their behavior that striving for efficiency actually results in inefficiency. Conscientiousness is related to impulse control and work ethic, and so those with low conscientiousness scores may exhibit antisocial or criminal behavior, or may simply be prone to procrastination. (As with most such statements, the tie between low conscientiousness and criminal behavior must be taken with a grain of salt; white-collar crime is actually moderately correlated with high levels of conscientiousness.)

Consensus

Consensus is a general agreement among a group, whether concerning a course of action or a sentiment held by the members of the group. Often it represents the decision or resolution that faces the least objection, rather than representing the first preference of a majority of the group. Various decision-making processes seek to find or build consensus, even if the final authority for the decision lies elsewhere (with a leader or group of leaders, for instance, or as determined by a vote). Building consensus may also be seen as minimizing dissent, which explains its appeal even when it is not required to take action, as dissent can lead to lingering resentment, frictions, and ongoing problems.

Consensus decision making

Group decision making sometimes seeks to find a consensus of the group, rather than an adversarial decision-making process like a majority vote that overrules the minority. In some cases this may be required of or by the group, as with a jury or the decision-making meetings held by the Occupy Wall Street movement. In other cases it may simply be the group's preference, whether explicitly expressed or not. Consensus does not mean that the decision made by the group is the preferred option of all group members, or even of any member, and may simply be the option that was the least objectionable. Each member "consents," but does not necessarily "agree." Decision-making processes that require a supermajority vote to pick an option are sometimes considered consensus processes, even though they do include dissenting votes.

Consent of the governed

The consent of the governed is a concept reflecting a particular view of political legitimacy, which argues that the only legitimate regime is one that has the popular support of the people, in contrast with the divine right of kings or the Mandate of Heaven. The first major historical example of such a regime is that of 5th-century B.C.E. Athens, though the political idea of the consent of the governed was not developed until the Enlightenment—in fact, ancient Greek philosophy like that of Plato was more frequently concerned with arguing against the Athenian model. John Locke in particular, in his Second Treatise on Government, argued that only a government operating with the consent of the governed would be able to satisfy the fundamental needs of the nation. This concept was reflected in the Declaration of Independence, and Jean-Jacques Rousseau later developed it as part of his social contract theory.

Consequential strangers

Consequential strangers are personal connections who are neither family nor close friends, and so include many work connections, as well as professionals with whom one interacts on a recurring basis, such as doormen or security guards, the receptionist in one's doctor's office, one's dentist, or the wait staff at a favorite restaurant. They may also include social acquaintances with whom one has not had much one-on-one contact, such as friends-of-friends who are often invited to the same parties, or the neighbors of relatives whom one regularly visits. Sociological and social psychological work has become increasingly interested in these peripheral, secondary, or weak relationships, because of the sheer bulk of social "space" that they occupy in our lives. For instance, social interactions at work may be superficial beyond the interactions that focus on work itself, but they can nevertheless be crucial to one's emotional health.

Considerate style of leadership

As described by Fred Fiedler, a considerate style of leadership is one that focuses on relationships among co-workers, typified by a leader who derives satisfaction from healthy and positive interpersonal dynamics. This is particularly appropriate to work environments in which workers need or want autonomy in determining the course of their work, such as in research groups or college faculty, as opposed to work that benefits from or requires a high degree of task structure, such as factory work, emergency or disaster response, or a political campaign.

Consideration

One of two factors identified by the Ohio State Leadership Studies, consideration is the level of concern a leader displays for the well-being of his followers. Leaders who focus on this factor make themselves accessible and approachable to their followers, treat everyone as equal without strict concern for a hierarchy of roles, and foster employee engagement in the workplace. *See also* authenticity

Constitutional monarchy

A constitutional monarchy is not simply a monarchy in which the monarch's powers are limited by a written constitution but rather a form of democracy in which the monarch is a head of state whose actual political powers are limited. Most political powers are instead held by other bodies or by an executive branch of government that coexists with the monarch. In the United Kingdom, for instance, the prime minister holds most of the executive political power and is determined through election. Most constitutional monarchies are in western Europe, though Japan and Thailand are notable exceptions.

Constructivism

Constructivism is a theory of epistemology that posits that knowledge and meaning are created—constructed—in the human mind by the interaction between the individual's ideas and his experiences, a process that begins in infancy. Constructivists tend to put greater emphasis on the learner's role in the process of learning. At Phillips Exeter Academy, for instance, the Harkness method was developed, named for the circular Harkness table (named for a donor) at which students would sit for a discussion they guide themselves.

Consultative system

One of Renis Likert's management systems, in the consultative system, upper management controls decision making impacting the whole organization and general policies, while lower level employees are given a degree of decision-making power over their own work. Lower levels are consulted as part of the decision-making process at the upper levels, while both rewards and punishments are used to motivate behavior.

Consumer confidence

An economic indicator measuring consumers' feelings about the national economy in general and their personal financial situation specifically, as a factor impacting their future spending activity.

Contagious shooting

In military and police experiences, in which multiple armed officers or soldiers are present in a potentially threatening scenario, "contagious shooting" is an observed phenomenon in which one person in the group shooting leads to the others doing so. Though there is no scientific study confirming the phenomenon, it has been used to explain situations in which a number of shots are fired that are disproportionate to the threat level, such as many instances in which dozens of shots are fired by multiple officers at a single armed suspect, even when this requires reloading.

Contingency theory

The contingency theory school of behavioral theory says that the best system of leadership or decision making is contingent on internal and external factors specific to the situation, and that there is no universal "best" system. This has been used to explain why approaches that were successful in one set of circumstances did not translate to success for a leader or business in a different set of circumstances.

Continuous improvement

Continuous improvement (CI) is an effort in management to constantly improve products, services, or the processes involved in their production. Incremental continuous improvement, for instance, is a key feature of Japanese manufacturing. Though many point out that "continual improvement" is preferred grammatically, "continuous improvement" is nevertheless the term that has been adopted in the management world.

Control freak

A control freak is someone who is too invested in controlling the circumstances around them and the actions of people working under or with them. The phrase was coined in the 1960s in contrast with the loosening of social and cultural mores at the time and is not a formal psychological term, but there is considerable overlap between the idea of the control freak, the disorder of the antisocial personality, and the behaviors of micromanagement and perfectionism.

Corporate climate

Corporate climate is closely related to corporate culture, and consists of an organization's employees' perceptions of properties in the work environment (physical, social, organizational, and so on) that influence employee behavior. Corporate climate has a significant effect on employee retention and absenteeism.

Corporate governance

Corporate governance consists of the entities, processes, and mechanisms that direct and control the operations and activities of a corporation. Duties of corporate governance include the equitable treatment of shareholders and non-shareholder stakeholders, integrity on the part of corporate leadership and the organization as a whole, and transparency in the roles and responsibilities of corporate leadership. The "Anglo-American" model of corporate governance, practiced in most American and British companies, uses a system of corporate officers overseen by a single-tiered board of directors, while much of the rest of Europe uses a two-tiered board, one made up of executives and the other of non-executive members representing shareholders.

Corporation for National and Community Service

A U.S. federal agency formed after the 1990 National and Community Service Act, responsible for operating several programs aimed at supporting "the American culture of citizenship, service, and responsibility." Corporation for National and Community Service is the largest provider of grants for service and volunteer work, and operates the intensive community service program AmeriCorps, which provides staff for public agencies and non-profit community organizations; Senior Corps, which provides aid to senior citizens through community programs; and Learn and Serve America, which provides service learning programs for students.

Coughlin, Charles

Father Charles Coughlin delivered frequent radio addresses while leading the Christian Front group. (Library of Congress)

Father Charles Coughlin is one of the better-known modern examples of a demagogue who was not himself a politician. The Catholic priest was an early adopter of mass media, addressing an audience in the Detroit, Michigan, area in 1926, on a radio program that was picked up nationally in 1930. His pre-Depression addresses covered mainly religious topics, and he was a staunch opponent of the Ku Klux Klan, which had adopted an anti-Catholic stance in its second incarnation. After the Depression, Coughlin became increasingly political, supporting the populist Huey Long and many of Roosevelt's New Deal reforms, but by the mid-1930s becoming known for his support of fascism, his anti-Semitism, and his claims that Jewish bankers had caused the Russian Revolution, while a "cash famine" had caused the Great Depression.

Counter-insurgency

The attempt by an incumbent government to resist and defeat an armed rebellion (or insurgency).

Court-packing plan

The court-packing plan was a strategy of President Franklin D. Roosevelt's, culminating in the failed Judicial Procedures Reform Bill of 1937. Because FDR's New Deal bills so drastically changed the scope of the federal government's powers and activities, he had faced difficulty with the Supreme Court, which heard several cases alleging that New Deal reforms were unconstitutional. Most were found in FDR's favor, but the experience soured his opinion of the judiciary branch, and he sought the power to increase the size of the court so that he could appoint enough new justices. Given the reverence the public possesses for the Constitution, and the widespread perception at the time of the court as guardians of that Constitution, it is a testament to Roosevelt's own popularity that his presidency was not more tarnished by this fairly clear overstep. The legislation failed, though notably while the bill was under discussion, the court ruled in favor on three New Deal cases Roosevelt had been concerned about. The fight over court-packing drifted from a conflict between FDR and the court into one between the president and factions within his own party; had World War II not brought many recalcitrants and resignees back to the fold, he might have permanently lost the support he enjoyed for the first half of his presidency.

Cowboy diplomacy

A disparaging term for foreign policy actions that involve heavy risk or provocation, especially with the implication that the cowboy diplomat in question lacks a mature and nuanced view of international relations.

Craft analogy

The ancient Greek philosopher Plato introduced the "craft analogy" of leadership in his attack on democracy (as practiced in Athens, where most public officials were selected by lottery). Plato wrote of the value of specialized training: physicians receive specialized training in order to be able to tend to the body's ailments, experienced sailors train new sailors in order to pass

on technical skills and accumulated knowledge of the sea, and so on. Leadership in Plato's view similarly benefited from, even required, specialized training, and was a true craft (that is, skill-based and teachable), rather than something that simply emerged from the would-be leader's personality and character.

Cravath system

The Cravath system is a law firm management system developed at Cravath, Swaine, and Moore, a New York City law firm, in the 19th century. It has since been adopted by many firms. The system encourages partners—who are the only tenured employees—to work together rather than in cliques, and adopts an "up or out" policy such that associates who are not made partner within ten years are dismissed. Similarly, partners are only hired from within the office, except when expertise is required that is unavailable in that pool. The partners lead the firm with a firm hand. The Cravath system also uses a lockstep compensation system for pay.

Creative class

The creative class as a socioeconomic class consisting of about 30 percent of the workforce was proposed by economics professor Richard Florida in 2002. Florida divided the creative class into the super-creatives, who are fully engaged in creative work for a living, and creative professionals, knowledge workers who solve specific types of problems in fields like healthcare, finance, and the legal sector. Florida's work was concerned in large part with predictions about the growth of the creative class, which were made before the 2008 financial crisis changed many of the important variables, and he has been criticized for not providing a clear definition of "creative." It dovetails with the rise of the term *quaternary sector* to refer to a fourth sector of the economy, based on information, knowledge, and knowledge-based services, and thus including media and culture businesses.

Creative industries

Creative industries, sometimes classed as part of the "quaternary sector" of the economy, include advertising, architecture, art, crafts, design, fashion, film, music, performing arts, publishing, research and development, toys, broadcasting, and video games. The more common European term is cultural industries, while some economic literature uses the term *creative economy*. The creative industries have risen in prominence in recent decades, as well as producing vital American exports at a time when manufacturing has declined. Richard Caves has proposed a list of properties characterizing the creative industries, including demand uncertainty as a result of the difficulty of ascertaining consumer reaction, much less predicting it, and "art for art's sake"—the fact that creative workers will work for lower wages and fewer rewards because the work itself is fulfilling.

Credentialism

Credentialism is the preferential status accorded to professional or academic credentials such as licenses, certificates, degrees, or organizational memberships, especially in hiring practices. The class effects of credentialism are well documented, since college degrees, for instance, are more easily available to the upper and middle class, and a college graduate will often be hired over a non-graduate even when the two candidates are equal in merit.

Creeping normality

Creeping normality is a phenomenon whereby a radical change, introduced incrementally, is accepted as normal because each increment is in of itself too small to inspire serious objection. It is often used in reference to climate change, for instance, in which any given change year to year is fairly small until accumulated changes cause a "sudden" disaster, or to the disappearance of the wetlands in coastal regions, the suburbanization and development of former farm towns, or the increase in cost of certain services and utilities.

Critical mass

In nuclear physics, critical mass is the level of fissile material mass needed for a nuclear chain reaction to sustain itself. In social dynamics, critical mass is achieved when an innovation has been adopted by a sufficient number of members of a social system that the rate of adoption can sustain itself.

Critical reflection

Critical reflection is a critical thinking process in which the individual examines and assesses the assumptions, presuppositions, and biases that inform his understanding of the world. S. D. Brookfield identified three phases of critical reflection: the identification of assumptions, the assessment of their validity, and the transformation of the individual's body of assumptions into something more appropriate. In some schools of thought in education, concepts similar to critical reflection are called reflective practice, reflective thinking, or reflexivity. In cooperative education, many educators recommend critical reflection assignments for students, in order to better guide the development of their understanding.

Critical thinking

"A well-trained man knows how to answer questions," sociologist E. Digby Baltzell wrote in

Harper's in 1955, "An educated man knows what questions are worth asking." He was addressing the goals of Bell Telephone's new liberal arts program for its executives, founded in order to develop leadership within the organization among managers who had primarily technical backgrounds. The curriculum focused on none of the technical issues their work addressed, but rather on developing their intellects and their critical thinking faculties. Critical thinking is disciplined thinking, by a rational agent who is able to evaluate the information available to them and the relationships among pieces of that information, and analyze and synthesize the results in the process of developing their views. Key to critical thinking is the awareness of the process, of one's own biases and the biases of others, and the ability to see multiple sides of a scenario, rather than responding from emotion or "going by the gut."

Croly, Herbert

One of the intellectual leaders of the late-19th- and early-20th-century Progressive movement, Herbert Croly co-founded the liberal magazine *The New Republic*. His books *The Promise of American Life* (1909) and *Progressive Democracy* (1914) were among the most most influential books on American liberalism, calling for stronger and more effective federal institutions, commercial reforms including the adoption of workplace democracy, and constituting the strongest articulation of an American liberalism that is neither anti-capitalist nor pacifist, advocating the protection of democracy abroad and an economic system that both respects the worker and encourages American ingenuity. His works were a strong influence on the New Deal, though he died shortly after the Great Depression began, without seeing his ideas adopted as policy.

Cross-cultural communication

Cross-cultural communication is a discipline that studies the ways people from different cultural backgrounds communicate, both among themselves and with one another, and the different types and strategies of communication found in cultures. It developed during the Cold War, when both the private sector and governments found that foreign language training alone was not sufficient preparation for expanding their operations internationally.

Crowd manipulation

Crowd manipulation is the attempt to influence or control a crowd's behavior or beliefs, in contexts ranging from sales pitches to large crowds to political campaign rallies.

Crystallized intelligence

Crystallized intelligence is one of two factors of general intelligence, representing the ability to use previously acquired skills and knowledge in order to solve problems or perform tasks. Crystallized intelligence is the ability to use and apply one's knowledge, whereas its counterpart, fluid knowledge, is the ability to perform in new situations based on methodologies like inductive or deductive reasoning.

Crystallized self

In contrast with the idea—prevalent in self-help books and the popular imagination, somewhat less dominant in psychology—that each individual has a single true and authentic self, the idea of the "crystallized self" is that of a faceted individual capable of showing multiple equally true selves. Notions of what constitutes the true self are particularly key to discussions of authenticity and authentic leadership, and more broadly to the idea of identity as explored by the social sciences.

Cult of personality

The "cult of personality" is the phenomenon that arises around a particular leader to create an idealized and heroic image. The term is especially associated with the state-sponsored idealization of such leaders, through propaganda, media influence, and even policy issues, and so the classic modern-day examples are Kim Il-Sung and Kim Jong-Il of North Korea, and Joseph Stalin of the Soviet Union. The term is sometimes used—though rarely by political scientists—more loosely to refer to the lionization of a leader or the glorification of a leader, and in this sense has been used in reference to people like Gandhi and Martin Luther King, Jr.

Cultural determinism

Cultural determinism states that key elements of an individual's psychological makeup, including aspects of behavior and emotional responses, are determined by the culture in which they are raised. Not every aspect is culturally determined, and the extent of variation in any given aspect varies from culture to culture as well. For instance, rural New Englanders are certainly not all identical in behavior or psychology, but most would agree their stoicism is a behavior common to the culture. Because culture is itself the collective product of individuals, cultural determinism paints a picture of individuals collectively creating a structure that perpetuates certain values and behaviors.

Cultural diplomacy

Cultural diplomacy is diplomacy conducted through the exchange of cultural products of the nation, as a way of encouraging understanding of and even emotional investment in one's own country on the part of the targeted country. The United States, as the chief exporter of culture for much of the 20th century, essentially stumbled into cultural diplomacy without a plan; South Korea, on the other hand, has engaged in a specific program of cultural diplomacy in recent years, called Hallyu.

Cultural diversity

Cultural diversity is the presence of multiple cultures, especially the healthy coexistence and mutual respect of such cultures. Just as biodiversity, the wide variety of life on Earth, is thought to be necessary for and an indicator of the quality of the health of the planet's ecosystem, so too have organizations like UNESCO argued that cultural diversity is necessary for the health of humanity. By extension, cultural diversity can be valuable for an organization in introducing a greater variety of viewpoints and competencies. Ideally, diversity is integrated into the organization, rather than grafted onto it through a separate program.

Cultural heritage hypothesis

The cultural heritage hypothesis is one attempt to explain the origin of cultural differences in decision making. The hypothesis explains these and other cultural differences with reference to the major philosophies and values forming the basis of a culture—Confucian thought, for instance, for much of Asia, and Aristotelian thought for much of the West. The differences between these philosophical systems trickle down into differences in behavior, values, and priorities. This seems to discount the relevance of philosophical developments since, or at least to subordinate their relevance to that of the earlier schools of thought.

Cultural schema

Cultural schema are schema that exist throughout a culture rather than just for the individual. While an individual's schema are formed by experience, cultural schema are formed by shared experiences and represent norms, expectations, and shared knowledge. There are basic schema consisting of facts, like what the capital of the United States is, and more complex schema representing information individuals might have trouble explaining the origin of, like the toppings that could potentially taste good on a pizza, a schema that differs significantly by country and sometimes region. Other schema deal with social situations, social roles, etiquette, and values attached to certain behaviors or traits.

Culture and affect display

The expression and display of emotion varies considerably by culture, and seems to be most noticeable in the difference between Eastern and Western displays (very little work has been done on affect display or emotions in the cultures of sub-Saharan Africa or the indigenous cultures of Australia or the Americas). Generally speaking, affect display is subtler and more moderate in Asia than in Europe and the Americas. This difference is sometimes chalked up to the Eastern tendency toward collectivist cultures, compared to the Western sacralizing of individualism, with the implication that in an individualist culture, broader displays of emotion are encouraged and accepted. The relative stoicism of Eastern cultures historically contributed to the Western caricature of Asians as "inscrutable" or "mysterious." There are notable exceptions to these generalizations, and Finland in particular is noted for cultural norms discouraging broad affect display in public. Differences in affect display can lead to cross-cultural misunderstandings, as well as impact the extent to which an individual interacting with members of another culture is able to put his putative charisma and social skills to work.

Culture trust and distrust

Any culture may be thought of as a culture of trust or distrust. Cultures of trust are associated with greater well-being and economic growth, and members are better able to manage insecure situations. Individuals in cultures of distrust tend to perceive trusting individuals as naive or weak, and live in a culture of cynicism, exploitation, and corruption.

Cyber-harassment in the workplace

The sociological work on the effect of the Internet as a communication medium on the inhibitions and empathy of communicators is considerable, and at least some of this disinhibiting effect seems to hold even when the medium is not anonymizing—when the conversation is between people who know each other. Cyber-harassment and cyber-bullying are serious problems in modern culture, and the workplace is not immune to them. Messages sent by e-mail, messenger programs, or over social networks may bully their targets directly or may include sexist, racist, or otherwise offensive material that constitutes harassment. Further, the use of social networks, which are mediated outside the workplace, raises questions about the proper interaction between co-workers online, outside of work hours.

"Daisy"

"Daisy" was the most famous piece of Lyndon B. Johnson's 1964 presidential campaign against ultraconservative hawk Barry Goldwater. While its descendant in fear-mongering campaign ads, "Bear in the woods," positioned Ronald Reagan as the only president prepared for (presumably nuclear) conflict with Russia, "Daisy" warned against such conflict, and implied it would be much more likely under Goldwater. The ad depicts a 2-year-old girl picking the petals of a daisy while counting, fading into a missile launch countdown and a nuclear explosion. The final voiceover says, "Vote for President Johnson on November 3. The stakes are too high for you to stay home."

Dalai Lama

The Dalai Lama is a religious and sometimes political leader in Tibetan Buddhism, whose teachers are titled "lama." Certain lamas called tulkus are considered the reincarnations of enlightened beings of the past (before the Chinese invasion of 1950, there were thousands of tulkus in Tibet; there are now roughly 500). Tulkus, nearly all of whom are male, have specific lineages of reincarnation, and the current Dalai Lama is the fourteenth in the lineage, believed to be the manifestation of Avalokitesvara, the bodhisattva (enlightened being) who is the universal manifestation of compassion. At various times from the 1600s until the Chinese invasion, several Dalai Lamas served as the head of the Tibetan government. The 14th Dalai Lama has lived in exile since fleeing to India in 1959, and retired as head of the Tibetan government in exile in 2011. Though he mentioned in

Tenzin Gyatso, His Holiness The 14th Dalai Lama of Tibet (left), won the Nobel Peace Prize in 1989. The Dalai Lama is the longest-living incumbent. (Seattle Municipal Archives)

a 1970s interview that he expected to be the last Dalai Lama, he announced at the time of his retirement that the decision of whether or not to reincarnate would be made following discussions with other lamas and comment from the public of the Tibetan diaspora.

Decentralized decision making

Decision-making processes that are distributed across a group are called decentralized decision making, especially in large organizations where decision-making processes and authority can be distributed across multiple layers, so that workers have some amount of decision-making power over their own work, managers over the aims of the groups they manage, department heads over the purview of their departments, and so on.

Decision engineering

Decision engineering approaches organizational decision making from an engineering perspective, by incorporating best practices in order to provide a structured decision-making framework that is informed by complexity theory and systems thinking.

Decision making

The process of selecting a choice from multiple possibilities is one of the oldest areas of study in philosophy and the social sciences, and has been an important area of study in disciplines from political science and ethics to psychology and neuroscience. Studies may be, broadly, either descriptive—illustrating how individuals and groups make decisions—or prescriptive, presenting or justifying a preferred method.

Decision-making model of leadership

The decision-making model of leadership posits that leadership is fundamentally a decision-making activity (more than it is a relationship with followers, for instance). Like Situational Leadership Theory, this model is well-suited to leadership training because it supposes that leaders *can* be trained, and that leadership is a teachable skill.

Decision theory

Decision theory is the study of the underlying factors involved in making a decision, and of the optimality and rationality of the resulting decision. Decision theory is similar to game theory—and to a game theorist may simply appear to be a special case of game theory—and plays an important role in economics, philosophy, and the social sciences. It is correct both to speak of "decision theory," as in the field, and "a decision theory," as in the specific theoretical underpinnings of a decision-making methodology.

Deep blue sea

Wilfred Drath used the metaphor of the deep blue sea to explain the difference between leaders and leadership in leadership studies: leaders are the white caps of ocean waves, but they cannot be understood without understanding the mechanics of the deep blue sea below them. Drath differentiated these approaches as personal leadership (the Great Man–influenced study of the character and attributes of individual leaders) and relational leadership, the study of the deep blue sea, in the form of the system of relationships in which leadership takes place.

Defensive realism

An application of realism (cf.) in its international relations sense, defensive realism says that because survival is the main motivator of states and states act rationally, states will always act to maximize their own security and defenses.

Definition of the situation

In sociology, the definition of the situation consists of the characteristics of a given social situation, including the roles assumed by the participants, the norms and values governing or guiding their actions, and other elements. Successful social interaction requires agreeing to the definition of the situation, which is rarely explicit; in fact, in some situations, attempting to explicitly define the situation may be counterproductive or met with resistance.

Defense mechanism

In psychology, a defense mechanism is an unconscious coping strategy for dealing with anxiety. Common defense mechanisms discussed in Freudian psychoanalysis, for instance, include rationalization, in which the individual justifies his own bad behavior or impulses by concocting valid reasons to support it, turning it into "good" behavior and avoiding the anxiety of guilt; and repression, in which the individual buries an impulse or the feelings about a behavior rather than deal with them. Defense mechanisms are not inherently unhealthy, and become unhealthy only when they lead to unhealthy behavior or cause emotional damage. The presence of the defense mechanism is one of the factors explaining how people are able to behave in a way that is contrary to their stated beliefs and values. Defense mechanisms in the workplace can result in challenges for leaders. Workers may have developed unrealistic views of the quality of their work or their relationships with other people as the result of pathological defense mechanisms like the superiority complex, for instance, or may respond to stress in the workplace with passive aggression.

Healthy defense mechanisms include forgiveness—which relieves the individual of the anxiety of continuing to think about the wrong done against them—as well as emotional self-regulation.

Deformation professionnelle

The French phrase *deformation professionnelle* translates literally as "professional deformation," but might be better called "conditioning" or "socialization." The phrase captures the idea that one's profession, in part because it takes up so many waking hours and so many hours of concentration and engagement, shapes the way one views the world—not simply in positive ways by exposing one to valuable information about the workings of the world, but by distorting one's view. A common worry, for instance, is that police officers begin to see the world as one filled with criminals and victims, while the views of divorce lawyers on the virtues of marriage are the subject matter of a number of romantic comedies.

Deindividuation

Deindividuation is the phenomenon of diminished self-awareness and self-evaluation when in groups, often leading to a diminution of inhibitions.

Deliberative democracy

Deliberative democracy is a term coined by Joseph M. Bessette in his 1980 book of the same name, and refers to democratic government in which the decision-making process is committed to deliberation, not in lieu of voting but as a key component of the process. In the United States, the Green Party is the only party specifically committed to deliberative democracy, but various government and non-profit groups have encouraged deliberation in the run-up to specific legislative issues, notably health care reform.

Demagogue

The word *demagogue* originally meant a leader of the common people, with no specific connotation beyond that. The word comes from the ancient Greek, and in Athens the word came to be used to refer to violent and trouble-making lower-class citizens who were elected to office, usually after a campaign of emotional appeal, lies, and unkept promises. Demagogue has since come to mean a political leader who gains power by exploiting the fears, prejudices, and other negative emotions of the working class. Their political rhetoric is often marked by extremism, a call to action, and positions that eschew deliberation, compromise, and moderation in favor of decisiveness and easy to understand sound bites.

Demand control model

A model from positive psychology that promotes a workplace design of high demand and high control, in order to encourage employee learning and autonomy. Social support between managers and employees is important in this model, in order to place workers in positions that keep them active and interested in seeking out challenging situations.

Deming, W. Edwards

W. Edwards Deming introduced the Effiency movement to Japan after World War II, as part of the larger effort to modernize and Westernize aspects of Japanese industry. When Japan's postwar economy rebounded in the Japanese "economic miracle" of the 1950s, Deming was given much of the credit, especially by the United States, and he eventually returned to the United States to work as a consultant.

During the late 1970s and early 1980s, when economic competition with Japan's manufacturing sector was of chief concern to Americans, his expert opinion was sought to increase the efficiency of American industries, leading to a consultancy position with Ford (which in turn led to the launch of the Ford Taurus) and the publication of his book *Quality, Productivity, and Competitive Position*, later republished as *Out of the Crisis*. The book was the primary inspiration for the Total Quality Management movement, a revival of the Efficiency movement.

Democratic peace theory

Democratic peace theory, interdemocracy nonaggression theory, or mutual democratic pacifism are all terms to refer to the idea that democratic states are less likely to go to war with other democratic states. Explanations of the theory include the effect of war on reelection, the possibility of successful diplomatic institutions to resolve conflicts instead, and the inclination to view other democratic states favorably. Advocates of the theory sometimes conflict with the realist view that the world is in a constant state of war; on the other hand, critics of democratic peace theory point to the lack of a well-defined model of causality and the possibility that it is only an irrelevant correlation. Often relevant to the discussion is the much discussed fact that there have been no major European general wars since the end of World War II, an unprecedented period of peace that might be explained by the advent of the European Union or factors related to the Cold War and its dissipation. There have been some well-known wars between democracies, notably the Spanish–American and Mexican–American wars, the Boer wars, and the American Revolutionary War.

Depersonalization

In normal psychological context, depersonalization is the experience of watching oneself act with no sense of control, often accompanied with the feeling of being less real. It can be experienced by anyone and is often a response to trauma, but chronic depersonalization is associated with a variety of disorders. In social psychology, however, depersonalization is the perception of the self as the embodiment of a social stereotype rather than as a unique individual.

Descriptive

There is a divide in philosophy and many of the social sciences between the descriptive and the prescriptive. Descriptive work and research seeks to describe the world—descriptive approaches to sociology, for instance, model how people and institutions behave, while descriptive linguistic describes how people use language. Prescriptivism, in contrast, is occupied with defending the right way to do something, rather than showing the various ways people do that thing. Descriptive models of leadership focus not on recommending leadership approaches, but identifying what real-world leaders actually do (and, often, the effects of what they do).

Descriptive representation

Descriptive representation is the mathematical proportion of members of a given group who are elected or appointed to a given government body, such as the number of women in Congress. *See also* substantive representation

Design by committee

"Design by committee" is a pejorative term referring to a project that has been designed or managed with the input of multiple parties and has suffered for it. The pejorative dimension of an otherwise neutral-sounding, descriptive phrase may be a reference to the description of a camel as a "horse designed by committee," attributed to the automobile designer Alec Issigonis.

Deterrence theory

Deterrence theory was a military strategy used during the Cold War and was best articulated in Thomas Schelling's 1966 *Diplomacy of Violence.* The essence of the theory states that military strategy in the Cold War, because of the consequences of going to war, needed to be concerned with not just victory but with dissuading the other side from engaging in hostilities. Though Americans and Soviets spent most of the Cold War anticipating the beginnings of war, almost five decades passed from the end of their World War II alliance to the dissolution of communism without a single missile launched (though several proxy wars were fought, to neither side's satisfaction). Deterrence theory is essentially synonymous with nuclear deterrence: the amassing of a well-distributed and well-protected nuclear arms stockpile (though both of these adjectives have been questioned in hindsight) sufficient to dissuade the other party from attempting war due to the realities of Mutually Assured Destruction. Sixteen years after the end of the Cold War, several architects of deterrence theory—notably Henry Kissinger and George Shultz—disavowed it in a *Wall Street Journal* article in which they expressed their concerns about the threats posed by decades of nuclear weapons proliferation.

Dictatorial style

One of the leadership styles plotted on the managerial grid model, the dictatorial style was originally called the produce or perish style. Dictatorial managers have a high concern for production and low concern for people, and expect employees' pay to be sufficient motive to ensure performance and loyalty, or they risk being replaced. This is the same leadership style as Theory X (cf).

Dictatorship of the proletariat

In the works of Karl Marx, Friedrich Engels, and their followers, a dictatorship of the proletariat, in which the working class has seized political power, is a transitional step between capitalism—in which the capitalists possess the power—and communism, in which power is commonly owned. "Dictatorship" here means simply "rule," and modern translations of Marx sometimes reflect this, but the phrase entered the English language and fossilized before "dictatorship" became synonymous with "autocracy."

Differential psychology

Differential psychology is the psychological study of the ways and reasons that individuals exhibit different behaviors, including personality, intelligence and other mental capacities, skills and abilities, interests, self-concept and esteem, and morals.

Diffusion of innovations

Communications studies professor Everett Rogers introduced the theory of the diffusion of innovations in his 1962 book of the same name, which has remained in print and an important contribution in the study of ideas and technology. Innovations—new technologies or ideas—are, according to this theory, passed along through channels of communication by participants in the social system in which they have been introduced. Rogers helped popularize the term *early adopter*, in reference to opinion leaders who are among the first to adopt an innovation.

Diffusion of responsibility

Diffusion of responsibility is a phenomenon that occurs in groups, wherein any given individual is less likely to take the initiative to perform an action or resolve a problem if other people are present who could do so. In the workplace, this is one justification for the explicit division of labor and duties. In situations where someone needs help, this phenomenon is called the bystander effect, the most famous example of which is the typical portrayal of the Kitty Genovese murder. As it happens, that portrayal is inaccurate, but the idea of a woman having been murdered in full view of her neighbors, who did nothing to intervene or report the crime to the police, was the catalyst for much of the research into the diffusion of responsibility.

Dilbert Principle

The Dilbert Principle, introduced in the Dilbert comic strip by Scott Adams, states that the least competent people are promoted to management positions in order to shift them away from roles that actually perform work.

Diplomacy

Diplomacy is the art of negotiations that transpire between representatives of states, including trade and economics issues, human rights and environmental concerns, war and peace-making, as well as the everyday business of maintaining diplomatic relationships between states. In the modern world, diplomacy has arisen as a professional field, and ambassadors and their staffs are significant players in international affairs, largely unnoticed by the public. While the focus of history is often on the diplomats of the largest or most aggressive states, the role of small state diplomacy is slowly being recognized, as smaller states are so affected by the actions of larger states that diplomacy is one of the most vital tools available to ensure the protection of their interests. Diplomats act in accordance to policies over which they have no control—set by the executive and legislative branches—but nevertheless frequently take on leadership positions, negotiating terms of treaties, finding means of gaining strategic advantage over other states, and acting to avoid armed conflicts. Because of their importance, diplomats and their communication have long been considered untouchable by foreign powers, either by convention or—in the modern world—by international agreement.

Diplomat

See diplomacy

Diplomatic history

The history of international relations between countries, diplomatic history tends to focus specifically on the relevant foreign policy and trade relations of the countries involved, and the official negotiations between states, rather than cultural exchanges and informal contact between citizens. Diplomatic histories tend to focus on leaders, having been influenced by the Great Man histories, though some focus on the important role played by individual diplomats and the choices they make. Diplomatic histories go back as far as the ancient Greek Thucydides, but are especially associated with the 19th and 20th centuries; the 19th-century German historian Leopold von Ranke considered diplomatic history the most important field in history. Winston Churchill's 1948 history *The Gathering Storm* set the tone for even non-diplomatic histories of World War II in its portrayal of appeasement policies.

Direct democracy

Direct democracy is a form of democratic governance in which actions and policies are determined by the group, whether through voting, consensus building, or other means, rather than by elected representatives, as in representative democracy. Direct democracy invites the danger of the tyranny of the majority, concerns over which led to the framing of the U.S. government as a representative democracy. However, direct democracy practices are used in many American communities, as well as for specific kinds of laws and policies in every state (proposed constitutional amendments, for instance, and referred to the legislature by a vote of the people in almost every state, while 19 states give the people the power to recall an elected official through popular vote). Concerns with the electoral college, even before the controversial 2000 presidential election, have motivated a push for direct elections of the president, and technological advances have led some to advocate electronic direct democracy, facilitating participation in policy votes through computers.

Disney method

A problem-solving and idea-generating strategy developed by neuro-linguistic programming pioneer and motivational speaker Robert Dilts, the Disney method calls for the use of four different thinking styles, undertaken in sequence as the group adopts different roles: that of outsiders, to gain an external objective perspective; that of dreamers, to brainstorm creative solutions; that of realists, to examine the brainstormed ideas and their possible implementations; and that of critics, to evaluate the plan of the realists. Key to Dilts's method is that the same people perform these four roles, rather than distributing them to different people.

Dispositional affect

In psychology, dispositional affect is the personality trait that reflects an individual's general tendency toward positive or negative views and responses. It is not the same as optimism versus pessimism, though that is a convenient comparison. An individual with a high positive affectivity will tend toward optimism but also experiences positive moods more often and in a larger variety of circumstances, while experiencing generally high energy. Someone with high negative affectivity may be a pessimist but is also more easily upset, tends toward low self-esteem, becomes distressed when challenged, and tends to exhibit high levels of negative moods like nervousness, annoyance, fear, or melancholy. Dispositional affect is sometimes called the lens through which the individual sees the world—pink (as in rose-colored glasses) or black—and has a clear effect on the individual's interpersonal relationships and presence. Dispositional affect has experimentally demonstrated effects on both decision making and negotiation, as well—high-positive individuals are more open to cooperation, flexibility, and "outside the box" suggestions. Contrary to expectation of some researchers, risk aversion does not seem to be affected.

Dispute system

See complaint system

Dissanayake, Ellen

In her 1995 book *Homo Aestheticus*, anthropologist Ellen Dissanayake argues that there is an innate human need to "make special," and that accordingly, artistic activities should be considered in the same light as rituals and festivals, as ways in which humans approach aspects of their experience to "make special." The singling out of individuals as leaders is similarly "making special."

Dissident

A dissident actively opposes the power of a particular status quo. Although the term originally referred to those who separated from the Church of England, since the 1940s it has been used in political contexts, first to refer to critics of communism in eastern Europe. More recently it has been applied to Americans acting in opposition to key activities of the American government, such as Edward Snowden.

Divide and conquer

To "divide and conquer" is to break a group into smaller parts over which power can be maintained, or obtained, more easily than the whole, and to continue to prevent those smaller groups from consolidating. It is especially associated with imperialism, beginning with ancient Rome and practiced by the colonial powers during the 18th and 19th century, when European powers would create or encourage social divisions in African and Asian nations over which they held sway.

Divine right of kings

The doctrine of the divine right of kings states that the monarch receives his authority and legitimacy directly from God, and is thus bound by no earthly authority. This was the justification for absolute monarchy in Europe, though Catholics and Protestants tended to differ on the role of the church in such an arrangement, with the Catholic Church tending to favor a view of the pope as possessing an authority greater than those of any king (which created a check against the power of monarchs), as the representative of God, while Protestants were more likely to favor treating the church as an institution that answered to, or operated completely independent from, the state. The alliance between the pope and various monarchs of western Europe was an important one; the pope's endorsement of a monarch as chosen by God validated the power of each of them.

In Asia, a similar concept was the Mandate of Heaven.

Dollar diplomacy

Dollar diplomacy began as an American foreign policy in the late 19th and early 20th centuries, in which guaranteed loans were extended to foreign governments as enticement to get them to agree to American requests. It was especially key in American relations with Latin America.

Dominant minority

A dominant minority is a minority group that is sufficiently powerful to be politically or economically dominant in a country. This usually refers to ethnic minorities who, often for historical reasons, control the political or economic institutions of a country, such as the Russian-speaking Ukrainians of Ukraine, the Basque-Chileans of Chile, and the Americo-Liberians of Liberia. In the age of imperialism, it was also true of whites in South Africa and Rhodesia, the Dutch in the Dutch East Indies, and the French in Vietnam. On a smaller scale, dominant minorities may be found in cities where most of the key leadership and law enforcement positions are filled by the same ethnic minority, such as the whites of Ferguson, Missouri.

Draft

The draft is an informal U.S. term for the practice of military conscription—the compulsory enlistment of young men (almost exclusively) in the military, one of the oldest methods for populating an army. Since the political, cultural, and military failures of the Vietnam War, reviving the draft has been perceived as a political impossibility, but it was a driving force in the culture of young American men for over a century.

Dramaturgy

Dramaturgy is a framework in sociology, introduced by Erving Goffman in his 1959 *Presentation of Self in Everyday Life*, which describes social interactions in theatrical terms, and constructs them as dependent on time, setting, and audience. In particular, individual identity in dramaturgical sociology is presented as fluid, shaped in response to interactions with others, and scenes that are played out.

Drive theory

Drive theory is one of the "four psychologies" forming the foundation of modern psychology. Building on the work of Sigmund Freud, it studies psychological drives—the drive to meet a psychological need—and the phenomena that arise from the tension of unmet needs and the manner by which the individual meets those needs.

Drucker, Peter

Peter Drucker was a management consultant and author best known for his development of management by objectives, or management by results. His first major work, 1946's *Concept of the Corporation*, is an examination of General Motors and its relationship to society. His delineation of the interpersonal interactions within the company, the political environment, decision-making processes, and power structures, provided a new way to look at a business, arguably the most significant change in approaches to management since scientific management. He wrote 39 books in addition to running his management consulting firm, and his work became popular enough in Japan that a 2009 best-selling novel, *What if the Female Manager of a High-School Baseball Team Read Drucker's Management*, was adapted into both animated and live-action films. The Global Peter Drucker Forum is an annual international management conference devoted to his philosophy.

Dunning-Kruger effect

The Dunning-Kruger (DK) effect is a cognitive bias whereby an individual who is unskilled in a given area not only overestimates his ability in that area, but has difficulty recognizing the genuine ability of others in that area. It is named for David Dunning and Justin Kruger, Cornell University researchers who first conducted experiments testing it in 1999. Experiments also demonstrated that the bias is not permanent—learning the skill in question leads to recognition of one's previous incompetence. Media coverage of the DK effect focused on the tendency of people to overrate their abilities in areas where they lack skills and training, but equally interesting—and differentiating the cognitive bias from a superiority complex or the overconfidence effect—is the inability to recognize skill in others. The combination easily leads to circumstances in which someone continues to make poor choices informed by their own incompetence even when they have been advised otherwise by competent people, because they lack the grounding in the relevant area to recognize competence when they see it.

Dyad

In sociology, a dyad is the smallest possible social group, consisting of two people. Any two people who interact in some way constitute a dyad, and the strength and stability of the dyad is the result of their efforts, intensity, and the amount of time they spend together, as well as the relative rewards and costs that are incurred.

Early adopter

The term *early adopter* was introduced in Everett Rogers' 1962 book *Diffusion of Innovations* and has become well-known in the 21st century. Early adopters are among the first individuals who either (in the original coinage) become customers of a new product or (in the recent broader sense) adopt a new technology, process, approach, or idea. One may speak both of an individual being an early adopter of an iPhone and of a business being an early adopter of pay-by-smartphone-app technologies. Rogers described a bell curve, consisting (in order of adoption) of innovators, early adopters, early majority, late majority, and laggards. In this bell curve, it is important to note that early adopters are the second group to adopt an innovation; they are characterized by being choosier than the innovators (who are attracted to novelty), but still tend to be wealthier and more technologically literature than the majority. Their choosiness makes them important opinion leaders. In some cases, early adopters are an important part of the business model behind a new product: their purchases at higher prices, before the mass release of a cheaper model, essentially subsidize the cost of the product for later adopters; in other cases, the product they purchase is buggier or lacks key features introduced in the later version the majority will adopt, and their user experiences and feedback help to improve the product's design (which is not to say that they are acknowledged as beta testers).

Eating your own dog food

Eating your own dog food is the practice of a company using its own products as evidence of their faith in those products. In 1981, for instance, Apple Computer eliminated the use of typewriters in their offices, in favor of Apple computers for all word processing, spreadsheets, etc. In contrast, the adoption of AOL e-mail by Time Warner after the 2001 merger of the two companies was seen as disastrous,

because there was no way to import old e-mails, which were lost as a result.

Economic history

Economic history uses both historical and statistic methods to study historical events, trends, and institutions from the perspective of modern economic theory. This may encompass areas of labor history or international relations. Often a goal is to demonstrate the validity of economic theories with reference to the past, or to increase understanding of economic theory through an economic understanding of the past.

Educational psychology

Educational psychology is the branch of psychology that studies learning, especially but not limited to the study of formal educational settings and the ways to optimize the experience. The study of learning encompasses individual, group, and organizational learning and experiences, memory, cognition and conceptualization, instruction, and the impact on the learning experience of other psychological factors. For instance, developmental psychology and educational psychology share an interest in how young children learn.

Efficiency movement

The Efccciency movement was a decentralized movement in business practices, especially in the industry and the public sector, in the late 19th and early 20th centuries. In the United States, the Efficiency movement (which had the support of many of the age's business tycoons, like Andrew Carnegie) was part of the larger Progressive movement which was inspired by the scientific and technological advances of the 19th century to seek scientifically informed improvements to as many aspects of life

A PRACTICAL FORESTER
(A subject that had attention all through Mr. Roosevelt's Presidency.)

A 1908 editorial cartoon featuring Theodore Roosevelt, who was staunchly committed to conserving natural resources. The conservation movement came to prominence during the Progressive era. (Public Domain)

as possible. One of the most far-ranging social movements in the United States, Progressivism encompassed efforts as varied as modernizing facilities for the mentally ill in light of the new psychological science, improving services to the poor and sick in order to reduce poverty, creating state- or nation-wide standards for free public education, increasing the rights of workers and women, and creating professional standards and governing bodies for roles like doctors and lawyers. The Efficiency movement sought to maximize the utility of the advances of the Industrial Revolution, by making factory work as efficient as possible through scientific management (cf.), and to create a class of trained bureaucrats. Chicago, for instance, was the first of several cities to create an Efficiency

Division in 1910, examining city employees' performance and standardizing procedures for maximum efficiency. Schools of business administration offered management training programs for both the public and private sector, and Efficiency spread even to the use of natural resources, thanks to Theodore Roosevelt's staunch commitment to conservationism. The Efficiency movement finally fell out of favor due to Herbert Hoover's failure to adequately deal with the Great Depression of 1929; Hoover was the president most strongly associated with the movement, in part due to his background as an engineer.

Effort heuristic

The effort heuristic is an idea in psychology saying that people assign a value to a thing based on their perceptions of the effort that went into it, rather than simply its quality or function. This also affects the efforts people put into their work: if the goal does not seem valuable, their efforts will be diminished. Similarly, people observing their work will undervalue it if they believe it came easily, independent of their performance quality.

Ego psychology

Ego psychology is one of the "four psychologies" forming the foundation of modern psychology. It consists of the study and elaboration of Sigmund Freud's model of the mind as being divided into id, ego, and superego: instinct (id), judgment (superego), and the mediator between them (ego).

Egocentric advice discounting

In the social science study of advice, egocentric advice discounting is the tendency of a decision-maker to prioritize advice they receive that is closely aligned to the preconceptions and opinions they had formed before seeking advice. This is functionally similar to confirmation bias.

Elites

In political science, the elites or power elite are a small group of people with disproportionate political power or wealth. Leadership studies in political science have typically focused on members of this group, including heads of state, government officials, and leaders of political movements. C. Wright Mills's 1957 book *The Power Elite* discussed elites in America as primarily a group of prep school and Ivy League educated–WASPs from well-established wealthy families, from which group a disproportionate number of political and military leaders have come. Mills distinguishes the power elite from the more British idea of a ruling class because its power is consolidated through association with wealth-generating and -preserving organizations rather than through the British class system, which is more concerned with social ties and family prominence than with wealth.

Elitism

Elitism is the belief that a particular group of people, because of a particular kind of superiority (usually based on class, wealth, or education), generates opinions and judgments that should be lent greater weight than those of others. It is compatible with ideas like Plato's philosopher kings, but when the elite group is defined broadly enough, it is also at the heart of such things as literacy tests for voter registration.

Elizabeth I

The Queen of England from 1558 until 1603, Elizabeth I was the last monarch of the Tudor dynasty, and the daughter of Henry VIII. She came to the throne as a young woman in a tumultuous time, the third monarch in a five-year span, succeeding her half-brother Edward VI and half-sister Mary, the latter of whom had attempted to remarry the Church of England back to Rome after Henry had severed its ties, and had imprisoned Elizabeth for suspected conspiring with Protestants. Despite or because of this, Elizabeth was a moderate both politically and religiously, reestablishing the Church of England, reducing factionalism in her government, and playing it safe in foreign affairs. She never married and was believed to remain a virgin all her life. The Elizabethan era now named for her included the dramas and poetry of William Shakespeare and Christopher Marlowe, the voyages of Francis Drake, the first English settlements in the New World, and the music of composers like William Byrd and Thomas Campion. It is still considered a golden age for the country.

Emerson, Harrington

Inspired by Frederick Winslow Taylor, management consultant Harrington Emerson adopted scientific management principles—originally developed for factory labor—for the Santa Fe Railway, creating a division between staff employees, who worked as managers, and line employees, who did most of the labor. Bonuses were paid for better-than-average work, as well as to foremen, and time studies were performed in order to set standards for each task (after first standardizing equipment throughout the railway).

Emotional aperture

Emotional aperture is the ability to perceive group emotions, rather than focusing only on the affect display of a single person. Leaders skilled at emotional aperture are able to perceive the affective diversity of their group and the relative high positives and low negatives of the moods in play, in addition to "taking the temperature of the room" and determining the most common emotion in the group. This is an aspect of emotional intelligence, but most tests and studies of emotional intelligence have focused on one-on-one interactions.

Emotional competence

Emotional competence is related to emotional intelligence, and consists of the ability to express and vent one's emotions, rather than suppressing or ignoring them. Psychologists believe emotional competence is an important component of well-being.

Emotional contagion

Emotional contagion is the unintentional emulation or reflection of one person's emotions by another person, especially beginning with mimicry of their emotional expressions, followed by reflections of the emotions themselves. Emotional contagion has been subject to extensive research that has found people's emotions are heavily influenced by the non-verbal emotion-indicating cues of others, such that they can reflect emotions they are not even aware the other person is feeling. Neuroscientists have theorized that mirror neurons may be implicated in the mechanism of emotional contagion. Emotional contagion received considerable press in 2014 after the revelation that Facebook had carried out an experiment on over half a million users by manipulating their news feed to measure the extent to which exposure to negative emotions in others' status feeds would result in posting similar emotional statuses.

Emotional intelligence

Emotional intelligence is the capacity to perceive, understand, and manage emotions. The concept was developed in the 1990s, and

various attempts have been made to quantify emotional intelligence in individuals, as well as to link high scores to leadership ability. There is disagreement as to whether emotional intelligence measures something distinct from existing personality tests and metrics, or if it represents something already described by models like the Big Five. The term was first coined by Daniel Goleman, in whose formulation it consists of five components: self-awareness, self-regulation, internal motivation, empathy, and social skills.

Emotional self-regulation

Emotional self-regulation is the ability to have emotional responses to changing circumstances that are honest and authentic while at the same time remaining within the bounds of social norms and continuing to function in one's life. Although to some degree this means keeping an even keel—not giving in to drastic sways in mood or wallowing in emotional extremes—it also entails modulating behavior even when internal emotions are strong. For instance, upon hearing of a death in the family, an individual may wait until they are home, or at least no longer in a public setting, before bursting into tears. And tears or no, emotional self-regulation allows that individual to deal with the pragmatic post-mortem processes like funeral arrangements, notifying friends and family and employers, dealing with the will, and so on, without simply repressing grief and anger. In leaders, emotional self-regulation is an important part of professionalism.

Emotional tyranny

Communication Studies professor Vincent Waldron coined the term *emotional tyranny* in 2000 to refer to the use of emotions and emotional displays by leaders and influential members of a group in ways that are cruel, damaging, or are motivated by seeking control. Tactics of such tyranny include using emotional language to describe employees, rather than describing their behavior or the results of their work; using emotional displays as a punishment or threat, such as subjecting workers to angry tirades or displays of disappointment, especially as a way to manipulate their behavior; and including emotional language in workplace communications. Emotional tyranny is especially associated with aggressive displays of emotion, but Waldron's description would also be consistent with a manipulative form of passive aggression in a supervisor whose employees work not under threat of an enraged outburst, but the threat of crying, guilt, or panic at the prospect of goals not being met.

Emotions in the workplace

The importance of the emotional states of the workplace and the emotional impact of events and processes at work has enjoyed greater attention in research since the publication of Arlie Hochschild's 1983 *The Managed Heart*. Emotions of individuals and groups play a role in the social health of the workplace and the engagement, absenteeism, and satisfaction of individual workers, while the negative use or expression of emotions is consistently associated with poor leadership.

Empathic accuracy

Empathic accuracy is a specific measure of empathy, measuring the accuracy with which an individual can determine the feelings and emotional state (and possibly the causes and contexts thereof) of another person. The term was coined in 1988 and has been the subject of neuroscience research, which has shown that the two areas of the brain most associated with it are (1) affect sharing, the ability to share the emotion the other person is feeling; and (2) mentalizing, the ability to think about and label that emotion. The increased public awareness of autism spectrum disorders and Asperger's syndrome in the 21st century has, in turn, increased awareness of how fundamental processes like empathy are to the everyday social interactions of people who are not on the spectrum.

Empathy

Empathy is the human ability to recognize and understand the emotions felt by another, and to be influenced by them—to feel happy because of another person's joy, for instance, or be moved to anger by another person's rage. It includes the ability to emotionally engage in fiction or other representations (including movies, music, nonfictional biographies, and other works in which individuals' emotions are portrayed). Empathy is not an all-or-nothing capacity—we may sometimes perceive that someone is feeling a negative emotion, but have difficulty, especially if we lack the context of what has brought them to this state, pinpointing whether it is anger, guilt, or sadness. Empathy is not the same as sympathy—recognizing emotion, even understanding its sources, does not require feeling tender toward them or perceiving them as in need. It is the precursor to emotional contagion, however. Empathy is a significant factor in interpersonal interactions, one that has been extensively studied but for which extensive study yet remains. It is key to certain forms of intelligence, and likely to charismatic and authentic leadership styles.

"The Emperor's New Clothes"

"The Emperor's New Clothes" is one of Hans Christian Andersen's fairy tales, first published in 1837 as the third booklet in his *Fairy*

Tales Told for Children series, along with "The Little Mermaid." The story is perhaps his most familiar today: the Emperor, motivated by his vanity, purchases new clothes from con men who convince him that they are invisible only to the stupid and incompetent. Though they present him with nothing at all, the Emperor pretends to be impressed by them so as not to seem stupid; his ministers do likewise, as do the townsfolk when the Emperor parades before them. Only a naive child who does not understand the desire to conform cries out that the Emperor is naked. Often told today as a parable about groupthink, in its time it was likely also a criticism of the growing bureaucracy and the hopeless leaders who were led by their advisers.

Empire building

Empire building is the acquisition of resources outside a country's borders for the purpose of expanding that country's size, power, or influence, and is used figuratively to refer to the territorial expansion of individuals and groups in a corporate culture by exerting control over increasing numbers of projects.

Employee

An employee provides labor to a business on an ongoing basis, almost always in a specific job role. In American labor law, "employee" has legal dimensions of meaning that are more specific than "worker," bearing on certain protections and rights as well as the taxes paid by an employer, compared to the situation faced by, for instance, independent contractors, who receive pay but not benefits, and are technically operating their own business which sells labor to the client business. Nevertheless, in this volume "employee" and "worker" are used synonymously except when otherwise noted.

"Employee engagement," for instance, describes a concept frequently relevant to independent contractors as well, but is more commonly found in the literature than the more inclusively phrased "worker engagement."

Employee engagement

Employee engagement is a positive outcome of a healthy relationship between an organization and its employees, resulting in employees who are interested in their work and feel a sense of satisfaction when it is done well or achieves positive results. Employee engagement requires a good match between the employee's role in the organization and their self-image, as well as between their beliefs about their role and the actual day-to-day work they do. That is, they should intuitively understand not only why the work is being done, but why they are the ones doing it.

Employee morale

Employee morale is the well-being and satisfaction of an employee and is a significant contributor to productivity, while low morale is correlated with absenteeism and turnover.

Employee silence

Employee silence is the withholding of information relevant to an organization by its employees, either by choice or because proper communication channels have not been established nor use of them encouraged.

Employee survey

An employee survey is one distributed to employees throughout an organization and is used to monitor employee feelings about their compensation, their job role, their working environment, and any problems in the course of their work. Employee surveys are a valuable diagnostic tool but also a source of resentment if they do not lead to a satisfying response when problems are reported.

Employeeship

Employeeship is a Swedish management philosophy in which a partnership between managers and employees replaces the traditional leadership hierarchy, in order to cultivate a supportive work environment in which managers act as facilitators for employees' skills and ideas.

Empowerment

Empowerment is the process of increasing the strength and engagement of a group or individual. In the last few decades, employee empowerment has become an increasingly popular concept in management theory, and empowerment is often considered one of the leadership competencies. Increasing the strength of employees means giving them greater authority, responsibility, and autonomy in the performance of their jobs, without overburdening them with tasks for which they are not prepared. Communication is important, as are clear boundaries so that the employee does not feel adrift rather than empowered. Many people stress the importance of mentoring here as well. Medical leadership researcher C. A. Rajotte, in the 1996 *The Kansas Nurse* article "Empowerment as a Leadership Theory," listed educating, leading, structuring, providing, mentoring, and actualizing as the methods of empowering, in combination with team-building and power-sharing.

Engineering management

Engineering management is an approach to management that brings an engineering mindset to business management. While there is overlap with industrial engineering, industrial engineers are not always managers, whereas engineering managers are typically trained in both engineering and business, often earning a degree in each. (A small number of programs teach engineering management as its own discipline, including Rensselaer Polytechnic Institute, George Washington University, and West Point.)

Enhancers

In substitutes for leadership theory, enhancers are workplace factors that increase the effectiveness of leadership. These include experienced followers, non-routine tasks, group norms that encourage cooperation, and leaders who have the ability to reward followers with a reward that is relevant and valuable to them.

Entrepreneur

An entrepreneur is a person who starts a business and bears responsibility for its success or failure. Economic studies of entrepreneurship are among the antecedents to modern leadership studies, as there have been debates and theories about the traits, qualities, and behaviors of entrepreneurs, and the effects of these factors on the success of their businesses since at least the 18th century, when Richard Cantillon described the entrepreneur as a risk-taker who made his fortune by identifying and taking advantage of new opportunities despite their uncertain outcome. Similarly, in the 1960s, Peter Drucker described the entrepreneur as one who looks for changes in the marketplace or available technologies and develops them into profitable ventures. Many economists have described entrepreneurs as necessary to or healthy for the economy, as they pioneer new areas of business that can later be entered by more risk-averse organizations. Barriers to entrepreneurship have thus largely been viewed as unhealthy restrictions.

Entrepreneurial leadership

Entrepreneurial leadership consists of using the skills of an entrepreneur in order to lead an organization, and when advocated, is often contrasted with a "corporate mind-set" that has become stagnant through risk aversion and hidebound fixation on procedure. Entrepreneurs, in contrast, are risk-friendly, innovative, and adept at managing change. The classic example is Apple's Steve Jobs, who led his company from the early days of personal computing when not everyone in the industry was even convinced of the long-term demand for personal computers to an age of mobile devices that his company virtually created.

Environmental psychology

Environmental psychology is an interdisciplinary branch of applied psychology that examines the relationship between individuals and their surrounding environment, including the natural and built environments as well as the social world. Environmental psychologists are concerned with improving built environment design, especially workplaces, housing, and public spaces, in order to improve human well-being.

Episcopal ordination

Episcopal ordination in the Catholic Church is the process of elevating a priest to the position of bishop, a role conferring greater responsibilities and duties, notably the administration of the Catholic community in specific bishopric regions (called dioceses in the Roman Catholic Church and eparchies in the Eastern Catholic Churches). Less numerous than priests, more numerous than cardinals, bishops constitute an important part of Catholic leadership, and a shortage of bishops at various times and places (such as during the colonizing of North America) has been considered a serious concern.

Equal consideration of interests

The principle of equal consideration of interests states that the interests of all involved or affected parties should be considered equally when determining the correct course of action in a situation. Though the concept dates back at least as far as utilitarianism, the principle was coined by Peter Singer in his 1979 *Practical Ethics*, which explores the ramifications of the principle in dealing with equality, disability, embryo experimentation, euthanasia, political violence, overseas aid, refugees, and (in the third edition) climate change, as well as addressing whether there is a moral obligation to help others.

ERG theory

Existence, Relatedness, and Growth (ERG) is a psychological theory formulated by Clayton Paul Alderfer and based on Abraham Maslow's hierarchy of needs. ERG theory reclassifies Maslow's five-tiered hierarchy into three groups. The Existence group of needs consists of those things needed for basic material existence, such as a safe environment in which to live, food, sleep, and security, and so includes Maslow's Physiological and Safety tiers. The Relatedness group combines Belongingness and Esteem, and includes the human needs related to social interaction. The Growth group overlaps with Maslow's Esteem tier and includes his Self-Actualization tier, and includes the needs that address the human desire for personal growth.

Escalation of commitment

Escalation commitment or irrational escalation is the phenomenon whereby decision-makers continue to pursue a course of action despite new evidence suggesting it should be abandoned or re-evaluated, as in the proverb of throwing good money after bad. The phenomenon often results from cognitive biases like the overconfidence effect, overplacement, and the Dunning-Kruger effect, all of which cause people to put too much faith in their own judgment and skills. Gambling is a common example of escalation of commitment, as are the American government's commitments to the Vietnam and Iraq wars, but the phenomenon is seen in numerous areas.

Ethical leadership

Ethical leadership is leadership that is guided by a moral code that both informs the decisions they make and their approach to leading, in their interactions with and treatment of followers, colleagues, superiors, and others. While other theories of leadership do not specifically advocate immorality, many approaches to leadership have been essentially amoral, focused on the bottom line—which is one source of the "Hitler problem" (cf.), as it complicates the evaluation of a leader who meets goals but is morally abhorrent, or one whose goals themselves are morally abhorrent. The tendency toward a people-focused approach to leadership naturally leads to the advocacy of ethics in leadership, which is compatible with many different leadership models. The founder of the Center for Ethical Leadership, Bill Grace, proposed the 4-V Model of Ethical Leadership, consisting of Values, Vision, Voice, and Virtue, with additional elements including Service (connecting Vision and Values), Polis (political engagement, connecting Vision and Voice), and Renewal (the reevaluation of one's actions, connecting Voice and Values).

Ethics

Ethics, ethical theory, or moral theory is the branch of philosophy that addresses moral values of conduct. Unlike most areas of philosophical inquiry, most ethics work is normative or applied—devoted to determining the best way to determine the right course of action, and the right course of action for a given situation—whereas most philosophy is more concerned with theory than its applications. Ethics is not a school or approach to philosophy, but rather an area of inquiry; it is more important to some philosophers and schools than others.

Ethology

Ethology is the study of animal behavior under natural conditions (as opposed to behaviorism, which studies the behavioral responses of animals in controlled studies, such as the famous example of Ivan Pavlov's dogs). Since E. O. Wilson's 1975 *Sociobiology: The New Synthesis*, especially, ethology has been concerned with the behavior of and within animal social groups, rather than of individuals. This trend in ethology occasionally dovetails with the rise of evolutionary psychology, which seeks evolutionary explanations for human social behavior, and serious attention is given to parallels between human and animal behaviors. Recent work such as that of Roberto Bonanni's group finds commonality in leadership behavior among humans and free-ranging dogs.

Evaluating leadership

Lewis Edinger, in a 1975 article in *Comparative Politics*, categorized evaluations of leadership as using two kinds of criteria: intrinsic and extrinsic. Intrinsic criteria examine how the leader's group performed relative to its objectives, and perhaps measures like profit, cost, efficiency, customer or employee satisfaction, and so forth. Extrinsic criteria compare the leader's performance to the observer's own values and ideas of how leading should be conducted.

Evaluation

An evaluation is an assessment of an employee's, group's, department's, or project's performance relative to goals, along with feedback and other details.

Evolutionary leadership theory

At the intersection of evolutionary psychology and organizational psychology is evolutionary leadership theory, which presumes that significant traits related to the leader–follower relationship are evolved adaptations. Parallels between human leadership relationships and leadership in the animal world, especially primates, are important, but so is the distinction between leadership and simple social dominance, which is typically motivated by competition for limited resources. In its prescriptive mode, evolutionary leadership theory focuses on the importance of developing followers rather than subordinates.

Evolutionary psychology

Evolutionary psychology is an interdisciplinary intersection of basic psychology and evolutionary biology, concerned with the role of human evolution in mental and psychological traits, from personality to the functions of memory and language. Evolutionary psychology does not propose that all psychological traits within humanity are evolved adaptations, but rather seeks to uncover which traits are. Most evolutionary biologists are adaptationists, meaning that they consider natural selection to have exerted considerable power on the development of human psychology, through psychological traits that are the products of adaptation.

Executive

"Executive," "leader," and "manager" are used quasi-synonymously, but when distinctions are made, "executive" typically refers to someone in upper-level management at a tier consisting of the top 10 percent (or less) of an organization. Executives often have roles with greater autonomy than lower-level managers, and include department heads and vice presidents.

Executive development

Executive development is any activity aimed at fostering and developing the skills and behaviors of the executives of an organization, or those who are on track to be appointed to such positions. Many larger organizations have a dedicated executive development process or team, which may include training seminars, training in skills such as processes and operations of the company, or team building and communication exercises.

Executive education

Executive education programs are operated for business executives and high-level managers. Usually offered by a graduate school arm of a business school, they are rarely degree-granting or credit-bearing, but teach skills for upper-level management, ranging from leadership and communication skills to corporate finance and management theory. The fastest-growing sector of the market is customized executive education programs, which are constructed for a single company's executives as part of their executive development activity.

Expectancy theory

Expectancy theory, first proposed by management professor Victor Vroom in 1964, says that an individual's behavior is motivated by their expectations of the outcome of that behavior, especially as compared to alternatives. (A lottery ticket buyer does not expect that purchasing a ticket will lead to winning, for instance, but *does* expect that purchasing a ticket increases their odds of winning, compared to not buying a ticket.) Vroom proposed this theory in order to point out the need for organizations to directly tie worker rewards to performance, and to ensure that they are of a type appropriate to motivate the worker. The basic variables involved in expectancy theory are valence, the desirability of a given outcome; expectancy, the individual's belief that his effort at attempting a task will be successful; and instrumentality, the individual's belief that succeeding at a task will lead to the given outcome. Difficult goals like winning the lottery or setting a sales record have a low expectancy, which lowers the individual's motivation even when the valence is very high.

Expectancy violations theory

Expectancy violations theory (EVT) is a communications theory explaining peoples' reactions to unexpected behavior from other people. Violation refers to the transgression of a rule or norm, possibly explicit but more often implicit and sometimes specific to the individuals involved, as when a friend suddenly seems to act out of character. EVT originated in communication research on reactions to violations of personal space, such as in Judee Burgoon's 1976 Nonverbal Expectancy Violations Model. Like expectancy theory, EVT focuses on expectancy and valence. Violation valence is the positive or negative value the individual assigns to another person's breach of expectations, while communicator reward valence is the value the individual assigns to the person himself, based on their ability to bring value to the individual in the future. For instance, a loved one, who is valued by the individual and has great power to reward the individual in the future through ongoing displays of love, is typically accorded greater access to personal space than a casual friend.

Expert authority

Expert authority is authority that a leader enjoys when his team respects his skills or knowledge in a given area and is confident in his use of those skills.

Expert power

Expert power is one of John R. P. French and Bertram Raven's bases of power, and one of Patrick J. Montana and Bruce H. Charnov's varieties of organizational power. Expert power is influence that can be exerted because of one's special skills or knowledge, especially as proven by credentials or reputation.

Experiential education

Experiential education is an approach to education that emphasizes the importance of experiential learning. Experiential education is a common approach to job training, and has become increasingly important in management training and organizational development. Several learning games have been developed for experiential education.

Experiential learning

Experiential learning is learning through direct experience and subsequent reflection on the experience. Building on the work of developmental psychologist Jean Piaget and educational reformer John Dewey, educational theorist David Kolb popularized experiential learning, and introduced a four-element model with Ron Fry: concrete experience, observation of and reflection on that experience, abstraction and conceptualization following reflection, and testing of new concepts.

Experimental political science

Experimental political science—the use of experiments for discovery in political science—is a newer area of political science than theory is, and even today many political scientists are skeptical about the utility of experimentation over analysis of existing data. Typically, experimental political science focuses on voter psychology, including polling methodology, effects of media coverage, and impacts on voter turnout, and the effects of different voting systems, both by the electorate and by legislators.

Exploitative authoritative

One of Rensis Likert's management systems, in the exploitative authoritative system, leaders motivate their workers through negative incentives like threats and punishment. Decision-making power is not well distributed through the hierarchy, with most decisions made at the top levels and most communication conducted one way from the top down.

Extra-role behavior

Extra-role behavior (ERB) was defined in 1995 by Linn Van Dyne, L. L. Cummings, and Judi Mclean Parks, building on the work of Dennis Organ and others on Organizational Citizenship Behavior. Both concepts refer to employee behavior that benefits the organization, but lies outside the behavior that is explicitly asked of the employee by organizational policies or the definition of his duties. Since the 1960s, studies have shown that these behaviors are key to an organization's overall effectiveness and well-being. However, ERB encompasses behavior that not only is not requested by the employee's role definition or policies but actually dissents. Principled organizational dissent, for instance, protests injustice in the organization, while whistle blowing reports wrongdoing within or by the organization, both of which are held to be for the good of the organization by correcting its behavior.

Extraversion

Extraversion is one of the "Big Five" personality traits, characterized by the individual's engagement with the outside world. Extraverts are perceived by others as full of energy or "the life of the party," and feel positive about their interactions with other people in social situations, including strangers. Extraversion and its opposite, introversion, exist on a continuum, though individuals because of their past experiences or other personality traits may feel more or less extraverted in specific types of social environments.

Extrinsic motivation

Extrinsic motivation is motivation to perform a behavior that is introduced from outside the individual. Both rewards and punishments are extrinsic motivations, whether explicit and agreed upon in advance (grades and detention for students) or implicit and assumed (the reaction of the crowd to sports or other performances). Certain approaches to education, parenting, and management favor extrinsic motivation as a way to condition individuals' behavior, and extrinsic factors can provide motivation in cases where no intrinsic motivation exists.

Eye contact

Eye contact is an important part of nonverbal communication, typically seen in Western cultures as a sign of confidence and honesty during conversation, as well as a way to direct another person's attention. Aversion to eye contact is often interpreted as insecurity or deviousness, which leads to misunderstandings due not only to cultural differences but different levels of social comfort among individuals within a culture.

Fa

In Chinese philosophy, fa is a concept sometimes translated as "law" or "model," as in a

Eye contact is thought to have a large influence on social behavior, and is often a sign of confidence and social communication, while a lack of eye contact can give the impression of insecurity or dishonesty. (Wikimedia Commons/Bild Bundersarachiv)

model for behavior. It originated in the Mohist school (cf. Mozi), in which fa were required to pass the "three tests" (or criteria): they must have precedence in the sage kings, who represented a Golden Age of the Chinese past; they must be logically sound; and they must benefit the people and the state. Though Confucianism displaced the Mohist school, the concept of fa remained important in Chinese thought and political philosophy.

Facial expression

Facial expressions are one of the major forms of nonverbal communication, and carry much of the weight of social information in face-to-face human conversation. Facial expressions carry so much meaning that according to some studies, a small percentage (less than 1 percent) of the population can detect lying based on facial expression without special training.

Facilitator

The role of the facilitator emerged in the business world in the 1980s, though it has been an important role in Quaker decision-making meetings since the 18th century, and in various protest movements for much of the 20th century. A facilitator runs a meeting but is not a chief decision-maker the way a department chair or business head is, and is not interested in presenting or persuading people to support a specific plan. Impartiality is part of their goal, and they simply guide the conversation, sometimes according to a specific predetermined protocol. Facilitators set the agenda for the meeting, call on those who are to speak and ensure that they have the space to do so, and moderate the discussion without commenting on its merits.

Family as model for the state

Since the ancient Greek philosophers, various thinkers have proposed an understanding of the operations and structure of the state with reference to analogous structures in the family unit. By extension this has meant a model of the leader as a parental figure—usually explicitly a father. Some models have focused on the family as a model of the relationship between the leader and his subjects, while others have used it to explain relationships within the state's leadership, such as between a monarch and the aristocracy.

Fayolism

Fayolism was a management theory developed by French mining engineer Henri Fayol, similar to but developed independently from scientific management, around 1900. Fayolism's key distinction compared to Frederick W. Taylor's work in scientific management is in its focus on management rather than on the task. The five principles of Fayolist management are planning, organizing, command (the implementation of the plan, with proper allocation of resources and motivation of employees), coordination (the harmonizing of activities among managers, and communication between elements of the organization), and control (the evaluation and improvement of performance and communication). Fayol also staunchly advocated face-to-face communication over written communication, contrary to the conventional wisdom at the time, which favored the formality of letter writing.

Fear mongering

The use of fear to influence the feelings or behaviors of others. While fear mongering could capitalize on reasonable levels of fear of legitimate dangers, it is more commonly associated with the creation or inspiration of hyperbolic fear. The most famous modern examples are found in political campaign advertisements, especially "Daisy" and "Bear in the woods" (cf.), but there are many cases of leaders and authority figures using fear as a motivator, from parents and educators exaggerating the effects of drug use or poor grades to influence their childrens' behavior to managers who keep employees in a state of fear for their jobs.

Ferguson, Missouri

Ferguson, Missouri, is a small predominantly black city in the Greater St. Louis metropolitan area. In August 2014, it became the first American site to which Amnesty International sent delegates to witness and gather testimony about human rights abuses, during protests following the fatal shooting of unarmed black teenager Michael Brown by local police. The police response to the protests, including the use of military equipment, widespread tear-gassing of nonviolent protesters, arrests of journalists, refusal by officers to provide their own names or badge numbers, and numerous incidents of police officers pointing loaded weapons at unarmed protesters and journalists even when they knew they were on camera, was widely held as a critical failure of leadership. Governor Jay Nixon and President Barack Obama both faced criticism for not responding more decisively in the first two weeks; Nixon in particular was berated for issuing a curfew rather than publicly taking disciplinary action against the various police officers and authorities at fault. The protests raised important issues about the continuing problem of personal and institutional racism in the United States, disparate treatment of blacks and whites by the justice system, the militarization of local and state police, and the proper limits on police power. In the aftermath, among the investigations launched by local, state, and federal authorities, the U.S. Commission on Civil Rights requested a Justice Department investigation into the racial makeup (nearly all white) of the Ferguson city council and police force.

Fiedler, Fred

Fred Fiedler is an influential organizational psychologist who introduced the contingency theory of leadership. Contingency theory is a behaviorist approach to decision making that says the optimum decision is contingent on situation specifics. Fiedler built on the work of the Ohio State and Michigan leadership studies, and used contingency theory to explain the failures of scientific management, which took a "one size fits all" approach to leadership. Fiedler was also instrumental in focusing on the role of stress in leadership and the way interpersonal dynamics can drive decision making as much or more than rationally perceived pros and cons.

Fiedler contingency model

The contingency model of leadership developed by Fred Fiedler describes the relationship between a leader and the favorableness of the situation in which he is leading, as determined by the relationship between the leader and his followers, the degree to which the group's tasks are structured, and the inherent power of the leader's role. Powerful leaders with healthy relationships with their followers, overseeing highly structured activities, are the most successful in Fiedler's model.

Figurehead

A figurehead is an individual with a title implying a leadership role, who exercises little to no actual power of authority—either by convention or due to structural limits on this exercise. The monarch of the United Kingdom is arguably a figurehead, possessing power that is principally ceremonial; then again, the financial resources of the royal family and the cost of maintaining their household is just as arguably a passive use of significant power, especially in the eyes of anti-monarchists. The term *figurehead* is also used as an insult to refer to a leader who could exercise power but is largely controlled by another figure.

"First they came . . ."

An untitled poem by Martin Niemoller deals with the blindness of Germans to the effects of the Nazis' rise to power. Niemoller delivered the poem as a speech in many variant forms in his career as a pastor, and so there is no official version. The familiar version reads:

> First they came for the Communists, and I did not speak out—because I was not a communist. Then they came for the Trade Unionists, and I did not speak out—because I was not a trade unionist. Then they came for the Jews, and I did not speak out—because I was not a Jew. Then

they came for me—and there was no one left to speak for me."

Flat organization

A flat organization is one with little to no middle management, which in a sufficiently large organization results in more decentralized decision making, as there are fewer supervisory layers between upper management and the workers. This is typically accomplished with self-managing teams, a model that has become common in software companies where it may help that most of the labor required is highly skilled labor. Flat organizations overlap with but are distinct from cooperatives, in which not only decision making but ownership is decentralized.

Flow

In psychology, flow is a mental state in which the subject is completely immersed in his activity: focused, energized, engaged, and perhaps most importantly, enjoying the immersion, in a way that is not necessarily true of the similar concept of hyperfocus. Flow is commonly described as "being in the zone," and is in many ways the opposite of the "autopilot effect" of performing a task expertly but without engagement as a result of frequent repetition, as often happens to commuters on their drive home. One of the goals of positive psychology is to increase the experience of flow for workers. Owen Schaffer listed seven conditions for flow: knowing what to do, how to do it, how well you're doing it, and were to go, with difficult challenges, well-developed skills, and sufficient lack of distractions. In a workplace context, flow is related to employee engagement: mere competence is not enough; flow responds to a reasonable challenge and the pleasure of mastering it. The idea of flow is well developed in eastern religions but new to Western psychology.

Fluid intelligence

Fluid intelligence is a factor of general intelligence, representing the capacity to solve problems in new situations, independent of knowledge. Inductive and deductive reasoning and logic skills are part of fluid intelligence, as opposed to crystallized intelligence, which is the use of already acquired skills and knowledge.

Follett, Mary Parker

Mary Parker Follett was a management consultant and one of the pioneers in management theory in the early 20th century. Her work focused on employee participation, negotiation, reciprocal relationships in a professional context, and the noncoercive power-sharing approach to leadership that she called "integration." She was a great critic of micromanagement, which she called "bossism."

Followership

Followership is the complement to leadership, the social process of and capacity to follow a leader or leaders. Robert Kelley's work has been at the forefront of the academic study of followership. In 1988's *Harvard Business Review* article "In Praise of Followers," he identifies four qualities of followership: self-management (including independence, critical thinking, self-awareness, and self-evaluation), commitment to the group goal, competence in the areas relevant to the follower's role, and the courage to be candid with superiors.

Followership patterns

Robert Kelley identified five patterns of followership, based on two behavioral dimensions: whether the follower is active or passive, and whether or not he is a critical thinker. Sheep are passive followers who require constant supervision in their work. Yes-People (or Conformists) are committed to their work, but do not question the leader or act on their own initiative. Pragmatics are not as devoted to the leader's directions as Yes-People, but neither will they pursue an action or idea until it has the support of the majority, which may make them slow to react in response to a change in information or circumstances. The Alienated resent the leader and constantly question his decisions or authority, and may try to slow down the group's progress. Star Followers (or Exemplary Followers) require little supervision and are engaged critical thinkers, sharing the leader's goals but evaluating courses of action before following them.

Fordism

Named for automobile tycoon Henry Ford, Fordism is an industrialized and standardized system of mass production, encompassing both economic and social dimensions. Fordism is sometimes compared to Frederick W. Taylor's scientific management, and Taylor himself apparently thought Ford had adopted his techniques, but many of Ford's practices were independently formulated. Fordism is most associated with the standardization of products and the tools and processes used to make them, which is the aspect most consistent with scientific management and the one that was eventually adopted by nearly all of American manufacturing, at least those industries that use assembly lines. But Fordism also called for higher wages for workers, specifically for the purpose of ensuring that they could afford the products they were making—in this case, automobiles. Ford was far more concerned than Taylor with absenteeism and employee turnover, which in a Taylorist system are solvable by hiring different employees. Of course, Fordism was tailored specifically for the automobile industry, a novel product that, however revolutionary, was more expensive than most manufactured household goods. Ford's success has been tied in large part to his workers' wages, because he was able to turn his employees into customers.

Forer effect

The Forer effect (named for psychologist Bertram Forer) is the tendency of individuals to perceive vague, general statements that could apply to most people as highly accurate if they are told the statements are tailored specifically to them. For instance, most descriptions of personality derived from various forms of divination—handwriting analysis, fortune telling, palm reading, astrology, etc.—contain multiple statements, often vague, so that the individual will identify with at least some of them. In his initial experiment, Forer used statements including "You have a tendency to be critical of yourself" and "At times you are extroverted, affable, sociable, while at other times you are introverted, wary, reserved." Avoiding the Forer effect is a criterion of well-constructed personality tests. Similar phenomena are seen in the workplace, such as when feedback is presented in general enough terms that it could apply to most situations or individuals.

Founder's syndrome

Founder's syndrome is a system of difficulties faced by an organization as a result of one or more of its founders retaining disproportionate influence on the organization. Especially in the cases of organizations that have grown much larger than when the founder first instituted them, there may not be a well-considered management hierarchy in place, or one of the founders may routinely ignore the hierarchy and its norms. Decision-making processes may seem opaque even to other members of upper management, and key employees and board members may have been selected for their support or connection to a founder and so serve the founder's interest rather than the organization's.

Four Frames

Lee Bolman and Terrence Deal introduced the Four Frames model in 1984's *Reframing Organizations: Artistry, Choice, and Leadership.* Each of the four frames represents a way people view the world, which influences their approach to organization and leadership. The Structural frame views organizations as machine-like and favors rules, policies, and technology, and leadership's task as providing social architecture suited to the organization's goals. The Human Resource frame views organizations as family-like, based on relationships, skills, and needs, and leadership's task as empowering employees and keeping organizational needs in line with human ones. The Political frame views organizations as jungles full of conflict and competition, where leaders need to support and advocate an agenda and consolidate a power base around it. And the Symbolic frame views organizations in theatrical or temple-like terms, responding favorably to narrative, ritual, and ceremony, and requiring their leaders to inspire them. Although individuals tend to favor one or two frames, most people adopt different frames in different situations, as no one frame is suitable for all situations. Each frame favors slightly different approaches to basic organizational activities like strategic planning (which the Political frame treats as an opportunity for conflicting views to be expressed, while the Human Resources frame treats it as an opportunity to encourage participation in the process), decision making, goal setting, communication, team meetings, and conflict resolution. These different frames also produce different types of leaders, whether effective or not: Structural leaders tend to be architects or tyrants; Human Resources leaders, catalysts or pushovers; Political leaders, negotiators or con artists; and Symbolic leaders, prophets or fanatics.

Four psychologies

The "four psychologies" are the areas of psychology that provide the foundation of modern psychology on which both therapists and theorists draw. They consist of self psychology, the school of psychoanalysis that focuses on empathy, mirroring, the disruption of developmental needs, and other areas as developed in Chicago by Heinz Kohut; drive theory, the analysis of different psychological drives and needs and the phenomena that result from them; ego psychology, which builds on Sigmund Freud's model of the mind as consisting of id, ego, and superego; and object relations, which proposes that family experiences in infancy shape the future adult's relationships with other people.

Freethought

Freethought is an ideological position that favors reason and empiricism over authority and dogma. Though sometimes associated with atheism or agnosticism today, "free-thinkers" originated in 17th-century England as people who rejected the authority of the Church of England in favor of their own personal study of the Bible, though the term quickly spread to encompass those who rejected the authority of the Catholic Church and of religious traditions in general. Over the 19th century, freethought became associated with humanism, a rejection of nationalism and ethnocentrism, and

especially a rejection of preserving traditional institutions on the basis of their traditional authority, and an insistence that traditional beliefs and values must be supportable by objective reason. In the United States, the Free Thought movement began in the early 19th century, supporting philosophical skepticism, humanism, and freedom of speech and expression, and played a major role in the development of utopian communities.

French and Raven's bases of power

Social psychologists John R. P. French and Bertram Raven studied power in social influence settings in 1959, resulting in a model proposing five bases of power (with a sixth added by Raven in 1965) representing the different forms it can take. Power in this sense refers to social influence—the ability to change another person's behavior, attitudes, or beliefs—which is fundamental to an understanding of leadership. The bases of power they identified are Coercion, Reward, Legitimacy, Expert, Reference, and Informational (added by Raven).

Freud, Sigmund

The founder of psychoanalysis and one of the founders of psychology, Sigmund Freud began his work in the late 19th century, helped to spread psychoanalysis in the early 20th century even as some of his earliest followers began to develop their independent psychological theories, and continued to publish until his death in the 1930s. The defining feature of his work was the treating of psychological conditions through dialogue between the patient and the psychoanalyst, combined with his revolutionary theories of the mind, including the scientific analysis of dreams, his theory of the unconscious and the importance of the unconscious mind, the use of free association as a therapeutic technique, the existence of a sex drive and a death drive, and the mechanism of repression. While few outside the humanities continue to adopt Freud's ideas without alteration—he has been deeply influential on literary criticism in that respect—much of modern psychology is still defined by reactions to Freud or refinements to his ideas. He was among the first to study the decision-making habits and patterns of ordinary people, as opposed to commenting on the wisdom of the decisions of powerful leaders, and notable in seeing little mechanical or cognitive difference between the processes of one man debating whether to ask for a raise and another man debating whether to lead his nation to war.

The friendship paradox and centrality

The friendship paradox is the fact that most people have fewer friends than their friends have, on average. This is true for other forms of social connection as well: most people have had fewer sexual partners than their sexual partners have had. The reason for this is the same regardless of the type of social connection: the people with the greatest number of connections have an increased probability of being among one's own connections. Those people are in an interesting position, as the exceptions to the friendship paradox's generalization: they have more friends than most of their friends have, and have greater than average centrality, referring to their position in a map of their social networks. Further, the greater their centrality, the more it influences their access to certain kinds of social information. One well-publicized study found that highly central people are aware of flu outbreaks two weeks before professional surveillance methods are, because their information access is superior to the sampling methods used.

Fuhrerprinzip

The Fuhrerprinzip (German for "leader principle") is a term from German political science, referring to a principle upon which a government can be founded, stating that the leader's will supersedes other sources of law. The term was introduced by social Darwinist Hermann Keyserling, who believed that certain individuals were born to rule, and that their followers should not restrict their freedom to do so. The Fuhrerprinzip was the foundation of Adolf Hitler's Third Reich, and was invoked in the post–World War II Nuremberg Trials to support the claim that those charged with war crimes were simply following orders.

Full Range Leadership Model

Developed by leadership scholars Bernie Bass and Bruce Avolio in the late 1990s, the Full Range Leadership Model describes six lower-order factors and three higher-order factors of laissez-faire, transactional, and transformational leadership. The model describes transformational leadership in terms of idealized influence, inspirational motivation, intellectual stimulation, and individualized consideration, and is measured by the Multifactor Leadership Questionnaire developed by Bass.

Functional leadership theory

Functional leadership theory is a behavior-based theory of leadership that focuses on the functions that leaders perform or are responsible for. Rather than focusing on what leaders are like, as with trait-based theories, functional leadership theory focuses on what leading is. Functional leadership studies often extend their focus beyond the titular leader to look at what leadership functions are being performed in an organization, regardless of the title or formal role of the individuals performing them. John Adair's work lists eight leadership functions: task definition, planning, team briefing, controlling production, evaluating results, motivating individuals, organizing groups, and setting an example. Functional leadership is influential in leadership training because it implies a set of leadership skills that can be taught.

Future orientation

One of the global leadership cultural competencies identified by the GLOBE Project, future orientation is the extent to which individuals in an organization, group, or culture keep the future in mind through behaviors like saving and investing, planning, or constructing long-term strategies, which likewise influences their ability to delay gratification. Projects like climate change mitigation, for instance, have substantial short-term costs, with very long-term benefits, and have proven politically and practically difficult because of the level of future orientation required of supporters (and because of the number of supporters required for a project of such scope and breadth).

Galbraith's *Anatomy of Power*

Economist and diplomat John Kenneth Galbraith is best known for his trilogy on economics: *American Capitalism* (1952), *The Affluent Society* (1958), and *The New Industrial State* (1967). In 1983's *Anatomy of Power*, he classified power into three types: condign power, gained through use or threat of force; compensatory power, in which obedience is bought; and conditioned power, attained through persuasion. Further, power stems from one of three sources: leadership or personality, wealth, or organization (by being the organization's leader).

Game theory

Game theory is the study of mathematical models to represent conflict, cooperation, and decision making by intelligent and rational decision makers. Integral to economics, game theory has also become important in biology and the social sciences. It began in the middle of the 20th century with John von Neumann's 1944 *Theory of Games and Economic Behavior*, which demonstrated the way economic activity could be modeled and studied by treating it as a game with strategies, rules, and rewards. Organizational psychology, political science, peace studies, and political economy make heavy use of game theory, and game theory has been used to explain the stability of government forms, candidates' performance in primaries and elections, and group behavior in cooperative or competitive settings. In biology, game theory frequently focuses not only on evolutionary game theory but on communication games, to explain and model both animal and human communication.

Gandhi, Mahatma Mohandas

Mahatma Gandhi was the most prominent leader of the Indian nationalist movement in the early 20th century, seeking freedom from British rule, and is generally considered the father of the modern country of India. He led nonviolent protest movements against British rule both in India and in the Indian community in South Africa, and became the leader of the Indian National Congress in 1921, where he worked for women's rights, religious pluralism, and the end of poverty, in addition to his overarching quest for Indian independence. When independence was finally granted in 1947, in the form of separate Hindu (India) and Muslim (Pakistan) states, Gandhi traveled to the regions affected by religiously motivated violence among the displaced, rather than partake in the official celebrations of independence. He undertook several fasts in the attempt to promote

Mahatma Gandhi (right) employed nonviolent civil disobedience to lead India to independence, inspiring movements for freedom and civil rights around the world. (Wikimedia Commons/Dave Davis for Acme Newspictures)

religious pluralism, and having attained independence at last, some Hindu Indians were offended by his support of Muslims. He was assassinated by a Hindu nationalist in 1948, less than half a year after independence.

Gantt chart

Henry Gantt was an engineer and management consultant who learned scientific management from Frederick Winslow Taylor in the 1880s and developed the Gantt chart in the 1910s. The Gantt chart is a bar chart illustrating a project schedule from start to finish, with a work breakdown of the various stages and processes of the project. Later additions to the Gantt chart included the use of shading to demonstrate completion percentage of various stages, and a precedence network showing the relationships between different processes. Gantt charts were adopted by the American military beginning with World War I, and today are commonly used in Web-based collaborative groupware.

Gardner, Howard

A professor of cognition and education at the Harvard Graduate School of Education, Howard Gardner is best known for his theory of multiple intelligences, and also published an analysis of leadership, *Leading Minds: An Anatomy of Leadership*, in 1995. In it, he argues that humans' expectation of being led is inherited from our evolutionary forebears among the primates. Gardner also focuses on leaders as storytellers, presenting and embodying a particular narrative.

Gemeinschaft and Gesellschaft

Gemeinschaft and gesellschaft are German terms for "community" and "society" and were used by German sociologists to name two opposed categories of social ties—those based on Gemeinschaft, or community, which are derived from personal social experiences and the values and beliefs that are developed as a result of those experiences; and those based on Gesellschaft, or society, which are derived from indirect interactions and formal values.

Gender and leadership

Leadership has historically been a male role in most human cultures, and women remain extremely underrepresented in both political and business leadership today: only about 16 percent of the directors of Fortune 500 companies are women, which is about the same percentage of delegates to the 2013 World Economic Forum who were women. There is no evidence to suggest that women are less effective business leaders—in fact, the less than 5 percent of

Fortune 500 companies with female CEOs out-performed the S&P 500 in a 2014 *Fortune* magazine study, returning an average of 103.4 percent compared to 69.5 percent. The research is inconclusive on the impact of gender on leadership style or effectiveness, with some studies finding no difference and others finding small but nontrivial differences.

Gender egalitarianism

One of the global leadership cultural competencies identified by the GLOBE Project, gender egalitarianism is the extent to which an organization or culture avoids, prevents, or works to stop gender-based discrimination and gender role differences.

Generation gap

The generation gap is a term in use since the 1960s to refer to the cultural differences between older and younger people, traditionally between parents and their college-age children; in discussions of voting trends, the gap discussed is sometimes wider, as in the gay marriage debate, in which the broadest support is found in the youngest tier of voters, and the least support in the oldest tier. But traditionally, it has referred to the tendency of young people to be more socially liberal than their parents (and by implication, to become more conservative with age), and more experimental in their lifestyle and fashion choices. Increasingly, the generation gap is also relevant when it comes to social media competence, as trends can live and die in a four- or five-year span.

Gesture

Gestures are bodily movements communicating specific information (as opposed to body language that is simply expressive). The use of gesture in language seems to be universal, but the extent to which gesture is relied upon varies considerably from culture to culture; Italians are notorious for their heavy use of it compared to Americans.

Gilbreth, Frank, Sr.

Frank Gilbreth was an early pioneer in the Efficiency movement, who extended the principles of scientific management first developed by Frederick Winslow Taylor by adding the concept of the motion study—a study of the physical process of performing a discrete task constituting part of a company's operations, in order to optimize that process for maximum efficiency. Frank's wife, Lillian, was the first organizational psychologist, and the two used their large family to conduct efficiency experiments, as later recounted in *Cheaper by the Dozen*, a book by two of their children, adapted into a film with Myrna Loy, and its sequel *Belles on Their Toes*.

Gilbreth, Lillian

Lillian Gilbreth was one of the first female engineers and is considered the first organizational psychologist. Her Ph.D. from Brown University was the first degree granted in industrial psychology, and she was the first engineer to bring psychological principles to scientific management by suggesting changes to Frederick Winslow Taylor's original work that were better-informed about human character and motivation. Gilbreth also worked as a consultant and marketing

Lillian Gilbreth, one of the first women to become an engineer, is best known for the management and efficiency techniques she and her husband devised. (Flickr/Smithsonian)

researcher, using psychology to craft marketing campaigns during the Great Depression, and created the modern "work triangle" kitchen design (still common today) as a way of applying scientific management to household work.

Global leadership

Global leadership is the interdisciplinary study of leadership throughout the world and in the context of globalization, with an emphasis on determining the competencies, skills, and knowledges that leaders in a globalized world should possess. The Institute for Global Leadership at Tufts University, for instance, is an incubator for innovative approaches to global issues. Social psychologist Geert Hofstede's 1980 research identified several global leadership dimensions: individualism vs collectivism, long-term orientation, masculinity, power distance index, and uncertainty avoidance index.

GLOBE Project

The Global Leadership and Organizational Behavior Effectiveness Research (GLOBE) Project began in 1991 under the leadership of scholar Robert House at the Wharton School and continued Geert Hofstede's work on cultural dimensions of global leadership. Researchers, including co-investigators in 62 different cultures, collected data from 17,300 managers in 951 organizations. The cultures were grouped into Anglo Cultures, Arab Cultures, Confucian Asia, Eastern Europe, Germanic Europe, Latin America, Latin Europe, Nordic Europe, Southern Asia, and Sub-Sahara Africa. When the data was analyzed, the group identified six dimensions of culturally endorsed implicit leadership (CLT): charismatic/value-based; team-oriented; self-protective; participative; human orientation; and autonomous. Further, they identified nine cultural competencies:

performance orientation (the extent to which excellence is rewarded), assertiveness orientation (the extent to which individuals are assertive in their social relationships), future orientation (the degree to which individuals plan for the future), human orientation (the extent to which individuals are encouraged to be altruistic, friendly, or kind), institutional collectivism, in-group collectivism, gender egalitarianism, power distance, and uncertainty avoidance.

Goffman, Erving

One of the most cited sociologists, Erving Goffman's work is central to American sociology in the 20th century, and largely concerned the sociology of everyday life, the self, and social interaction. His seminal work, 1959's *The Presentation of Self in Everyday Life*, uses the allegory of the theater to portray humans as in a state of constant performance, in which certain social practices are adopted to avoid embarrassment of the self or others, while private thoughts remain "backstage." Every person is both an actor and an audience. One of the key elements of the book is the necessity of actors agreeing to the definition of the situation (cf.).

"Good enough"

In software and systems design, the "good enough" principle says that products do not need to be optimal, they only need to be good enough to meet consumer needs. A product that's "too good" may wind up being too expensive, or simply fail to find sufficient consumers who have a use for its additional capacities. Though coined in a software design context, the principle has broad applicability. In some cases, as with basic point-and-shoot digital cameras, the Chromebook bare-bones laptop, and cell phones marketed at seniors, "just good enough" is even a marketing talking point.

Good Manufacturing Practices
Good Manufacturing Practices (GMP) are the manufacturing practices guidelines recommended by a regulatory agency in order to meet a minimum level of quality and to minimize safety risks. "Good X Practices (GxP)" exist in many fields, including Good Clinical Practices for clinical drug studies, Good Laboratory Practices for laboratory experiments, and other GxP recommendations or regulations.

Grand theory of leadership
The grand or general theory of leadership is a hypothetical theory that would represent the unified findings of scholars in the multidisciplinary field of leadership studies: a set of universal principles related to leadership–subordinate relationships. Leadership scholar James MacGregor Burns convened a group of scholars at the Jepson School of Leadership Studies in 2001 with the intent of developing such a theory. Some scholars in the field rejected the idea of a unified theory outright, but Burns and others believed that leadership studies was a fragmented field and risked being trivialized. The group never produced such a theory, but the attempt to do so constituted an energetic and lengthy discussion of leadership studies, its findings, and its methodologies.

Great Men
In the 18th and especially the 19th century, scholars treated history as the work of "Great Men"—often heroic, virtuous, or especially competent men, especially when history was considered from their point of view, but sometimes simply men of great influence or charisma. Though the Great Men approach was particularly popular in the United States (and lives on in the form of popular mammoth biographies like Robert Caro's multivolume work on Lyndon B. Johnson), and was perhaps influenced by the American fascination with individualism and with the role individuals played in the independence and industrialization of the nation, Scotsman Thomas Carlyle actually was the first to formalize the idea, when he said "The history of the world is but the biography of great men." In contrast, Herbert Spencer argued that these great men were products of larger social forces, while Leo Tolstoy argued that Great Men "are but labels that serve to give a name to an event."

Scottish philosopher, Thomas Carlyle, who popularized the Great Man theory when he said that the world's history "is but the biography of great men." (Public Domain)

The Greatest Salesman in the World
First published in 1968, Og Mandino's *Greatest Salesman in the World* became a best-seller translated into 25 languages. An insurance salesman who attributed his success and recovery from alcoholism and suicidal feelings to self-help and motivation books, he wrote his own, consisting of elaborations of ten declarative statements: "Today I begin a new life. I will greet this day with love in my heart. I will persist until I succeed. I am nature's greatest miracle. I will live this day as if it is my last. Today I will be the master of my emotions. I will laugh at the world. Today I will multiply my value a hundredfold. I will act now. I will pray for guidance." The book praises the value of work, and uses incidents from a life as a salesman to illustrate its points.

Group affective tone

An aggregate of the moods of the members of a group is called the group affective tone. Not all groups have an affective tone, if members do not share similar moods, but common social experiences, common experiences with the work environment, emotional contagion, and the stability of group membership all conspire to make mood similarity likely.

Group cohesiveness

Group cohesiveness is the nature and strength of the bonds linking members of a group to one another and to the group as a whole, and consists of their perceptions of unity in a joint effort, the social relationships among them, the task-related relationships among them, and members of the group's feelings about each other and the group. There are many schools of thought about how to achieve healthy group cohesiveness and whether certain types of group makeup are more inclined toward cohesion.

Group conflict

Group conflict is a conflict either between groups or within a group. Intragroup conflicts may result from disagreement over goals or the means of achieving those goals, or from personality conflicts between members. Some studies have suggested that a plurality of intragroup conflicts among upper management are personality-driven rather than based on issues related to the work of the group.

Group decision making

Group decision making is the process of making a decision collectively, sharing participation in the process and responsibility for the outcome. Studies have found that groups often make very different decisions than individuals do, the reasons for which are the subject of ongoing study.

While groupthink is the best-known phenomenon, in part because of the fame of the Bay of Pigs invasion, which was used to illustrate it in Irving Janis's work, there are others that impact group decision making, which is not to say that they always make it worse. Common problems include time management (Parkinson's law applies here, stating that "A task will expand to fill the time available for its completion"); difficulty in setting discussion priorities and getting bogged down in trivialities, nuances, side discussions that will not affect the final outcome or represent a single member's hobby horse; and the possibility of rushing through the process and allowing the most passionate or charismatic members to sway the rest of the group. On the other hand, a group can avoid the individual biases of any one of its members, and can contribute greater information and relevant experience to inform the decision-making process. *See also* Consensus decision making, satisficing

Group emotion

Group emotion is the collection of emotions and moods experienced by members of a group. Experiments have shown that people are affected by the moods of those around them; Facebook famously even experimented with the status updates Facebook users see, to demonstrate the impact on their own status updates. Group emotion can and often is discussed in terms of the aggregation of the moods and emotions of individuals, but it can also be looked at from the group-as-a-whole perspective, which posits the group dynamic as having an impact on the moods of the members, especially with reference to their interactions with one another.

Group narcissism

Group narcissism is excessive love of one's own group, be it a work group, ethnic group, national identity, or any other group. It is related to, or can be an expression of, ethnocentrism, nationalism, chauvinism, and elitism, and can lead to cronyism and nepotism. Some psychologists believe it is an extension of personal or individual narcissism: "I am fantastic; my membership in this group is important to my conception of the 'I' that is fantastic; therefore, membership in this group is evidence of being fantastic." However, there are certainly cases where group narcissism can coexist with a personal low self-esteem, as can sometimes be found with white supremacists or nationalists. Group narcissism can also be the narcissism of a group, that is, the feeling and view that emerges from a group made up of individual narcissists, as discussed in the work of Jerrold Post.

Group polarization

Group polarization is the tendency of individuals to voice stronger opinions in a group situation than in individual situations. As a result, decisions made by a group have a tendency to be more extreme or involve more drastic change than if an individual group member had made a decision. Group polarization is frequently used to explain the decisions of groups as diverse as juries, terrorist and hate groups, political parties, and committees.

Groupthink

Groupthink is a phenomenon that can emerge in a group of people making a decision, in which the desire to avoid conflict leads to a superficial consensus that is achieved without due consideration of other options. Despite this, members of the group may be as devoted in their advocacy of the decision as one reached through more rational means. When William Whyte Jr. coined the term in a 1952 *Fortune* magazine article, he called it "a rationalized conformity—an open,

articulate philosophy that holds that group values are not only expedient but right and good as well." Many different group dynamics can result in groupthink, but common among them are dynamics that encourage or enforce conformity, and groups that value group harmony over rational action and accuracy. Groupthink occurs in myriad situations both trivial and dangerous, from a group of friends deciding on where to go for dinner and arriving at a restaurant that was no one's preference (cf. Abilene paradox) to the mass suicides of cults. The John F. Kennedy administration's decision to invade the Bay of Pigs in 1961, based on a plan put together by the Dwight D. Eisenhower administration, was used as an example by psychologist Irving Janis in his early work on the concept.

Groupware

Groupware is software that assists people in collaborating through the creation and maintenance of a collaborative working environment in which files can be worked on and annotated by multiple members of the group, often with the addition of project management capacities like group calendars, messaging, and task assignment sheets. Though collaborative computing applications were envisioned early on, the first widespread applications were actually recreational—Colossal Cave Adventure and other MUDs (Multi-User Dungeons) allowed multiple users to play the same dungeon video game together from different computer terminals, in an antecedent to today's massively multiplayer online roleplaying games. PARC's Pavel Curtis, who had adapted the MUD concept to the online social environment—a sort of massively multiplayer chat room—of LambdaMOO in the early 1990s, later developed groupware that simulated an auditorium, which became the basis for a commercial package sold to the military. Key to MUDs, LambdaMOO, and modern groupware, as opposed to other early multiuser software packages like IRC, is persistence of data: information about each user and their activities is saved and restored in each session.

Guru

In the religions of the Indian subcontinent (Buddhism, Hinduism, Jainism, Sikhism), "guru" means "teacher," especially a mentor who passes on religious teachings as well as practical knowledge. In the United States, it has typically referred to a Hindu teacher who leads his pupils toward enlightenment, but "guru" often refers to a teacher of individuals or organizations in a specialized field. Management consultants, marketing researchers, and other outsiders brought in to advise an organization may, if they have made a name for themselves in their cottage industry, be referred to as a "management guru" or similar term. Likewise, "leadership gurus" have developed their own industry, offering leadership development services to organizations or operating leadership training seminars for individuals.

Habermas, Jurgen

Jurgen Habermas is a German philosopher of the Frankfurt school. He has written on the rule of law, social theory and epistemology, democracy, capitalism, and German politics, and is perhaps best known for his theory of communicative rationality. He participated in a famous published dialogue with Cardinal Joseph Ratzinger, a year before his election to the papacy, on philosophy, religion, and reason, and has spoken of the emergence of post-secular civilization and the need for the secular to be tolerant of the religious just as the religious must be tolerant of the secular.

Hallyu

Hallyu or the Korean Wave is a South Korean term for its increased export of culture since the 1990s. The South Korean government has made loans and credit available to entertainment and food companies in order to increase exports, and established a Presidential Council on Nation Branding in 2009. Many parts of the world—even those, like the United States, that already had a well-established Korean community—have seen a marked increase in recent years in the popularity or prevalence of Korean cuisine, Korean music, and Korean entertainment, while pop star Psy ("Gangnam Style") became an international sensation. Hallyu is an exercise of soft power or public diplomacy—an attempt to influence worldwide perceptions of Korea and of Koreans (who have been treated poorly throughout much of their immigration diaspora).

Halo effect

A cognitive bias by which an individual's feelings about a person influence their evaluation of that person's behaviors and competencies. Often this is used to refer to the Warren G. Harding effect—assuming that a physically attractive person is also competent—but the halo effect is a broader phenomenon that is not limited to leadership competency.

Hansei

One of the Japanese cultural terms introduced to the United States through cross-pollination of Japanese and American business practices, hansei means "self-reflection," and refers to making clear what one's errors were and planning to improve in the future. At Toyota and some other Japanese companies, a hansei meeting is held after each project's completion, even if it is considered a success, in order to critically evaluate and discuss one's own work on the project. An important aspect of hansei is the belief that a point will never be reached when there is nothing that could have been improved upon.

Happiness

In the workplace, positive psychology has repeatedly found correlations between happiness and productivity, as well as employee engagement and job satisfaction, and a negative correlation with absenteeism. Nevertheless, most management approaches treat happiness as a side effect rather than a goal. There is a growing movement to change this.

Haptics

Haptics is a form of nonverbal communication conducted by touch. While some forms of haptic communication are both easily noticeable and clear in their meaning—a kiss on the cheek or a handshake (whether in greeting or to denote agreement to a deal), for instance—other forms are more subtle and often conducted unconsciously, such as lightly touching the listener while speaking in order to underline a point, or squeezing the speaker's hand while listening to indicate support. Norms of haptic communication vary by culture, and because touch involves entering personal space, there are often different sets of unspoken norms based on gender and level of intimacy.

Hard power

Hard power is, in Joseph Nye's phrase, "the ability to use the carrots and sticks of economic and military might to make others follow your will." While "carrots" are positive rewards and the "stick" is the threat of violent punishment, such overt and tangible displays of power are considered "hard" in contrast with soft power, a term Nye coined to refer to forms of diplomacy.

Harvard Business Review

Harvard Business Review is a management magazine published monthly by Harvard Business Publishing, a subsidiary of Harvard University. Founded in 1922 and made more accessible to a general audience in the 1980s, it was one of the first venues to introduce concepts like the glass ceiling, globalization, and core competence, and has published many of the luminaries of the management and leadership studies world.

Hawthorne studies

The Hawthorne studies were a series of 1924 to 1932 psychological experiments conducted by Elton Mayo at the Hawthorne Works, a Chicago area factory. The studies initially suggested that improving lighting in the workplace improved productivity, but a later investigation by Henry A. Landsberger in 1950 pointed out that the productivity increases ended when the study did. Landsberger's belief was that the fact of a change, and the awareness of a study being conducted, was actually the driving factor behind the workers' increased productivity, rather than the specifics of the change. Novelty, in other words, caused a temporary increase, which has since been called the Hawthorne effect.

Hazing

A ritual of harassment and humiliation used to initiate a person into a group, hazing is especially associated with college fraternities, but similar behavior is evinced by other close-knit and particularly male groups, including sports teams, private schools, gangs, and military units. Rituals range from the lengthy pledge week of fraternities to the old practice of painting a printer's apprentice's genitals with ink, and proponents say that the shared experience of hazing creates close bonds among initiates.

Similar rituals are sometimes adopted in the workplace, though they rarely involve the sort of physical harassment common elsewhere.

The hedgehog's dilemma

The hedgehog's (porcupine's) dilemma is that he needs to huddle close to the other hedgehogs in the group to stay warm in the winter, and yet cannot get too close to them lest they hurt one another with their spines. They remain apart despite mutual intentions to be close. The image was first invoked by German philosopher Arthur Schopenhauer to illustrate the life of the individual in human society: intimacy is not possible without mutual harm, despite intentions, and knowledge of this (or the first brush against those spikes) causes people to engage in shallow relationships. Sigmund Freud later quoted and helped to popularize Schopenhauer's analogy in his work on group psychology. A common rejoinder to Schopenhauer is that he has supplied his own solution: the hedgehogs need to huddle close, but not *too* close; it is his own pessimism that supposes the distance dictated by the spines is sufficient to prevent warmth and intimacy.

Hedonistic relevance

Hedonistic relevance is an attributional bias whereby an individual explains a person's behavior, when that behavior negatively affects the observing individual, with reference to the person's character and disposition rather than external factors. The classic example is to assign motive and intent to someone who has accidentally bumped into you, dropped or broken something of yours, or spilled something on you.

Heifetz, Ronald

The co-founder of the Center for Public Leadership at the John F. Kennedy School of Government (Harvard), Ronald Heifetz is a leading leadership studies scholar who has promoted adaptive leadership in the education field. His best-known book, *Leadership Without Easy Answers*, was first published in 1994 and focuses on the difference between technical problems solvable through expertise and problems requiring adaptive leadership.

Herd behavior

Herd behavior is the behavior of people as a group without direction or planning. While common in the animal world, among humans herd behavior is a marked category because of our usual reliance on communication. In some instances, stock market bubbles and riots have been blamed on herd behavior.

Here Comes Everybody

Here Comes Everybody: The Power of Organizing Without Organizations is a 2008 book by Clay Shirky on group dynamics in the age of social media, crowdfunding, filesharing, and Wikipedia.

Heterarchy

A heterarchy is one of the major ways to structure an organization. Unlike a hierarchy, in which different elements of the organization are ranked in static tiers, the elements of a heterarchy are unranked or can be re-ranked in different configurations. Sociologist David Stark has explored heterarchies, their distributed intelligence, their emergence in postsocialist economies in eastern Europe, and their applicability to Western organizations.

Hierarchy

A hierarchy is one of the major ways to structure an organization, in which elements of the organization are arranged in static tiers ranked with respect to one another. The hierarchy is the form of the typical bureaucracy, with executive leadership at the top, followed by department heads who oversee tiers of middle managers and supervisors overseeing work groups and teams. In most business and government organizations, as well as in the Catholic Church, every entity in the organization except the topmost is subordinate to a single other entity, which is usually visualized as either a pyramid or a tree. The hierarchy is a common enough form of organization that the other two major forms defined by triarchy theory are little known, especially in the business world.

Hierarchy culture

One of four organizational cultures identified by Robert Quinn's Competing Values Framework, hierarchy culture is focused on the well-being of people in the organization and favors a controlled organization structure. Hierarchical organizations tend to be bureaucratic, with clearly defined policies, procedures, and roles.

Hinduism

The dominant religion of India, Hinduism developed as a synthesis of Indian religious traditions in the 1st millennium B.C.E., shortly after Buddhism. Hinduism encompasses religious, philosophical, and cultural dimensions, and is intertwined with India's caste system, though non-Hindus in India are also part of the system. Brahmans, the highest of the castes, are the Hindu priests and religious leaders, responsible for leading rituals and ceremonies and running religious buildings and institutions. Another traditional Brahman role is that of the guru, a teacher who imparts knowledge to his disciple through a close spiritual relationship. Gurus are not exclusively religious in nature and are found in the arts and practical

studies. Hinduism stresses authenticity, sincerity, and self-knowledge as keys to a guru's ability to work with disciples.

History

History is the study of the human past (while historiography is the study of how history has been written). Historical methodologies vary considerably with the area and era of study; the differences in documentation available for 1950s America compared to ancient Sumer necessitate differences in method. As a formal discipline, history grows out of the work of the ancient Greeks (beginning with Herodotus), most of whom focused on the recent past and its impact on or relevance to the present. The modern discipline and its commitment to objectivity begins more or less in the Enlightenment, as epitomized by the works of Edward Gibbon and Thomas Carlyle. Historiographical trends have varied over time: "Great Man" histories dominated the 19th and 20th centuries, while the last decades have seen a rise in social history, multi- and interdisciplinary approaches, and cultural studies.

The Hitler Problem

"The Hitler Problem" is Joanne Ciulla's term for a conundrum in leadership studies: the dichotomy between an effective leader (as Adolf Hitler could be considered) and an ethical one. The layman is familiar with the dichotomy in the form of the old saying about Hitler's fellow fascist dictator Benito Mussolini "making the trains run on time," and the implication that a tyrannical ruler can nevertheless get things done; this overstates Mussolini's actual effectiveness, however, not to mention the state of the Italian railways. The Hitler Problem can be used in support of defining leadership in a way that is at least broadly prescriptive.

Hofstede, Geert

Dutch psychologist Geert Hofstede is best known for his work on cultural dimensions and global leadership. Much of his work deals with cultural differences or cross-cultural studies, an interest inspired by his travels as a young man after World War II, including a voyage to Indonesia and an extended trip to England, both of which left him struck by culture shock. Before his work in psychology, he worked in management, with a background in engineering. Later he founded the Personnel Research Department at IBM, conducting opinion surveys of IBM employees throughout the world. He published his first major work on cross-cultural studies, *Culture's Consequences*, in 1980, the same year he co-founded the Institute for Research on Intercultural Cooperation. Critics of Hofstede's work focus principally on the level of cultural determinism that he assumes.

Hoshin Kanri

A Japanese management method, hoshin kanri ("direction management") is a strategic planning concept in which a group of employees contribute their own ideas, expertise, and experience to developing a strategy. The method is influenced by the work of W. Edwards Deming, who worked as a consultant in Japan after World War II, and systematizes the strategic planning process. One of its key elements is the use of quality storyboards: after a policy statement has been defined, each manager draws a storyboard illustrating their understanding of it, with managers discussing their storyboards with each manager above and below them in the hierarchy in order to smooth out differences and align approaches.

Hostile media effect

The hostile media effect is an error in perception in which one who is a strong partisan of an issue perceives media coverage of the issue as biased against them. Studies of the effect have been conducted since 1982.

Hostile work environment

A hostile work environment is one in which workers are reluctant or afraid to come to the workplace because of harassment or factors that create a deeply unpleasant environment.

Hot-cold empathy gap

The term *hot-cold empathy gap* was coined by psychologist George Loewenstein, and refers to a cognitive bias in peoples' perceptions of behavior. The gap represents the inability to empathize with and truly understand the effects of emotions one is not oneself currently experiencing. Further, the gap is such that the individual often underestimates its extent and may not realize it is there at all (in contrast with situations in which individuals who have trouble relating to a given situation are well aware of their difficulty). Not being aware of the gap results in ascribing others' behavior to factors other than the emotion or circumstance with which the individual is unable to empathize. While some of the most important ramifications of this gap impinge on interactions with other people—in the workplace, for instance, an employer may not understand the impact of emotional or physical trauma on an employee, and so may not approve a request for leave or a reduction in performance quality—the gap applies even to predicting one's own behavior. Loewenstein, for instance, wrote of a study showing that young men were unable to predict the level of risky sexual behavior they would accept while aroused. The empathy gap is also implicated in the tensions and frictions that result from members of an unmarked category being unable to relate to the effects of membership on members of a marked category, such as racial minority status, addiction, or disability. Social psychology experiments have found that those in power experience difficulty understanding or predicting the behavior of the comparatively powerless, but again, are largely unaware of the gap.

How to Win Friends and Influence People

How to Win Friends and Influence People by Dale Carnegie was published in 1936, based on self-improvement courses Carnegie had offered for some years. It became the first self-help best seller, incorporating elements of business books—the book promised to help readers become better salesmen or executives, win new clients, and increase their earning power, among other pragmatic goals—as well as books of moral instruction and pop psychology. The book was especially influential in its advice on influencing other people by flattering them and avoiding direct criticism. One of Carnegie's pieces of advice has virtually become standard behavior: making a request by asking "do me a favor" rather than explicitly asking for something, in order to make the target feel important and benevolent.

Human microphone

A method for delivering a speech, the human microphone involves the participation of a group of people who cooperate with the speaker. The speaker speaks a phrase at a time, pausing to allow the group to repeat the phrase in unison in order to amplify it. This can be repeated for several waves, with groups at the edge of earshot repeating what the first group said in order to carry the speech, a phrase at a time, farther out. The method was associated with the anti-nuclear protest movement in the 1970s and 1980s but became better known when used by Occupy Wall Street.

Human orientation

One of the global leadership cultural competencies identified by the GLOBE Project, human orientation is the measure of the friendliness, altruism, and compassion of the individuals in an organization, group, or society.

Human relations theory

Human relations theory is an area of organizational psychology that studies the behavior of people in groups, and the role of the worker in his organization in terms of his individual psychology rather than simply his defined duties and relationship to other workers.

Human resource management

Human resource management (HR) is an activity within an organization devoted to putting the organization's human resources—its employees—to best use in order to meet organizational goals. In large enough organizations, HR is typically its own department, and activities include recruitment and development, performance appraisal, and the pay and benefit system, as well as the handling of disputes and conflicts.

Human Resources frame

In L. Bolman and T. Deal's Four Frame model, the Human Resources frame is one of the distinctive frames through which people view the world. This frame is concerned with individuals, feelings, understanding others and one's own need to be understood, personal expression, and the view of the organization as a family.

Hundred Flowers Campaign

The Hundred Flowers Campaign was a 1956 initiative by the Communist government of China to entrap dissidents and counter-revolutionaries by inviting citizens to speak openly about their feelings about the communist regime, which

Mao Zedong and the Chinese Communist government enacted the Hundred Flowers Campaign, designed to entrap citizens with anti-communist views. (Public Domain)

was still young but had come to power through a decade-long civil war. Identified dissidents faced punishments ranging from the relatively minor to labor camp sentences and executions.

Hunter-gatherer societies

Before the Neolithic age—characterized by the development of agriculture—human societies depended on hunting and gathering in order to acquire food. Evolutionary leadership theory describes several means by which leaders in such societies (which tended not to develop the long-term institutions of Neolithic and later societies) had their power checked. The most extreme was murder, especially of a violent leader. But leaders could simply have their power limited through disobedience, departure of subgroups within the group, criticism to undercut the leader, and gossip to deplete the leader's prestige.

Identity negotiation

In sociology, identity negotiation is the process by which people reach implicit and unspoken agreements about the roles they assume in their relationships, which roles, once formulated, they are expected to maintain or violate the expectations of the other people in the relationship. Erving Goffman's work, such as in *The Presentation of Self in Everyday Life*, pioneered this view of identity in the mid-20th century, a time when many women were entering the workforce and implicitly "violating"

the housewife role they had been consigned to, while young people reaching adulthood began to challenge the roles assigned to them or from which they were asked to choose.

Identity shift effect

The mechanism by which peer pressure works has been called the identity shift effect by psychologist Wendy Traynor, building on the work of social psychologist Leon Festinger. In Treynor's model, the individual experiences distress at the prospect of social rejection as a result of not conforming to the social norm of his peers, resulting in a change in behavior. This change in behavior causes a new source of distress as a result of having compromised one's standards, leading to a change in self-image (or shift in identity) in which the peer norm is adopted as a personal norm, eliminating the conflict.

Idiosyncrasy credits

In social psychology, idiosyncrasy credits are a concept representing the ability of a member of a group to violate the social norms of that group without exceeding the threshold of the group's tolerance for deviation. Edwin Hollander first coined the term in the 1950s to represent the affect of accumulated positive feelings from the group, allowing for deviation from the norm for members who have in essence "proven themselves" and whose deviation therefore is not sufficient to call into question whether they belong in the group. Idiosyncrasy credits can also be used to explain how one member's deviation can be punished while another's deviation—even a deviation from the same norm—can be rewarded, and the way minority views can become influential within a group. Hollander argued that idiosyncrasy credits are particularly important in American corporate culture, in which the accumulation of such credits is necessary for leaders to climb the corporate ladder to positions of ever-greater responsibility, at which point they are given the leeway to behave idiosyncratically, changing the very norms they were promoted for honoring.

"If it ain't broke, don't fix it"

This maxim was popularized by Bert Lance, the banker who served as President Jimmy Carter's director of the Office of Management and Budget. In a 1977 article in the U.S. Chamber of Commerce's newsletter *Nation's Business*, Lance said the United States needed to take the "if it ain't broke, don't fix it" approach in order to cut spending. The maxim has since become associated less with frugality and more with the implication that introducing change to a working system may stop it from working.

Ignoratio elenchi

The ignoratio elenchi, or irrelevant conclusion, is a fallacy of relevance in which the arguer presents an argument that is irrelevant to the issue at hand. Closely related is the straw man, which presents an argument that refutes a point the other side has not actually attempted to make. Both fallacies are a type of informal fallacy—arguments that are fallacious for failing to support the conclusion.

Immune neglect

Immune neglect is a cognitive bias affecting an individual's ability to predict the emotional impact an event or decision will have on him. Specifically, it is the inability to properly account for the psychological immune system, which works to help people recover from negative emotions. As a result, people predict that they will feel badly for much longer than they actually do.

Impact bias

The impact bias is a cognitive bias affecting peoples' ability to predict their future emotional states (affective forecasting). Specifically, it is the tendency to overestimate the intensity or duration of these states, despite their previous experience with the same or similar emotional states. This affects decision making, since it seems to weight more heavily the emotional impact of outcomes.

Impeachment

Impeachment is the legal process of accusing a public official of illegal activity, possibly followed by civil or criminal proceedings or the removal of the official from office. In the United States, for instance, the Constitution defines federal impeachments as concerning "the President, Vice President, and all civil officers of the United States," and their impeachable crimes as "treason, bribery, or other high crimes and misdemeanors." The power to impeach is given to the House of Representatives, while the Senate tries the impeachment. Neither "other high crimes" nor "civil officers" is defined in the Constitution, and so many specifics of federal impeachment are unclear, including whether members of Congress are impeachable; the sole attempt to impeach a member of Congress (Senator William Blount in 1798) did not resolve the issue, though it did famously cause a fistfight to break out between two congressmen. The Senate dismissed the impeachment on the grounds that senators were not impeachable, but expelled Blount from the Senate anyway, and the ruling is not considered final.

In-group

In-group refers to a social group with which an individual identifies.

In-group collectivism

One of the global leadership cultural competencies identified by the GLOBE Project, in-group collectivism is a measure of the extent to which individuals feel pride in their group membership.

Inclusive management

In public administration, inclusive management is a management style that is similar to participatory management in the private sector. Under this approach, managers involve not only members of their organization but members of the public, politicians representing the relevant constituency, and experts in relevant fields, in the process of making decisions about policy or actions taken by the organization, and in addressing public problems within the organization's scope. Inclusive management is especially associated with the public managers of Grand Rapids, Michigan, who coined the "50/50 rule," stating that the process of making a decision or addressing a problem is equally important to public satisfaction as the outcome.

Inclusivity

Inclusivity is the organizational goal of ensuring that members feel they belong. Belongingness has been recognized as one of the most fundamenal human motivations, and as leadership and management have become more people-focused, the value has become clear of making group members feel accepted by and engaged in the operations of the group. Inclusivity in the workplace borrows practices from and reflects similar values to political inclusivity (which seeks to encourage the participation and inclusion of all citizens in politics and policy), in making sure members do not feel excluded because of their age, gender, sexual orientation, race or ethnicity, religion, disability, or other identity traits. Common to most organizational inclusivity programs is the goal of making employees feel valued and creating a supportive environment that benefits the quality of work and employee engagement of everyone.

Inattentional blindness

Inattentional blindness is caused not by a vision defect but by inattention and may be impacted by mental workload and attentional capacity.

Incrementalism

Incrementalism is a work method in which incremental changes are made to a project rather than large additions. Typically, incrementalist work is not as thoroughly planned as in traditional methods. Instead, the most pressing problem of the moment is dealt with. Though often criticized in American business culture, Denmark's wind energy industry was built incrementally from an agricultural origin as opposed to the smaller American wind energy industry, which developed out of the aerospace industry with heavy research institute involvement, and required significant up-front capital investment. Incrementalism is also popular in product design divisions of Japanese businesses.

Indifferent style

One of the leadership styles plotted on the managerial grid model, the style was originally called the impoverished style. Indifferent managers have a low concern for both production and people and are primarily interested in staying out of trouble and preserving their position.

Individualism

Individualism is an ideology that attaches significant value to the individual. Independence, self-reliance, personal freedom, and self-expression are all highly valued and receive precedence over concerns of a larger group like the state, and within reason need to be protected from interference by larger groups. Liberalism is founded on individualism, as are anarchism and libertarianism, and John Locke provided a motto for individualism when he wrote, "No one ought to harm another in his life, health, liberty, or possessions." Individualism is contrasted with collectivism and other ideologies that put the interests of the group or groups above those of individuals.

Individualism versus collectivism

One of the cultural dimensions of organizations identified by Geert Hofstede, individualism versus collectivism represents the organization's position on a spectrum with individualism at one extreme, as seen in the United States, and collectivism, in which members are emotionally dependent on and invested in their organization, at the other.

Industrial engineering

Industrial engineering is the branch of engineering dealing with complex systems of equipment, materials, information, and people. The term originated in the manufacturing sector, but industrial engineers are found in all kinds of organizations, including the health care industry, the military, theme parks, and publishing. Industrial engineering involves systems thinking and a holistic, top-down view of a business or organization, followed by an examination and streamlining of the processes of its operations.

Industrial psychology or I/O psychology

See Organizational psychology

Industrial sociology

Industrial sociology is the branch of sociology engaged in an examination and critique of ongoing trends in labor, employment, management practices, and related issues like globalization, the impacts of international trade, and outsourcing and offshoring.

Influence

Influence is the formal or informal, overt or covert, ability to affect the behaviors, decisions, or emotions of others, or the behavior or decisions of organizations. Influence is wielded in numerous ways, not always consciously and not always in ways that serve the influencer's interests—making a poor impression in a job interview enacts a negative influence on the organization's likelihood of hiring you, for instance. At a greater extreme, reactance is the psychological term for the motivation of someone responding to an attempt to influence them by adopting the opposite of the behavior or viewpoint toward which the influencer is pushing them.

Informal fallacy

An informal fallacy is an argument that fails to support its conclusion due to a flaw in reasoning, but unlike a formal fallacy, it is not the result of a flaw in logic.

Informational power

Informational power is one of John R. P. French and Bertram Raven's bases of power, and one of Patrick J. Montana and Bruce H. Charnov's varieties of organizational power. It was the sixth base, identified separately by Raven several years after he and French identified the first five. Informational power is power exerted by providing the target with information that results in a change in their attitudes or behavior.

Informational social influence

Informational social influence, or social proof, is a conformity-enforcing phenomenon in which individuals mimic the observed behavior of others in their attempt to behave correctly in a given situation. It is especially pronounced in ambiguous social situations in which the individual does not already possess a "script" for the appropriate behavior and has not already developed his own norms or habits. The effect may be conscious or unconscious and can lead to a large group confidently making an incorrect choice as a behavior or attitude cascades through it. This form of social influence is also sometimes blamed for the phenomenon of copycat suicide.

Initiating structure

One of two factors identified by the Ohio State Leadership Studies, the "initiating structure" factor refers to the way a leader organizes and defines roles within the group, delegates tasks among those roles, and organizes activities for the group. Setting specific performance metrics both for the group and for individual roles, establishing rules and procedures, and focusing on maintaining a schedule are behaviors associated with initiating structure.

Institutional economics

Institutional economics, beginning with Thorstein Veblen's work in the late 19th century, is the study of the role of institutions in economic behavior, incorporating in its classical form an evolutionary perspective, Veblen having been influenced by the work of Charles Darwin.

Institutional collectivism

One of the global leadership cultural competencies identified by the GLOBE Project, institutional collectivism is the extent to which the institutional culture of an organization or institutional cultures throughout a society encourage collective action and distribution of resources.

Instrumentality

In Victor Vroom's expectancy theory, instrumentality is an individual's belief that he will be rewarded if he performs a particular task. Instrumentality is affected by past history, trust in and consistency on the part of the source of the reward, and faith in the fairness or neutrality of the reward system.

Intelligence

Intelligence is a trait that is difficult to adequately define, as a mental capability that encompasses knowledge, memory, reasoning, creativity, capacity for abstract thought and synthesizing information, communication, learning, problem solving, logic, and critical thinking. Intelligence tests are widespread but generally measure only certain applications of intelligence and reasoning skills. The difficulty in defining intelligence in turn makes it difficult to establish the extent to which non-humans are intelligent, with some researchers distinguishing between animal instinct and the capacity for abstract thought, an understanding of consequences, and the ability to plan for the future based on past experiences, while other researchers ascribe intelligence or intelligence-like capacities not only to many animal species but to some plants. (Two common criteria for intelligence in a species are the ability to set goals and the ability to learn from past experiences.) Numerous studies have indicated that successful leaders have above-average intelligence.

International Leadership Association

The International Leadership Association was founded in 1999 and has a membership of about 2,000. Established with a grant from the W. K. Kellogg Foundation, it is headquartered at the University of Maryland, College Park, and is the principal member association for leadership studies. The annual conference is held in the fall and alternates between North American and non–North American host cities.

Instructional theory

An instructional theory is a framework describing methods of instruction: ways to help people acquire skills and knowledge.

Intellectual history

Intellectual history is the subfield of the history discipline that studies major ideas, the context in which they were developed and by whom they were developed, the social and cultural institutions relevant to their development, and the factors affecting these ideas' adoption or abandonment. Intellectual history has supplanted the earlier history of ideas, and is differentiated principally by its insistence that those ideas cannot be studied in historical context without reference to the individuals who formulated, popularized, and discussed them. Intellectual history includes and overlaps with many subfields, including the history of political thought, the history of philosophy, and historiography itself.

Internalized moral perspective

One of the qualities of authentic leadership, "internalized moral perspective" refers to the leader's possession of a strong sense of ethics that is well developed and resists external pressures.

Intrinsic motivation

Intrinsic motivation is motivation that is driven by factors within the individual, such as an enjoyment or personal interest in the behavior or task in question. Studies find, for instance, that students who are interested in increasing their knowledge or mastery of a subject perform better than those interested in earning a grade (or,

in younger students, a gold star, sticker, et cetera). Of course, there are cases where no intrinsic motivation exists and only extrinsic motivation will bring a behavior about.

Intuition

Intuition is a perceptive or cognitive capacity that does not rely on reason or inference, though it may draw on knowledge through processes inaudible to the conscious mind. Intuition has been studied extensively in psychology and cognitive science, and is associated with creative capacities and scientific innovation, but is not well understood even by the standards of cognitive science. The extent to which one relies on intuition over or instead of reason is one of the measures taken in many personality tests, and empathy is often treated as an aspect of intuition, at least insofar as its role in anticipating or sensing the emotions of others.

Iroquois Confederacy Grand Council

The Grand Council is the ruling assembly of the Iroquois Confederacy, a group of Native American nations in the northeast that historically included the Mohawk, Oneida, Onondaga, Cayuga, and Seneca, with the Tuscarora joining in 1722. Long before European contact, as early as the 12th century and no later than the 15th, the Grand Council made its decisions through consensus represented by a 75 percent super majority of its delegates. This system of government was a significant influence both on early New England colonies and later on the Articles of Confederacy and the Constitution.

Jepson School of Leadership Studies

The Jepson School of Leadership Studies in Virginia was founded in 1992 at the University of Richmond, with a donation from Robert S. Jepson Jr. Co-founder Joanna B. Ciulla has described

Jepson as "a liberal arts school with an explicit focus on the study of leadership," and its commitment to liberal arts is a distinct one, resulting in students studying history, philosophy, and literature as part of their growing understanding of leadership. This was a significant statement about the school's position on leadership studies, as at the time most of the literature in the field came from management and psychology. This characterization is also meant to differentiate Jepson from leadership training schools, the founders having decided to avoid that route.

Jesus as leader

Jesus of Nazareth is often used as an illustrative example of exemplary leadership, though the exact lessons to be drawn from his example vary from usage to usage. German sociologist Max Weber used him as an example of a charismatic leader with un-everyday-ness (cf.), one who repeatedly used the formula, in reference to the scripture that came before him, "It has been written . . . but I say unto you . . .," asserting his authority as the source of the law.

Joan of Arc

Joan of Arc is a Roman Catholic saint who was born to a French peasant family in the early 15th century. As a teenager, she claimed to experience visions of Saints Margaret and Catherine and the Archangel Michael, telling her to support Charles VII, the king of France whose legitimacy was questioned by England, a conflict forming part of the Hundred Years' War. When Joan's participation in the siege of Orleans led to a fast and decisive victory, she rose quickly to fame, and Charles was crowned not long after. When she was captured by the English, she was tried and burned at the stake for her claims of visions, at the age of 19. A Catholic court later debunked the trial and declared her

a martyr; she was canonized in the 20th century, becoming one of France's patron saints.

Job Characteristics Model

The Job Characteristics Model (JCM) is a work design theory that has influenced workplace-based positive psychology. Designed to create personally enriching jobs, in its original formulation it addressed five job characteristics (autonomy, feedback, skill variety, task identity, and task significance) and five work-driven outcomes (absenteeism, motivation, performance, satisfaction, and turnover). Though related in some ways to the old theories of scientific management that emphasized efficiency, versions of JCM have more recently been proposed that emphasize workplace happiness as a route to productivity.

Job enrichment

Job enrichment is a strategy to motivate employees by defining their job to include a variety of tasks and responsibilities, coupled with feedback, encouragement, and sufficient communication to make their tasks feel meaningful and contextualized.

Job rotation

Job rotation is the practice of assigning a worker to different roles within the organization in succession, often over a period of several years. Job rotation is used to train employees and help locate their ideal role, especially young employees fresh from college who have academic credentials but little relevant previous work experience. Job rotation can also be used to alleviate boredom or to reduce the risk of injuries resulting from repetitive task performance. A similar practice is used in the training of medical students, wherein the last two years of their four-year education are spent rotating through multiple medical specialties, in which they work full-time jobs under supervising physicians. Often they are required to rotate through internal medicine, pediatrics, obstetrics and gynecology, family medicine, radiology, neurology, emergency medicine, and surgery, as well as a sub-internship in their chosen specialty.

John F. Kennedy School of Government

The John F. Kennedy School of Government is a public policy graduate school at Harvard University, offering graduate degrees in public policy, public administration, and international development. Approaches to public policy studies vary considerably by school, and Harvard Kennedy School (HKS) is characterized by its leadership-based approach.

Judge-adviser system

A judge-adviser system is an advice structure studied in the social sciences, in which the judge is the individual with decision-making power in a situation, while the adviser is a second individual providing a recommendation or relevant information. Experimental studies of advice usually focus on the judge-adviser structure, with participants taking randomly assigned roles.

Judicial activism

Judicial activism is a usually pejorative term referring to judges whose rulings are motivated not wholly by interpretations of the relevant body of law, but by personal considerations, including political, ethical, moral, and religious beliefs. The term is especially used in reference to Supreme Court decisions with wide-ranging effects, from those upholding or banning segregation to recent decisions like *Bush v. Gore* and *Citizens United v. FEC*. Though the term is associated with complaints about the Court overstepping its authority, judicial activism

Seated in the front row are Sigmund Freud, G. Stanley Hall, and Carl Jung. Abraham A. Brill, Ernest Jones, and Sandor Ferenczi stand in the back row, in a 1909 photograph. (Public Domain)

need not be constructed as a wrong, and there are defenders of such activism who see it as a valid aspect of judicial review. Right or wrong, judicial activism amounts to a sort of leadership from the bench.

Jung, Carl

The Swiss psychiatrist Carl Jung was an early colleague of Sigmund Freud, though the two had a falling-out over their conceptions of the libido. Dismissed by Freud as too mystical, the more mystical and stranger elements of his work and his interest in alchemy and astrology did prove influential to the New Age movement and the new religious movements of the 1960s—but he also introduced the ideas of the archetype, the collective unconscious, and synchronicity, and his work on personality types was the basis for the Myers-Briggs Type Indicator, as well as influencing much of personality psychology and trait-based theories of leadership.

Juran, Joseph

One of the American engineers who traveled to Japan after World War II to help restore and modernize Japanese manufacturing, Joseph Juran became an influential management consultant, especially in the area of quality management. He was the first to apply the Pareto principle to quality control issues and among the first to draw attention to the cost of poor quality, a concept referring to the costs an organization could save by improving the quality of its performance.

Jus ad bellum

The Latin phrase for "right to war," jus ad bellum refers to the criteria that determine (in advance of engagement) whether a war is a just war.

Jus in bello

Latin for "right in war," jus in bello refers to the criteria of a justly conducted war.

Just war

A just war is one that is morally defensible, as defined by meeting at least two sets of traditional criteria: those showing that there is a moral reason to go to war, and those showing that conduct during the war is moral. Jus post bellum refers to a third set of criteria more recently proposed: the moral nature of postwar actions like reconstruction. The idea of a just war assumes that war is not always the worst possible choice, an assumption that is rejected by some pacifists. The pacifist Ben Salmon, for instance, was sentenced to death for desertion during World War I, writing to President Woodrow Wilson that there was no such thing as a just war. (His sentence was later commuted to 25 years hard labor, and along with other conscientious objectors, he was pardoned in 1920 in response to public demand.)

Juvenal

The 2nd-century Roman poet Juvenal was a satirist of ancient Roman society. He is best remembered for contributing two phrases to Western culture, which have survived across many languages: "bread and circuses," in the sense of the appeasement offered by a ruling power (in the form of food to nourish their bodies and entertainment to occupy their minds) to the populace as distraction from tyranny and injustice; and "quis custodiet ipsos custodes," "who will guard the guardians themselves," often translated into English as "who watches the watchmen?" This latter question is asked as a criticism of dictatorships and oligarchies, even the benevolent ones such as proposed by the philosopher Plato: without a system in check by which rulers can be removed from office, such as in a democracy, what means is there to ensure that rulers will abide by the law and rule justly?

Kaizen

"Good change" in Japanese, kaizen is a term with slightly different connotations in many areas of life, from banking to psychotherapy. It was introduced to Americans via Japanese management practices, in which kaizen refers to the continual reassessment and, when possible, improvement of business processes and job functions. The key difference between kaizen in this usage and other forms of structural change to an organization's business processes is the sense that kaizen is a continuous process rather than a one-time event. More drastic change is called "kaikaku."

Kellerman, Barbara

One of the founders of the International Leadership Association, Barbara Kellerman is a professor of public leadership at the Kennedy School of Government at Harvard University. Her work focuses on followership as well as the leadership styles of women.

Keynesian Revolution

After the publication of John Maynard Keynes's *General Theory* in 1936, inspired by his study of the factors leading to the Great Depression, the orthodox view in the field of economics shifted quickly from the neoclassical economics that had prevailed to the new Keynesian view. The key difference was Keynes's insistence that the driving factor behind employment levels was demand, not supply, whereas prior to the unemployment crisis of the Great Depression, economists believed that in an unregulated free market, full employment equilibrium would naturally occur. After Keynes, regulation of the market was seen as necessary for the safety of the economy. Keynesian economics lost much of its influence on policy in the late 1970s as a result of that decade's economic travails and the rise of the deregulation-happy Ronald Reagan Republicans, but saw a resurgence after the 2008 financial crisis. Keynes's Biercean definition of capitalism remains important: "the astounding belief that the most wicked of men will do the most wicked of things for the greatest good of everyone."

Kinesics

Kinesics is the area of nonverbal communication related to movements of the body, including gestures, posture, and facial expressions, and the study of that area. The term was coined by anthropologist Ray Birdwhistell, who considered the term *body language* inaccurate. Examples of kinesic communication range from a nod of the head meaning "yes" (or "I am listening") to a student shifting in their seat indicating a wandering attention. Kinesic communication varies greatly from culture to culture.

King, Martin Luther, Jr.

The Reverend Martin Luther King, Jr., was one of the most prominent leaders of the African American Civil Rights movement in the 1950s and 1960s. A Baptist minister, he helped found the Southern Christian Leadership Conference in 1957 after organizing the Montgomery bus boycott after the arrest of Rosa Parks. A famously powerful speaker, he was considered a radical by J. Edgar Hoover and the Federal Bureau of Investigation, though today he is often contrasted with other civil rights leaders like Malcolm X who were less moderate in their views of how equality was to be achieved. For 13 years, King was one of the most prominent figures in the country, leading marches and other demonstrations, affirming his commitment to nonviolence, and speaking out against the Vietnam War. He was assassinated in 1968 by James Earl Ray; in 1999, Loyd Jowers, who owned a restaurant near the site of the attack, was found responsible by a Memphis jury for a conspiracy to murder King, but the details remain vague.

Knew-it-all-along

The knew-it-all-along effect is a cognitive bias in which people misremember and overestimate the extent of their past knowledge, such that they project backward onto their conception of their past self the understanding that they currently possess.

Knowledge

Knowledge is information and understanding that is acquired through experience or education. Knowledge includes both practical understanding—usually acquired through hands-on experience—and theoretical understanding. Knowledge must be acquired, which requires exposure to new information (though existing knowledge can be preserved or strengthened through repeated exposure, and connections between pieces of acquired knowledge can be discovered). The philosophical study of the nature of knowledge is called epistemology, while cognitive science, neuroscience, and psychology all approach the mechanisms and processes of knowledge acquisition and retention.

Kritarchy

Kritarchy is rulership by judges, as for example in ancient Israel as depicted in the Old Testament Book of Judges in the era before the appointment of Saul as the first king.

Lacan, Jacques

The most significant figure in psychoanalysis after Sigmund Freud, Jacques Lacan was one of the principal French intellectuals of the 1950s, 1960s, and 1970s. He held annual seminars in Paris from 1953 to 1981, which helped spread his ideas. Chief among them was his interrogation of ego psychology and rereading of Freud in light of the developments of the last half-century, and his extension of Freud's work on drives (psychological motivations that are inherently unsatisfiable and thus account for much of human behavior).

Laissez-Faire

Laissez-faire, "let them do/let them be," is perhaps the best-known French phrase in economics. It represents an approach to economic policy that calls for avoiding restrictions, regulations, tariffs, and subsidies as much as possible, limiting the government's involvement to the protection of ownership rights and, in most formulations, protection from fraud and other basic crimes. (Some do not even call for fraud protection, arguing that market forces are sufficient to disincentivize it.)

Lateral communication

Lateral communication in an organization transpires among participants at the same organizational level, such as between members of the same department. Lateral communication is more direct and effective, and studies have found that when members of an organization need to rely on lateral communication to solve a problem, information sharing and task coordination are easier than when vertical communication (between participants on different levels of the hierarchy) is required. On the other hand, it can invoke its own special pitfalls, notably territoriality as departments and teams work to protect their respective turfs.

Lateral thinking

Lateral thinking is a problem-solving approach that applies creative thinking and indirect reasoning rather than "vertical" step-by-step logic or "horizontal" brainstorming. Maltese physician and author Edward de Bono introduced the term in 1967. One of its methods is called "disproving" (or "the black hat," in de Bono's later *Six Thinking Hats*), in which statements accepted as common knowledge or obviously true are challenged and assumed to be wrong.

Law of the instrument

The law of the instrument is a maxim first stated by philosopher Abraham Kaplan in 1964 and rephrased by psychologist Abraham Maslow, more famously, in 1966. Kaplan's "law of the instrument" stated, "Give a small boy a hammer, and he will find everything he encounters needs pounding." Maslow rephrased this as, "If the only tool you have is a hammer, it is tempting to treat everything as if it were a nail." The popular adage derived from this is "If all you have is a hammer, everything looks like a nail," which naturally has been widely attributed to Mark Twain, who said no such thing. In any formulation, the maxim reflects a certain common and dangerous narrow-mindedness that views the

American prisoners captured in Ardennes, Germany, in 1944. The law of war concerns acceptable wartime conduct, including the treatment of prisoners. (German Federal Archives)

world in terms defined by one's own capabilities and competencies, and so insists on solutions that make use of those capabilities.

Law of war

The area of international law concerning acceptable actions in war and justifications for going to war, including issues like the treatment of prisoners, civilian casualties and civilian targets, prohibited weapons, proportionality, and the acceptance of surrender.

Leader Authenticity Scale

The Leader Authenticity Scale (LAS) was the first method developed to measure authentic leadership, and was introduced in 1983 by education researchers James E. Henderson and Wayne K. Hoy. The three areas most closely examined were accountability, avoiding manipulation of followers, and "salience of self over role"—the leader's ability to behave the same regardless of his job title, rather than assuming a role.

Leader–member exchange theory

Leader–member exchange or LMX theory is a leadership theory that is concerned with the dyadic relationship between leaders and followers, called leader–member exchanges. Each of these exchange relationships influences factors that impact the follower's work, including their resource access, influence on the decision-making process, and overall performance. Thus, healthy relationships with followers leads to better organizational performance. LMX theory grew out of role theory in the 1960s and 1970s, and posits three stages of the leader–member relationship: role-taking, role-making, and routinization. Role-taking occurs when a member first joins the group. Role-making occurs as new members take on tasks, and as a result of their performance at work, are subconsciously perceived by their supervisors as either in-group (a "team player" who fits in with the group) or out-group (as a result of lack of motivation or work quality). Routinization is the stage in which routines and habits develop in the relationship between a team member and a supervisor, with in-group members developing a healthier relationship with their supervisor while out-group members may have trouble earning trust back. One prescription growing out of LMX theory is for managers to identify the workers they have subconsciously treated as out-group, and reevaluate whether they still deserve that classification or have simply become alienated as a result of the unhealthy leader–member exchange.

Leadership

The act of being in charge of the decisions and actions of a group, of setting its goals, of issuing instructions to its members or to delegated go-betweens, and of evaluating the outcome of decisions. Leaders may be formal or informal, chosen by the group or appointed by an outside party, even selected at random, as with the jury foreman in some jurisdictions. The duties and powers of a leader naturally vary as well. When undertaken deliberately and skillfully, leadership can be seen as both an art and a science, and studied from either perspective.

Leadership (journal)

Published by Sage since 2005, *Leadership* is a scholarly journal of leadership studies. It is distinct in its solidly interdisciplinary approach, whereas the leadership studies journals preceding it were grounded primarily in psychology and management.

Leadership accountability movement

In the 21st century, there has been a loosely connected movement or trend to hold leaders of various institutions accountable for the harm caused by their actions or inaction. Clear examples include the growing dissent over the Catholic Church's handling of priestly sexual abuse, and the role that dissent may have played in the retirement of Pope Benedict; the establishment of the International Criminal Court and the United Nations Convention Against Corruption; protests greeting G8 meetings; the Arab Spring protests, and similarly motivated protests in Europe and Africa; and possible changes in the American demeanor toward Israel's treatment of Palestinians.

Leadership Behavior Description Questionnaire

A questionnaire designed by the Ohio State Leadership Studies team in the 1940s to measure nine different areas of leader behavior. Questionnaires were distributed to various groups whose members were asked to identify how frequently their leader engaged in each of 150 different behaviors. The two areas that showed the most variation were labeled

Consideration and Initiating Structure, which provided a framework for early leadership studies that moved away from a focus on leader personality in favor of leader behavior.

The Leadership Challenge

The Leadership Challenge is a 1987 book by James Kouzes and Barry Posner, which introduced their model of "the five practices of exemplary leadership," as supported by case studies. Their studies began with surveys of leaders, asking what practices they associated with their personal best performance. Rejecting trait-based models of leadership, they present a number of common personality traits and explain how people with these personalities can learn leadership skills and practices. The five practices they identified were labeled "Model the Way," "Inspire a Shared Vision," "Challenge the Process," "Enable Others to Act," and "Encourage the Heart," the least common of the five in their studies. "Encourage the Heart" combines authentic leadership, inclusivity, and taking pains to recognize employee successes and contributions. One of the most influential leadership books, *The Leadership Challenge* has been published in several editions (the 5th was released in 2012 on its 25th anniversary) and 20 languages, and Kouzes and Posner have become more prescriptive over time, developing self-assessment tools based on their book that have been adopted by government agencies and the Red Cross.

Leadership development

Leadership development is the attempt to improve leadership behaviors and abilities in individuals. This may take the form of a college program, such as some offered at business schools, or smaller-scale events like weekend seminars or executive retreats.

Leadership Institute at Harvard College

The Leadership Institute at Harvard College was founded in 2005 by four undergraduates. It is a student-run leadership development program, offering workshops, forums, and speaking engagements through the Leadership Development Initiative and the Presidents' Forum.

Leadership presence

Leadership presence is a concept that shows up in many discussions of leadership, and may at least in some cases be the same as charisma. In his *Three Levels of Leadership*, James Scouller uses the term to refer to a "something" that the most effective leaders have that allows them to command attention and trust, a "something" that varies from leader to leader—which in Scouller's view accounts for the failures of trait-based leadership theories.

Leadership pedagogy

Leadership pedagogy is the science of teaching leadership or leadership studies, which involves an introduction to various theories and models of leadership, group psychology, management theory, and other areas.

Leadership philosophy versus leadership theory

The distinction between a leadership philosophy and a leadership theory is sometimes useful. Though both may be normative, the former advocates specific values, as in ethical leadership or servant leadership, while the latter focuses on maximizing effectiveness. This should not be confused with the difference between normative (or prescriptive) leadership theory, which advocates a specific approach to leadership, and descriptive leadership theory, which merely describes how leadership is performed in the world.

Leadership psychology

A cross-disciplinary field, leadership psychology examines leadership as something that occurs in a complex system of individual and group behaviors. It is influenced both by positive psychology and by adaptive leadership, and studies the ways leaders work with followers to identify goals, assign roles, build consensus, and collaborate on projects. Leadership in introducing or adapting to necessary changes is also an area of interest.

Leadership Quarterly

The *Leadership Quarterly* (LQ) is the oldest scholarly journal for leadership studies, having been published in affiliation with the International Leadership Association since 1990. One of the highest-ranked journals in management and applied psychology, it primarily publishes scholars from those fields, though it is interdisciplinary in scope and open to submissions from other disciplines. In 2014, amid complaints about the quality of research in the leadership studies field and the increase in articles of specious quality, LQ retracted five articles from a Florida International University researcher whose work had been met with a flurry of reader complaints.

Leadership Series

Since 2003, the central event of India's Symbiosis Institute of International Business has been the Leadership Series, a three-day series of events attended by prominent speakers and participants from the worlds of business, politics, and international affairs.

Leadership studies

Leadership studies is a multidisciplinary field examining the phenomenon of leadership, the roles of leaders and followers, and the many styles of leadership. Leadership studies grew out of psychology and management, but history, philosophy, and the social sciences have long addressed leadership issues, while questions raised in education, public policy, and international relations have often had relevance to leadership. Today the field draws on numerous disciplines and includes researchers from diverse academic backgrounds.

Lean

Lean, short for "lean production" or "lean manufacturing," is an approach to production that builds on Frederick W. Taylor's scientific management from the early 20th century and Toyota Production System developed mid-century in focusing on the elimination of any resource expenditure that is not represented by added value for the end customer. Lean government takes a similar approach to the provision of government services, seeking to eliminate waste and inefficiency in public programs. Lean government had been implemented in Cape Coral, Florida; Grand Rapids, Michigan; and Fort Wayne, Indiana, among other cities.

Learning by doing

Learning by doing refers to experiential learning, and in economics, it refers to an organization or its employees learning to improve productivity as a result of performing its work, and in the course of that performance, streamlining or improving certain processes or becoming more adept through practice.

Learning by teaching

Learning by teaching is a method of education in which students are selected to teach part of a class's lesson, choosing their own methodology and approach (rather than simply making an oral presentation within a rigid didactic

formula). This has long been practiced to deal with labor shortages: in early European schools, older students sometimes taught younger ones, passing on what they had learned only a few years earlier, while today in American universities much of the labor burden in the teaching of introductory courses is borne by graduate students. The emphasis of learning by teaching, though, is the benefit to the student-as-teacher and the way it engages them with the material.

Learning theory

A learning theory is a framework describing the absorption and handling of information during learning processes, and forms the underpinning of an educational, instructional, or management approach.

Least preferred coworker

In Fiedler's contingency theory of leadership, the least preferred co-worker (LPC) is the co-worker with whom the leader has had the least success in work relationships. The importance of the LPC measurement is not how it reflects on the individual the leader considers their LPC, but rather on how they rate and describe their LPC, which in Fred Fiedler's view indicates their approach to work. Those who are motivated mostly by interpersonal dynamics will view an LPC less favorably regardless of that co-worker's productivity, while someone with a more "bottom line" orientation will forgive interpersonal frictions if the co-worker contributes something to the work group's productivity.

Legalism

In Chinese philosophy, the legalist school was a 1st millennium B.C.E. philosophical movement concerned with advocating the running of the state according to a strictly followed system of laws. Legalism was essentially pragmatic, but heavily influenced by the values promoted by both Confucianism and Mohism (though those schools differed strongly in some important areas). A key aspect of legalism was the *shi*, or mystery of authority, with which the emperor was imbued, and which entitled him to the unquestioning obedience of his people. The leader, in turn, was not supposed to be too showy or overt in his demands—a leader who needs to make threats is one who is not confident he will be obeyed, which calls into question his possession of *shi*. Because the emperor was supposed to remain mysterious and low profile, this also necessitated an elaborate bureaucracy, which in turn helped to justify the necessity of an elaborate system of rules for its operations.

Legitimacy

Legitimacy literally means "lawfulness," but in politics refers to the general acceptance of a ruling authority by the populace. Many regimes may be legal but considered illegitimate, especially if free elections were not held to put the regime in power; even in such cases when elections were held, if there are concerns about voter access, restrictions on the right to vote, or the vote-counting process, the elected regime may be considered illegitimate. The controversy over the 2000 U.S. presidential election is an obvious example of this. In the political philosophy of John Locke, the source of legitimacy is the consent of the governed.

Legitimacy (French and Raven)

Legitimacy is one of John R. P. French and Bertram Raven's bases of power, and one of Patrick J. Montana and Bruce H. Charnov's varieties of organizational power. Legitimate power originates from being elected, appointed, or otherwise put in a position of power by means that accord to social norms and expectations, or from being put in a position in which social norms say that they are entitled to power (though saying so explicitly may be unfamiliar). Influence is exerted because the target feels obligated. This includes not only the power of elected or appointed officials, for instance, but the influence on an individual's actions when they see someone in need and feel obligated to offer assistance because the values they have taken in from the social norms of their surroundings tell them to.

Leveling

In the work of existential philosopher Soren Kierkegaard, leveling is a social phenomenon in which all human activities are assigned equal value, smoothing out the complexities and whorls and grooves of individual experience until abstraction overtakes the uniqueness of the individual. Leveling is a communication process that occurs during organizational socialization. Idle talk and gossip leads to creating secondhand needs and definitions of selfhood, an abstract concept of "the public" with which the individual compares himself and loses his individual definition of the self in the process, adopting the societal definition in its place. This in turn leads to the individual renouncing responsibility, which instead rests with the crowd. Similarly, adopting organizational beliefs and values as part of organizational socialization distances the individual from his authentic beliefs, and in so doing, reduces his feelings of personal responsibility. Kierkegaard condemns leveling because it reduces personal responsibility, self-reflection, and individual authenticity—the basic requirements of authentic leadership—and so condemns the idle talk and gossiping that he feels create the process. Self-reflection and introspection act as checks against the effects of leveling.

Lexical hypothesis

One of the key hypotheses in the psychology of personality, the lexical hypothesis was first proposed by English psychologist Francis Galton in the 19th century. The lexical hypothesis states that because our encounters with personality traits are such an important part of our experience, major personality traits are inevitably reflected in our language—that is, a natural language always develops the capacity to discuss these personality traits—and the most important or prominent personality traits may be referred to with a single word. Numerous theories and methodologies in the psychology of personality depend on the lexical hypothesis, including most personality tests and metrics, which depend on description (by the self or other) and therefore take as a postulate the capacity of language to accurately discuss personality traits. There are many criticisms of the hypothesis, despite its widespread use. It seems predicated on a more precise use of language than laymen apply to personality-descriptive terms, for one thing. For another, there has been considerable debate throughout the history of philosophy as to whether language is sufficient to fully describe human experience. What's more, language does not account for the whole of human communication, and by extension even a rephrasing of the lexical hypothesis itself could suggest that while all major personality traits are reflected in human communication, some of them could be indicated only by body language, vocal tone, and other paralinguistic cues.

Liberal arts

The concept of the liberal arts is inherited from classical Greek education, in which Aristotle believed they represented the disciplines and areas of knowledge necessary for free people. In medieval Europe, this developed into the trivium (logic, grammar, and rhetoric—the verbal arts) and the quadrivium (mathematics and its three classical applications: music, astronomy, and geometry). Much of what we now associate with the liberal arts—history, the social sciences, the study of literature—did not yet exist as a formal field of study. This focus on education as individual development, as distinct from job training (the purpose to which the liberal arts have been shoehorned today), in many ways presages the development of leadership studies and explains the identification of leadership studies institutes like the Jepson School with the liberal arts.

Liberum veto

The Liberum veto was a unique feature of the Polish-Lithuanian Sejm (the legislature) in the 16th through 18th centuries. It allowed any legislator to end the session and nullify the legislation that had already passed by shouting out his veto. The legislature operated on the principle that if nobles were all equal, the legislation they passed could only be passed unanimously. In later years the Liberum veto was held up as an emblem of an ineffective system.

Life coach

A life coach works one-on-one with clients (though they may also publish work detailing their views and methodology, or offer seminars) in an attempt to help them develop and pursue their personal and professional goals. Unlike a therapist or analyst, the life coach does not offer counseling or psychological analysis but may recommend seeking out such services as a step in realizing a goal. Nevertheless, they occupy a similar cultural niche occupied by analysts and encounter groups in the 1960s through the 1980s and have not coincidentally become popular as the therapy field has shifted away from long-term relationships in favor of short-term crisis interventions. In most states, life coaches are not subject to licensing or other restrictions, though in some they are classed as mental health professionals and bound by relevant regulation.

Lifestyle guru

A type of life coach that developed in the 1990s, a lifestyle guru is an individual who combines religious advising with hands-on guidance to change one's lifestyle. Like life coaches and personal trainers, lifestyle gurus primarily work one-on-one with clients, and are especially associated with the idle rich, but may also air their views in books, magazine articles, or Web sites.

Likert, Rensis

A University of Michigan professor in the Institute for Social Research, Rensis Likert (1903–81) was an early pioneer in leadership studies. He led Michigan's Leadership Studies group in the 1950s and developed Likert's Management Systems—four broad descriptive styles of management he had observed in his work, which he later expanded to describe educational institutions as well as business organizations. Likert also developed the Likert scale, which is still used in social science and marketing surveys. Instead of asking respondents to answer "agree" or "disagree" to various statements, the Likert scale uses a five point scale of agreement from "strongly agree" to "strongly disagree" in order to weight response according to strength of feeling.

Likert's management systems

Leadership studies pioneer Rensis Likert identified and described four management systems, originally based on the management styles he found in his studies of supervisors of an insurance company and later revised to apply to educational settings as well. Each system assigns roles to leaders and their followers and defines the relationships between them: exploitative authoritative, benevolent authoritative, consultive system, and participative system.

Lincoln, Abraham, as leader

When Barack Obama ran for president in 2008, he named *Team of Rivals: The Political Genius of Abraham Lincoln*, Doris Kearns Goodwin's 2005 book about President Abraham Lincoln's leadership, as the one book other than the Bible that he would bring to the White House, in answer to a question journalists ask of presidential candidates to elicit answers that symbolize their values and views of the presidency. But although there is widespread consensus among historians that Lincoln was an exceptionally capable leader, there is little agreement on what lessons can be drawn from his leadership. Goodwin's study, which won the Pulitzer Prize, stressed Lincoln's desire to hear multiple points of view before making a decision and his choice of political rivals as his cabinet

Abraham Lincoln was a highly capable leader, aided by his strong communication and persuasion skills. (Library of Congress)

members. In 2008 Goodwin presented a keynote address to the Society for Human and Resource Management titled "The 10 Qualities that Made Lincoln Great," applying Lincoln thinking to modern management. Others have pointed to the relationship between the presidency and the Constitution, which defines and limits its powers, and Lincoln's recognition that leading a constitutional government was a unique challenge that required self-restraint. Still others pointed to his performance in the Lincoln–Douglas debates, and drew attention to his skills of communication and persuasion and his ability to regulate his emotions.

Lockstep compensation

A compensation system associated with the legal profession, lockstep compensation determines an employee's salary based on their seniority in the organization, regardless of merit or other considerations. In legal firms, this may be true of all attorneys (with separate base pay levels for associates and partners), just partners, or just partners and partner-track associates.

The Lonely Crowd

David Riesman, Nathan Glazer, and Reuel Denney's *The Lonely Crowd*, published in 1950, is one of the most influential sociological studies of the United States, and is particularly focused on the position of the country in the middle of the 20th century, when the middle class that had arisen after the Industrial Revolution began to dominate the country with its "other-directed" culture. The third of three cultural types analyzed in American history by Riesman, other-directed individuals define themselves in relation to others, and are accommodating and malleable as a result. It was this type that proved necessary for the rise of corporations and large organizations in the post–World War II years. *The Lonely Crowd* functions as an unintended perfect companion to *White Collar* and *The Organization Man*.

Long- versus short-term orientation

One of the cultural dimensions of organizations identified by Geert Hofstede, organizations and other cultures tend to be primarily concerned with either the short term or the long term. Long-term-oriented cultures are more able to adapt to changing conditions, as well as being more inclined toward perseverance; short-term cultures are more invested in their current values as representing absolute truth, and more likely to believe that a current practice is the best practice.

Lucretius

The Roman philosopher Lucretius, writing in the 1st century B.C.E., is best known for his epic poem "De Rerum Natura" ("On the Nature of Things"), which argued that belief in the gods was the source of human unhappiness, because humans conceived of bitter and wrathful gods; that the universe was governed by material laws, not supernatural whims; and that death is neither good nor bad for the deceased, representing a simple and complete cessation of being, without the continuation of consciousness in an afterlife. In ancient Rome, this was not necessarily revolutionary, as philosophers explored a wide variety of ideas; when the poem was rediscovered, translated, and circulated in Europe in the 15th and 16th centuries, it played a key role in catalyzing the humanistic revolution of the Renaissance.

Lyndon B. Johnson School of Public Affairs

The Lyndon B. Johnson (LBJ) School of Public Affairs is a graduate school at the University of Texas at Austin (UTA), offering master's and doctoral degrees in public affairs and related fields (as well as dual-degree programs in conjunction with other UTA schools). The LBJ School includes the Center for Politics and Governance, devoted to leadership development in the political sphere.

The Man in the Gray Flannel Suit

In many ways the fictional companion to *The Organization Man*, 1955's *The Man in the Gray Flannel Suit*, by Sloan Wilson, captured much of the zeitgeist of the 1950s. In the novel, Tom Rath and his wife Betsy struggle to find meaning in a business-dominated world.

Management consulting

Management consulting is the business of improving an organization's performance by introducing changes to its management practices. Organizations may hire a management consulting firm to deal with a specific problem or concern, or simply seek an evaluation of their performance and the ways it can be improved. Management consulting dates to Arthur D. Little Inc., which formed as a partnership in 1886, and experienced periods of significant growth in the 1930s (due to the changes introduced by the Glass-Steagall Act) and the 1980s. Many consulting firms specialize in specific industries or specific areas, such as human resource consulting or information technology consulting. Around the turn of the 21st century, the management consulting industry shifted from a time-and-materials-based pricing model to results-based pricing, with some consultants working for a fixed price based on specific deliverables and others working for a fraction of the value of the performance improvement that is introduced. Some corporations instead hire internal management consultants, who work on a full-time rather than project basis.

Management development

Management development is the increase of competence in managers by various means, including training, seminars, executive education programs, mentoring, self-evaluations, and other possibilities.

Management fad

"Management fad" is a pejorative term for a change introduced by management, with the implication being that the change has not been well considered or is not well suited to the organization, or that it will be replaced by a newer incompatible change when the next fad sweeps through the industry. Management fads are generally associated with changes to terminology, including new or rephrased job titles and new terms for existing business processes and practices, and a cottage industry of consultants whose job is to implement the fad. Similar fads are found in education, though the relatively greater organizational inertia of the education industry slows their adoption and consequently reduces their population.

Management by objectives

See Management by results

Management by perkele

A Finnish style of authoritarian leadership ("perkele" is a Finnish deity whose name is shouted in roughly the same contexts as "frak!" or "dang it!") originally associated with the Finnish army, in which no dissent is tolerated, but now used especially by the Swedish to refer to the use of such authoritarian approaches in the private sector where they are less appropriate.

Management by results

Management by results is an approach to management that focuses on defining an organization's goals through participation by both management and workers and setting policies and practices that are clearly appropriate to those goals, such that employees have an understanding of the results that are intended by their labors.

Management by wandering around

In the Japanese business world, the *genba* or *gemba* is the shop floor or wherever most of the organization's production takes place, and "going to the genba" means managers walking through the production area to observe and interact. In the United States, "management by wandering around" similarly calls for managers to physically interact at the site of production, not simply visiting in response to a problem or at appointed times, but at random impromptu points, in order to experience a random sampling of the production process.

Managerial grid model

Developed in 1964 by Robert Blake and Jane Mouton, the managerial grid model is a model of situational leadership, influenced by Theory X and Theory Y (cf.). The model portrays a grid with two axes, concern for production and concern for people, with a range from one to nine, and five styles of leadership plotted on the resulting graph: indifferent (or impoverished), accommodating (or country club), dictatorial (or produce or perish), status quo (or middle of the road), and sound (or team). Two other styles were later added: the paternalistic style, which discourages dissent and supports followers through praise; and the opportunistic style, which adopts whichever position on the grid suits its purposes.

Mandate of Heaven

The Mandate of Heaven is a concept in Chinese political philosophy that derives the legitimacy of an emperor's rule from the will of Heaven. The mandate is bestowed upon a just ruler, but may be withdrawn if he ceases to be just, resulting in an overthrow by rivals. Therefore, calamities experienced by the people of ancient China, including natural disasters and famines, were taken as signs that the Mandate of Heaven had been withdrawn. The principle was first used to justify the overthrow of the Shang dynasty by the Zhou dynasty and was invoked thereafter as a way to discourage abuses of power.

Mandela, Nelson

Nelson Mandela was one of the leaders of the anti-apartheid movement in South Africa, and the first black President of South Africa, elected in 1994 in the country's first fully multiracial election. A lawyer and activist in the 1940s and 1950s, he was imprisoned in 1962 for his campaign of sabotage against South Africa's apartheid regime. The apartheid policy, a system of legally classified racial groups segregated into specific residential areas, had been formally instituted in 1948, though racial segregation in general dated to the colonial era. While Mandela was in prison, apartheid was strengthened; basic services like education and health care were segregated, and blacks were denied South African citizenship and assigned citizenship to one of 10 tribes instead. Mandela became the public face of anti-apartheid resistance and was released in 1990 after international pressures. His negotiations with South African President F. W. de Klerk saved face for the latter and led to the abolition of apartheid and the first multiracial elections. As president, Mandela worked to undo apartheid and address its damages, while expanding health care. He declined a second term and instead became an international activist working against poverty and AIDS until his death in 2013.

Market culture

One of four organizational cultures identified by Robert Quinn's Competing Values Framework, market culture is externally focused on the well-being of the organization as a whole and favors a controlled organization structure. Leaders in market culture organizations motivate employees with rewards contingent on performance.

Martin, John Levi

University of Chicago sociology professor John Levi Martin's work suggests microscale cultural institutions result in the emergence of macro-scale social structures.

Maryland School of Public Policy

Part of the University of Maryland, the Maryland School of Public Policy is located inside the Capital Beltway and is one of the highest-ranked policy schools in the country. It offers master's programs in public policy and public management, including a specialization in management and leadership in which students study the relationship of government to the private and nonprofit sectors, as well as theories of leadership.

Marxism

Marxism is an ideology founded on historical materialism and Marxist dialectics, concerned with class struggle and a critique of capitalism. It may be more accurate to speak of Marxisms, or of Marxist ideologies, than a single interpretation of Marxism, which began with the work of German philosophers Karl Marx and Friedrich Engels in the mid-19th century. It is especially concerned with the development of society around the means by which people provide for their material needs, and thus an economic basis for the discussion of cultural, social, legal, and political institutions and phenomena. Marx's view of an ideal society is best summed up by the maxim often erroneously attributed to him, but which was actually coined by Louis Blanc: "From each according to his ability, to each according to his need." In this way, maximum value is created, and everyone's needs are attended.

Masculinity versus femininity

One of the cultural dimensions proposed by Geert Hofstede, masculinity versus femininity represents the way emotional roles are distributed between the genders. In masculine cultures, gender role differences are drastic and there is little flexibility, as in parts of the Arab world. In feminine cultures, men and women play similar roles and hold similar values.

Maslow's hierarchy of needs

Maslow's hierarchy of needs is a theory of human motivation proposed by psychologist Abraham Maslow in a 1943 paper, and later expanded. It is often represented as a pyramid, with the most basic human needs at the base level. From the most to least basic, the hierarchy of needs consists of physiological needs (air, food, water, sleep, etc.), safety (including the physical safety of the body from harm or ill health as well as safety of the family, access to resources, and employment), belongingness, esteem (including the needs for self-respect and respect by others), and self-actualization and self-transcendence (including the need for creative outlets, moral systems, and intellectual pursuits). The model provides a way to think of human needs that acknowledges the psychological need for things like self-respect or creative outlets while also explaining why these things may be sacrificed in the service of more fundamental needs. Maslow was also instrumental in the work recognizing the importance of belongingness as a human motivation. Though Maslow's work is less prominent in modern psychology than attachment theory, it remains influential and well-known in sociology, management, and leadership studies. Geert Hofstede has criticized the hierarchy for being culture-specific, arguing that the arrangement of needs actually differs from culture to culture, and that in particular the Maslow hierarchy reflects the values of an especially individualistic society.

Maternalism

Maternalism is an ideology that promotes a particular model of femininity and femaleness, and based on that model promotes the involvement of women in specifically female-appropriate roles in society. Arguably, maternalism helped involve women in roles outside the home in the 19th century, when women were prominent in the leadership of social reform movements, but the notion of there being male- and female-appropriate roles in working life is at odds with the goals of second-wave feminism and gender equality, and is at least in part responsible for the underrepresentation of women in leadership roles in nearly every industry.

Matriarchy

A matriarchy is a social, political, or cultural system in which women occupy all or most of the leadership roles. Unlike a patriarchial society, there is no real historical evidence for the existence of true matriarchal cultures, the 19th century theories about prehistoric matriarchal cultures having long since been discredited. The prevalence of matrilineal systems—systems in which descent or membership is traced through the mother's lineage, as with Jewishness today and numerous cultures throughout the world in the pre-modern

An elderly Hopi matriarch. The Hopi Native American tribe in northeastern Arizona had a gender ideology based on female superiority, with women central to the institutions of clan and household. (Public Domain)

era—strongly suggests that egalitarian cultures were once more common.

Maxwell School

The Maxwell School of Citizenship and Public Affairs, in Syracuse, New York, was founded in 1924 and was the first school to offer a graduate degree in public administration.

Mayo, Elton

Elton Mayo was an Australian psychologist whose work influenced the young field of organizational psychology in the early 20th century. Mayo pioneered human relations theory and innovative studies of productivity, including the impact of workplace lighting choices on employee productivity, and conducted the Hawthorne Studies. One of the key findings of Mayo's work was that the desire to feel a sense of belonging in the group impacted workers more than financial incentives or working conditions.

MBA

The master of business administration (MBA) is a graduate degree in business administration, which was introduced in the United States in the early 20th century against the background of scientific management. The first graduate degree in business was the Master of Science in Commerce, offered by the Tuck School of Business at Dartmouth, the first graduate business school in the United States, in 1900. The

Harvard Business School opened in 1908 with an MBA program. The prestige of the MBA, especially in American institutions, was seriously damaged by the financial crisis of 2008 and the role played by the worlds of finance, management, and academia.

Men's rights movement

The men's rights movement originated in the 1970s as a countermovement to second-wave feminism. Early men's rights groups in the 1920s opposed the entrance of women into the labor market, in part because it was another group with which white male workers would have to compete; labor parties and unions had previously opposed immigration and child labor for the same reason, to preserve the value of white male labor. With that battle essentially lost, the 1970s men's rights movement instead opposed other initiatives of feminists, both real and imagined, especially the alleged "feminization" of American culture.

Mentoring

Mentoring is a relationship between two people, in which the more experienced or knowledgeable of the two helps to guide the other and develop good habits. Mentoring is distinct from tutoring in that it typically differs substantially from teaching, as mentoring tends to be not only less formal but as concerned with the transmission of norms, social capital, traditions, and frames of reference as with knowledge. Where once the terms *protege* and *protegee* were used to refer to the less experienced member of the relationship, today "mentee" has become more common. Mentoring has enjoyed healthy growth since the 1970s in the business world, and is a standard part of the academic world, in which graduate students work with a thesis or dissertation adviser who typically acts to introduce the student to the world of professional academia and the norms and behaviors thereof, in addition to helping shape the thesis or dissertation.

Mentoring techniques

A 1995 survey of mentoring in the business world by Bob Aubrey and Paul Cohen found that most mentoring activities were represented by five techniques. In "accompanying," the mentor takes part in the learning process with the mentee. In "sowing," the mentee is given information that they are not ready to put to use or understand yet, in anticipation of the situation in which it will finally become clear. In "catalyzing," the mentor drops the mentee into the deep end of the pool, so to speak, forcing them to work and learn under pressure. In "showing," the mentor demonstrates the thing they are teaching. And in "harvesting," the mentor asks the mentee questions about their progress so far, especially with the intent of guiding the conversation so that the mentee makes connections they had not been able to articulate previously.

Metamotivation

Metamotivation is a psychological concept from the work of Abraham Maslow, best known for Maslow's hierarchy of needs. In that hierarchy, the highest tier—the least pressing of the basic needs—is devoted to self-actualization, such as creative outlets. In Maslow's framework, "motivation" describes any drive concerned with meeting the basic needs of the hierarchy, while "metamotivation" is the motivation of individuals who have met their basic needs, including self-actualization, and are now striving to transcend that hierarchy in order to fulfill their potential as humans. The "metaneeds" beyond the hierarchy include

Wholeness, Perfection, Completion, Justice, Richness, Simplicity, Liveliness, Beauty, Goodness, Uniqueness, Playfulness, Truth, Autonomy, and Meaningfulness.

Mexican standoff

"Mexican standoff" is a term, first coined in the 19th century, for a confrontation among three parties, each of whom is hostile toward the other two. Originally coined to refer to armed conflicts in the age of revolvers, this scenario meant that any one party who acted on his aggression—fired his weapon—would be left vulnerable to attack by a minimum of one of the other two parties. From the perspective of any given participant, A, the most advantageous possibility is for B to kill C, freeing A to kill B. Because all three are in this identical position, it is not safe for any of the three to act, nor is there a means of safely withdrawing.

Michigan Studies of Leadership

A series of leadership studies by Rensis Likert at the University of Michigan in the 1950s, the Michigan studies focused on identifying which leadership styles most benefited job satisfaction and productivity. Likert's team sorted leaders into two broad styles (employee-oriented and production-oriented), of which an employee-oriented approach without close supervision led to the best results. Likert's team also identified task-oriented behavior, relationship-oriented behavior, and participative leadership as critical characteristics of effective leadership.

Micromanagement

Micromanagement is a management style conducted through close observation of employees' work coupled with frequent input or intervention. Micromanagement results when supervisors are unable to commit to delegating the workload, instead assigning duties to employees without trusting them to carry those duties out. A manager and an employee may not always agree on the line between attention to detail and micromanagement, of course, but even the perception of being micromanaged interferes with employee engagement, satisfaction, and security.

Milgram, Stanley

Yale professor Stanley Milgram is best known for his 1961 experiment in which participants were asked to administer electrical shocks to subjects answering test questions incorrectly. In actuality no shocks were administered, and the test centered on participants' willingness to follow orders. Milgram wanted to use the test to answer moral questions raised by the war crimes trials of Nazi participants in the Holocaust in the aftermath of World War II (Adolf Eichmann's trial began shortly before the experiment), and whether there was anything unusually immoral about those participants or if it could be surmised that anyone in their position would have been just as willing to follow orders. Milgram is also known for the "small world experiment," which examined the path length of social networks and led to the concept "six degrees of separation."

Milgram experiment

The Milgram experiment, named for Yale professor Stanley Milgram, is one of the most famous experiments in social psychology. First conducted in 1961, the experiment was published in 1963, with further detail in a 1974 book. The experiment put participants in a position in which an authority figure ordered them to administer mild (but increasingly less mild) electrical shocks to another subject after each wrong answer in a simple test. In actuality no shocks were administered; the recipient of the imagined shocks was a confederate. What the experiment really tested was participants' willingness to follow orders, with the result that 65 percent of participants continued through the end of the experiment (administering an imaginary 450-volt shock, sufficient to be fatal), though every single participant paused at some point and did not continue until being told to. The ethics of the experiment have been called into question, with some critics predicting long-lasting psychological trauma to the participants.

Minority influence

Minority influence is social influence wielded by a minority group over the majority—sometimes constructed as the opposite of conformity. Minority influence requires that the group itself be unified in its viewpoint, which can lead to infighting between factions of the minority group. Latane and Wolf's social impact model states that the influence of a minority decreases as the size of the minority increases. In a group decision-making scenario, a minority of one wields considerable influence over the majority. Solomon Asch's experiments demonstrated "the magical number three," showing that although a minority of three wields drastically less influence than a minority of one, increasing the size of the group beyond that decreases influence only small amounts.

Mintzberg, Henry

Henry Mintzberg is a Canadian professor of management studies who is critical of both management education and the management consulting industry. He is best known for his organizational configurations model, which describes possible organizational configurations: the simple structure (associated with entrepreneurs), the bureaucracy, the professional organization, the diversified organization, and the innovative organization or "adhocracy."

Mirror neuron

A mirror neuron is a neuron (nerve cell) that activates or "fires" both when an action is performed and when that same action is observed being performed by another. Mirror neurons are present in both humans and animals, and their discovery has led to numerous theories of human behavior and social cognition. However, it is likely that more claims have been made about mirror neurons than will find support in further research; there is as yet no explanation for how mirror neurons could "feed into" cognitive functions like imitation and mimicry, for instance.

Mirrors for Princes

A genre of instructional political writing in Europe in the Middle Ages and the Renaissance, mirrors for princes were books on governance. Most were written as textbooks, but some were written as histories with pointed references to what historical figures had done right or wrong, in order to use them as instructive examples. Some were written for specific rulers: *John of Ireland's Mirror of Wisdom* was written for King James IV of Scotland, for instance, while *Erasmus's Education of a Christian Prince* was written for King Charles V of Spain. When composed for a specific ruler, the work was usually presented to him either in anticipation of his coronation or not long thereafter.

Mirroring

Mirroring is the mimicking of one person's behavior by another, especially while interacting with them, including the copying of body language and gestures, word choice, tone of voice, facial expressions, accent, and affect. Mirroring frequently occurs even between casual acquaintances or strangers, as listeners often mirror the smiles, frowns, and other expressions of the speaker. In most cases mirroring is unconscious and unnoticed by the speaker. It may help to build rapport and trust between people.

Mismatch hypothesis

In evolutionary psychology, the mismatch hypothesis says that some problems in human groups and human society are the result of a mismatch between our current needs and the needs for which certain psychological traits were developed. The chance of such a mismatch increases in inverse proportion to the amount of significant change the brain has undergone since the development of those traits, and so this hypothesis depends on a reasonably slow-evolving brain and reasonably early dates for the development of the relevant traits. A common example is the observed preference for young, physically vital leaders, despite the fact that leaders are no longer expected to exert physical power over either the group's enemies or their subordinates, and in fact will be less effective leaders if they do so.

Mission Accomplished speech

In 2003, President George W. Bush's televised address from the USS *Abraham Lincoln* aircraft carrier, in front of a banner reading "Mission Accomplished," declared an end to major combat in the Iraq War. The sentiment was considered premature and over-the-top posturing even at the time, and the Iraqi insurgency soon offered the proof, as U.S. troops did not withdraw for another eight years (during which time an Iraqi civil war was fought), with the insurgency continuing even after that. Like Bush's father, President George H. W. Bush, his words were used against him as evidence of incompetent leadership. In the elder Bush's case,

Sailors returning to port on the USS Abraham Lincoln, *sporting the Mission Accomplished banner that President George W. Bush was photographed in front of.* (U.S. Navy)

his famous campaign promise "Read my lips: no new taxes," made after an eight-year period of significant tax decreases under Reagan and against the inevitability of raising taxes to make up for the resulting budget deficits, was abandoned two years into his presidency.

Mission creep

Mission creep is the undesirable expansion of a project beyond its original goals or scope, and is especially used in cases where there is a perceived danger of failing as a result of the project's reach exceeding its grasp. Coined in reference to the United Nations peacekeeping mission in Somalia in 1993, the term has since itself expanded its mission to encompass non-military projects (both public and private sector), and has been retroactively applied to the Korean War.

MIT Sloan School of Management

Established in 1914 as the engineering administration program, the Sloan School of Management is the business school of the Massachusetts Institute of Technology. Like its parent institution, MIT Sloan emphasizes innovation, and its faculty has contributed some of the best-known theories in finance and management, including Theory X and Theory Y, System Dynamics, the Black-Scholes model of derivative markets, and the random walk hypothesis of stock market prices. MIT Sloan is also home to the MIT Leadership Center.

Modes of leadership
Psychologist David Wilkinson developed his "modes of leadership" in 2006's *Ambiguity Advantage*, describing leaders' responses to ambiguity. Wilkinson discussed four modes, each a different viewpoint and way of thinking: technical leadership, favored by dictatorial and risk-averse leaders, who deal with ambiguity by denying it and acting with certainty; cooperative leadership, which seeks to reduce uncertainty and mitigate risk through the distribution of power to teams; collaborative leadership, which seeks agreement from followers and deals with ambiguity through group discussion; and generative leadership, which seeks opportunity in ambiguity.

Monarch
A monarch is a head of state, usually one who inherits their rulership or is selected from among a number of potential heirs, and who typically rules for life. Today, most monarchs have limited powers or act as ceremonial heads of state while elected officials serve as heads of government, but historically monarchs controlled the national government in conjunction with regional leaders, religious authorities, and parliamentary bodies. Common titles for monarchs include emperor, king, queen, grand duke, sultan, emir, caliph, raja, khan, and pharaoh.

Monitoring competence
Monitoring competence is the process of remaining aware of the extent of one's knowledge and skills. More self-aware people are generally also aware of their skills and limitations.

Monopoly on violence
The monopoly on violence, from the German *Gewaltmonopol* ("Violence-Monopoly"), is Max Weber's term for the idea that the state is in sole possession of—has a monopoly on—the legitimate use of physical force, which it delegates to instruments like the police force, the military, and the institution of capital punishment. This concept is the basis for criminalizing other uses of violence without implying any guilt on the part of the state for its own violence, or any hypocrisy in the case of the state executing a murderer. The existence of the monopoly does not itself absolve the state of its responsibilities in the use of physical force or the need to have strict regulations on the type and extent of force used in specific circumstances; the use of force by the police, for instance, is strictly bound by law and behavioral codes, and even war against other countries abides by international law.

Monterey Institute of International Studies
The Monterey Institute of International Studies in California is a graduate school of Middlebury College (Vermont), offering programs in international policy, international business, translation and interpretation, and environmental policy, as well as operating five research centers. The institute specializes in training leaders for the cross-cultural, multi-lingual world of international affairs. One of its research centers is the Center for the Blue Economy, training future leaders in the sustainable management of the oceans.

Moral development
Moral development is the study of the emergence of morality in children and through

adulthood, and of the beliefs, attitudes, emotions, and behaviors that make up moral understanding. Sigmund Freud, for instance, believed morality developed as the child learns to repress his selfishness and is socialized by his parents. Jean Piaget, in his work on the psychological development of children, posited that children shift from focus mainly on obeying authority to developing their own moral beliefs. Lawrence Kohlberg expanded on Piaget's work, beginning as a graduate student in 1958. In Kohlberg's work, moral reasoning develops over the course of six stages as the individual becomes more adept at handling moral dilemmas. The first two stages, the pre-conventional level, are obedience and punishment orientation, and self-interest orientation. At this level, individuals are focused mainly on the consequences of their actions on themselves—avoiding punishment, in the first stage, and gaining a reward in the second stage. The conventional level consists of conformity, and social-order-maintaining orientation. This level represents the moral reasoning of adolescents and many adults, who derive morality from their understanding of society's expectations of them. Stage three, for instance, seeks to conform with expectations, while stage four focuses on the need to abide by laws and conventions in order for society to function. Finally, the post-conventional level consists of social contract orientation and universal ethical principles. At this level, the individuals truly own their own morals, and are better able to perceive the difference between law-abiding behavior and moral behavior and to advocate for changes in the law in order to better reflect their moral understanding. Kohlberg sometimes noted moral stage regression in individuals, in which case he may note them as "stage five and a half," possessing characteristics of both stage five and the abandoned stage six.

Moral hazard

Moral hazard is the problem that results when a party is protected from the consequences of risk taking to a sufficient degree to make them likelier to take risks. The classic example of moral hazard is in the insurance industry, in which insurers have to deal with the possibility that the possession of insurance will lead the insured to risk-taking behaviors. In recent years, the impact of moral hazard on the financial sector has become obvious. But on a smaller scale, the concept has bearing in many leadership situations, from parenting—many parents having to weigh the pros and cons of bailing a child out of a difficulty versus letting them learn from their errors—to management. Nepotism and other managerial biases in favor of certain employees create a condition of moral hazard; so does the security of an employee's position due to factors other than the quality of his work, whether this means tenure in an academic setting or internal political factors. Above all else, when the corporate culture of a workplace does not hold each worker and manager accountable for the consequences of their work, moral hazard is invited. In some cases the problem may be simply that there are so many steps between the worker and the negative outcome of their work that there is no easy path for the consequences to take.

Motivation

Motivation is the force driving an action. Exploring the roots of human motivation has been a large part of the focus of psychology, from Sigmund Freud's discussion of the sex drive to Abraham Maslow's hierarchy of needs. Motivation may be intrinsic—driven by an appreciation of the task itself—or extrinsic, in which the task is less important than the outcome resulting from performing the task. Most theories of motivation are pluralistic, and may differentiate between conscious and unconscious motivations. The understanding of motivation is important in predicting and modeling human behavior, especially given that self-interest alone is not enough to explain behaviors, nor do humans act with perfect rationality.

Motivation crowding theory

According to motivation crowding theory, the addition of extrinsic motivations related to a behavior can diminish or negate existing intrinsic motivations. "Overjustification effect" is the term for when this happens by an extrinsic reward being offered for a behavior, removing the intrinsic motivation so that the reward becomes necessary to motivate the behavior. But it is true of punishments as well, and punishing a given behavior can result in removing the intrinsic motivation to avoid that behavior.

Motivation-hygiene theory

Motivation-hygiene theory is a psychological theory developed by Frederick Herzberg and influenced by Abraham Maslow's hierarchy of needs. According to the theory, one set of workplace factors is associated with job satisfaction, while a separate set is associated with job dissatisfaction, and the two phenomena are independent of one another. In other words, increasing job satisfaction does not decrease job dissatisfaction—the two do not represent different ranges on the same metaphorical thermometer, but are rather two completely separate measures. This idea grew out of Herzberg's initial work on the insufficiency of lower-level needs (like salary and job security) in providing job satisfaction. The name of the theory comes from the separation between *motivators*, intrinsic conditions of a job that provide job satisfaction, such as being given responsibility or engaging in a challenge, and *hygiene* factors that do not provide job satisfaction

but do cause job dissatisfaction if they are absent, such as job security, salary and benefits, social status benefits, and working conditions.

Mozi

Mozi or Mo Tzu was a 5th-century B.C.E. Chinese philosopher in the early Warring States period. Mohism, the school of thought he developed, fell out of favor when both legalism and Confucianism gained more influence, but some Mohist concepts remained embedded in classical Chinese philosophy. Authenticity and self-knowledge were crucial to Mozi, and he argued against obedience to ritual and the traditional attachment to family and clan, contrasting in this respect with Confucius. Much of what Mozi proposed amounts to a model of enlightened self-interest, one that demanded equal respect and love for all, not just those to whom one had a personal bond. His system of ethics was similar to Western utilitarianism, except that the goal was not happiness but public goods in the form of wealth, population growth (a concern in a civilization accustomed to periodic famine), and domestic tranquility.

Multifactor Leadership Questionnaire

The Multifactor Leadership Questionnaire (MLQ) was developed by Bernard Bass in 1985, as part of his work extending the theories of James MacGregor Burns on transformational and transactional leadership. The MLQ has gone through several revisions, and measures leadership behaviors as perceived both by the leader himself and his followers. Bass later developed the Full Range Leadership Model to complement the MLQ.

Multiple Constituency Framework

Anne Tsui's Multiple Constituency Framework is a behavioral complexity model of leadership that examines the way managers deal with multiple constituencies, both internal (subordinates, peers, and superiors) and external (investors, customers, competitors), with different and possibly conflicting demands. Key to the framework and others like it is the premise that organizational effectiveness is measured not by the pursuit of a single goal but by serving multiple interests represented by the relevant constituencies. Tsui built on the work of multiple theorists, dating back to Eric Rhenman's introduction of constituencies (referred to as stakeholders) in his work on industrial demography in 1968. Different subunits of the organization have different sets of constituencies; the human resources and materials management departments of a manufacturing plant, for instance, serve different constituencies and pursue different goals in their activities. In Tsui's approach, the effectiveness of the organization is measured by the subjective perceptions of the constituencies served.

Munsterberg, Hugo

Hugo Munsterberg was a pioneer in applied psychology in the early 20th century. Initially influenced by William James, he rejected James's acceptance of mysticism and psychoanalysis and focused more on practical aims. He became interested in Frederick W. Taylor's scientific management, and applied himself to adding a psychological dimension to the approach, including guides to the types of employees to hire for various roles, and psychological methods for increasing motivation and performance or improving advertising and marketing efforts.

Murray, Henry

Henry Murray was a Harvard psychology professor and one of the first to teach psychoanalysis at Harvard. His work focused on the theory of personality he called Personology, according to which people are driven by both latent and manifest needs, as well as extrinsic factors in the form of "press" (discrete external influences) and "thema" (patterns of press and need).

Mushroom management

Mushroom management is the phenomenon of management doing a poor job of communicating with employees, who are expected to thrive while "being kept in the dark and fed manure."

Mutually assured destruction

Mutually assured destruction (MAD) is a nuclear deterrence doctrine that prevailed for much of the Cold War. Grounded in game theory, the doctrine states that once both sides of a conflict are armed with sufficiently destructive weapons, neither side has an incentive to initiate armed conflict because of the assurance of the level of damage both sides would take. Though the American government has since said that MAD was only one element of its strategy, the doctrine can be seen at work in the nuclear arms race, as well as in the expensive development of a sea-based nuclear force that would survive an attack on land targets.

My Lai Massacre

The My Lai Massacre was the mass killing of 300 to 500 unarmed Vietnamese civilians in U.S.-allied South Vietnam by U.S. Army soldiers, in 1968. Initially reported as a firefight with Viet Cong soldiers, it was discovered that American troops had not been fired upon, nor did they show any interest in ceasing their killing of civilians they had forced into a ditch when an American helicopter crew intervened in an attempt to stop them. When an attempted cover-up failed, 14 officers were court-martialed for suppressing evidence (largely to have the charges dropped), while Lieutenant William Calley, the ranking officer on-site of the massacre, was convicted to life in prison. Calley claimed to be following orders of his commanding officer, but no sufficient evidence of this was found, and the commanding officer was acquitted. Though not as broad in scope as the war crimes that were the subject of the Nuremberg Trials, the My Lai Massacre has a place in discussions of rank, authority, and responsibility.

Myers-Briggs Type Indicator

The Myers-Briggs Type Indicator (MBTI) was developed by mother and daughter Katharine Cook Briggs and Isabel Briggs Myers, based on the work of Carl Jung. The MBTI is a psychometric questionnaire intended to reveal the ways the respondent makes decisions and sees the world. From Jung it took the idea that four major functions—sensing, intuition, feeling, and thinking—provide our experience of the world, and that at any given time, one of them is dominant. The MBTI sorts respondents into one of 16 categories based on four dichotomies: Extraversion (E) or Introversion (I); Sensing (S) or Intuition (N); Thinking (T) or Feeling (F); and Judgment (J) or Perception (P). About 5 percent of the population are an INFP, for instance, characterized by sensitivity to criticism, low assertiveness, a strong sense of right and wrong, and a creative drive. About 10 percent of the population are an ESTJ, characterized as being matter-of-fact and pragmatic, good at and enjoying organizing and administration.

Narcissism

Narcissism is obsessive or preoccupying vanity, named for the Greek myth of Narcissus, a young man who became obsessed with his own reflection. Narcissism has been an area of study of psychology since Sigmund Freud, who devoted a book to the trait. Many modern psychologists consider some amount of healthy narcissism—which pursues self-interest but balances aggression, and is truthful about the self's traits—to be a necessary component of a healthy life, and even unhealthy levels of narcissism are not necessarily the same as Narcissistic Personality Disorder, which tends to feature grandiosity, self-obsession, and the pursuit of behaviors that validate one's sense of self.

Narcissistic defense

A narcissistic defense is a defense mechanism that acts to preserve an idealized self-perception. All people, especially as children, are susceptible to narcissistic defenses, not just narcissists. They usually operate unconsciously, and deal with information that reflects negatively on the self and could cause feelings of shame, guilt, or anxiety. In addition to defenses that simply bury the facts in question—unconscious repression, for instance, or conscious denial—there are defenses that construct a new narrative around the facts. The significance of an individual's failure or wrongdoing may be minimized, for instance, or justified through rationalization. Alternately, the individual may see someone else as bearing the blame for what is actually the individual's failing. In the workplace, narcissistic defenses make it difficult for people to accurately self-evaluate their own competence and performance, even when they believe they are being honest. Similarly, they complicate identifying the problem in a dysfunctional or unproductive work team or work environment.

Narcissistic parent

A narcissistic parent, whether it is highly developed enough to constitute Narcissistic Personality Disorder or not, poses an emotional danger to their children. Such parents may feel threatened by their children's eventual independence, and their lack of empathy may cause them to treat their child as a person who exists for the parent's benefit. These children often grow up narcissistic themselves, both to defend themselves from the manipulation of their parent and because they have learned from observing their parents that selfishness leads to getting one's needs met.

Narcissistic Personality Disorder

Narcissistic Personality Disorder (NPD) is a personality disorder classified in 1968, and known in earlier psychological literature as megalomania. The disorder involves an obsession and preoccupation with one's personal virtues, especially outwardly perceptible virtues like power, influence, prestige, and appearance. While the *Diagnostic and Statistical Manual of Mental Disorders* does not recognize official subtypes, many psychologists differentiate between exhibitionist narcissists who tend toward unsafe sexual behaviors and pathological deception, charlatan types who exploit others, narcissists compensating for low self-esteem, and so on. Many believe NPD is associated with charismatic leadership.

NASA Academy

Founded in 1993, the National Aeronautics and Space Administration (NASA) and NASA Academy is a leadership training program for college students, consisting of a 10-week summer program at a NASA center (including Ames Research Center, Marshall Space Flight Center, and Glenn Research Center). The program consists of research, team-building activities, visits to NASA labs and centers, and lectures by and socializing with aerospace industry leaders, across a long workday scheduled from 7:30 A.M. until 9 P.M. Eric Anderson, chairman of the Commercial Spaceflight Federation, is an alumnus.

National Youth Leadership Council

The National Youth Leadership Council (NYLC) is a national non-profit group formed in 1983 and based in Saint Paul, Minnesota. The NYLC promotes service learning in the United States through workshops, service projects, research publications, and hosting of the annual National Service Learning Conference.

"The Nature of the Firm"

A 1937 article in the journal *Economica* by British economist Ronald Coase (only 27 at the time), "The Nature of the Firm" was an exploration of the economic reasons individuals form partnerships and companies, notably the transaction costs of using the market.

Need for achievement

A term introduced by Henry Murray's Personology theory, need for achievement is a motivation driven by the desire for mastery of skill, accomplishment, or victory, and is rewarded by recognition of this achievement. This motivation is moderately risk-friendly and interested in innovation, but needs goals precisely defined.

Need for affiliation

A term introduced by Henry Murray's Personology theory, need for affiliation is a motivation driven by belongingness, the desire to feel involved with a group. People with a high level of this motivation do not always make effective leaders but are engaged team members, and require regular approval from and interaction with their co-workers and supervisors.

Need for cognition

In psychology, the need for cognition (NFC) is a personality factor that makes people seek challenging cognitive activities like problem solving, engaging debates over ideas, and activities that involve evaluating ideas (which includes many leadership roles). People with a low NFC score are more susceptible to believing stereotypes and broad generalizations, but those with high NFC scores have been found to be more susceptible to the creation of false memories.

Need for power
A term introduced by Henry Murray's Personology theory, need for power is a motivation driven by the desire to influence and dominate others. The motivation is associated with risk-friendliness, aggression, and competitiveness.

Negative selection
Negative selection is a phenomenon seen in certain kinds of leaders (including both political and business leaders) in which incompetent subordinates are deliberately selected in order to prevent them from presenting a threat to the leader's power.

Negativity effect
The negativity effect is a set of attributional biases that cause an individual, when considering the behavior of someone they do not like, to blame that person for any negative behaviors or outcomes associated with them, while explaining away any positive behaviors as the result of the environment or other external factors.

Negotiation theory
Negotiation theory is the formal study of negotiations, a special class of conflict resolution, using decision analysis, game theory, and other frameworks. Negotiation theory defines negotiation as the process that is engaged in when one party requires the other party's agreement in order to take action or accomplish a goal, such as when negotiating the terms of a treaty, which does not exist unless all parties agree to the same terms,

or negotiating the salary for a potential new employee. Different theories of negotiation describe the negotiation process differently. Strategic analysis uses game theory and describes it as a series of games. Integrative analysis describes it as a series of procedural stages. Structural analysis examines the distribution and use of power between the negotiating parties.

Nemawashi
The Japanese term *nemawashi*, introduced to Americans mainly via the Toyota Production System, refers to the preparations for an upcoming change in an organization, including the beginning of a new project. Such preparations include collecting comments and feedback, getting "the lay of the land" and discovering what response to the change will be, and—particularly important in Japanese business culture—informing highly placed members in the organization of the proposed change, regardless whether it will affect them or their work. In Japan, one of the privileges of rank is the expectation of being consulted on any change being considered.

Nepotism
Favoritism in hiring or appointment practices, especially toward relatives or people known through family connections. Nepotism was coined to refer to the appointment of cardinals who were the nephews (*nepos* in Latin) of bishops or popes, a widespread practice in the Catholic Church, but has application in politics and the private sector. In many contexts it is considered a form of corruption—a serious one, if it is suspected that the appointment is a way for the appointee to make money from the position—while in other contexts it may be frowned upon or mocked but does not constitute an ethical breach.

Neuromanagement

Neuromanagement is the study of management, leadership, and economics from a neuroscience perspective, and overlaps with the similar science of neuroeconomics in its reference to neurological explanations of behavior. It is particularly concerned with discovering the brain activities and processes implicated in decision making, the neural basis of preferences and game modeling, and the modeling of decision making. Zhejiang University in China founded the Neuromanagement Lab in 2006.

Neuroticism

Neuroticism is one of the "Big Five" personality traits, characterized by feelings of envy, anxiety, and moodiness, and a poor ability to cope with stress. While neuroticism is not the same as neurosis, high scores of neuroticism are a risk factor for the panic and anxiety disorders which have historically been labeled neuroses.

Neutralizers

In substitutes for leadership theory, neutralizers are factors in the work environment that reduce the effectiveness of leadership. These include the leader not having the power to reward subordinates for performance, and subordinates being indifferent to the reward.

NIMBY

NIMBY stands for "Not In My Back Yard," used to characterize an individual's position on a project when the individual supports the project's necessity or desirability but wants it located someplace where he or she will not be exposed to its negative side effects. It is especially associated with discussions of chemical plants and waste dumps, which historically are more likely to end up located in or near poor neighborhoods whose residents lack the influence to

This tower in Washington, D.C., was later removed due to complaints from residents of the neighborhood. Local citizens had adopted a "Not In My Back Yard" position regarding the structure. (Wikimedia Commons/Kate Mereand)

prevent it, but is also used in reference to the placement of infrastructure and services ranging from homeless shelters and institutional housing to highways, airports, and strip malls, and is sometimes used more figuratively to refer to financial sacrifices like layoffs or budget cuts. Executives who speak of the necessity of belt-tightening due to a financial crisis, leading to layoffs, canceled bonuses, or other negative effects felt by the lower levels of a company, while receiving bonuses themselves for reducing expenses, are an example of the latter.

Nirvana fallacy

The nirvana fallacy is an informal fallacy identified in 1969, in which the individual focuses on an idealized but unrealistic solution to a problem to such a degree that the realistic and adequate alternatives available seem unacceptable. Rather than choose between real available options, they thus perceive any choice as a choice between the perfect and the adequate, and reject the adequate.

Noble lie

The noble lie is an untruth propagated by the ruling class to maintain harmony and civil peace. As originally described in Plato's *Republic*, it often takes the form of a religious belief—Plato's example is a myth explaining the origins and justifying the continued existence of the social stratification of ancient Greece in such a way as to preserve the hierarchy of the classes and discourage class revolt, while inspiring devotion to the nation. Since the Enlightenment, some thinkers have considered religion itself as a noble lie—a fictional story told for the purposes of social control, in order to encourage belief in specific values.

Non-concurrence

IBM, which pioneered the computer industry, developed a decision-making tradition called "non-concurring," according to which any department head had the power to veto a proposed company strategy or policy if it was not aligned with his department's needs or strategy. When Lou Gerstner became the new chief executive officer in the 1990s, he saw non-concurrence as part of IBM's "Culture of 'no,'" in which too much energy was spent blocking changes rather than moving forward, and that this had contributed to the company's losing ground to competitors. He ended the non-concurrence policy quickly.

Nonverbal influence

Nonverbal influence is the influence one person wields over another through means other than verbal communication, such as through cues imparted by tone of voice, facial expression, or body language. This influence may take the form of intimidation—which includes not only physical intimidation but the threat of anger, disappointment, or tears—or may appeal to attraction or similarity. For instance, some studies of mirroring have found that people tend to mirror each others' body language and tone of voice, even accent, which increases the sympathy accorded to them. Nonverbal displays of power and status include accent, demeanor, clothes and accessories, and may also factor into influence.

Normative model of decision making

The normative model of decision making was developed by Yale leadership studies professor Victor Vroom, beginning in the 1970s. The model proposes to predict the effectiveness of a given decision-making process, and identifies five types of such processes, in order from most to least level of leader participation: Decide (in which the leader alone decides), Individual Consultation (in which members are individually consulted for input), Group Consultation, Facilitation (in which the decision is made by group consensus, with the leader leading the discussion), and Delegation.

Normative social influence

Normative social influence is a conformity-enforcing phenomenon in which the individual is influenced by the desire to be accepted, respected, liked, and approved of by other people, and so adjusts his behavior or attitudes accordingly. Belongingness is a powerful human motivation, universal throughout cultures, and the desire to belong to a group influences the individual's behaviors and attitudes in order to help him fit in with his group, or find one with which he fits.

Northhouse, Peter

Peter Northhouse is a leadership studies scholar and the author of *Leadership: Theory and Practice*, now in its sixth edition. His work has covered ethical leadership, leadership assessment, and leadership and group dynamics, as well as work on contingency theories of leadership and path-goal theory.

Not invented here

"Not invented here" is a shorthand phrase referring to the tendency in institutional and corporate cultures to avoid the adoption, use, purchase, or reliance on products, standards, or practices that were developed elsewhere. Sometimes the external costs associated with such adoption are the primary reason, particularly if adopting the product means purchasing or licensing it from a competitor. But the phrase is especially associated with the form of tribalism that rejects such products and practices not for pragmatic reasons but out of spite or fear.

Novelty seeking

Novelty seeking is a personality trait that drives the individual to seek out new experiences, leading to impulsive decision making and associated with a quick temper. Novelty seeking is correlated with extraversion, and inversely correlated with conscientiousness.

Nut Island effect

As coined by Paul Levy in a 2001 article on Boston Harbor pollution, the Nut Island effect is an organizational phenomenon in which a group experiences a catastrophic loss of their task-completion ability because the organization's skilled assets—the employees necessary to complete the task—have become isolated from the leadership overseeing the project. This is typically the result of leadership that is primarily engaged with activities other than seeing the task through to completion. Forced into autonomy, the employees may lack key resources or situational knowledge required to do their work.

Oakes, Len

An Australian psychologist and former cult member, Len Oakes used an "adjective checklist" of 300 items in his dissertation on charismatic leaders of new religious movements, seeking patterns in the responses. Published in 1997 as *Prophetic Charisma*, the study proposed two types of cult leaders: messianic prophets and charismatic prophets. Oakes ascribes some similarities in leaders with otherwise dissimilar backgrounds and beliefs to narcissistic personality disorder.

Obedience

Obedience is the following of instructions from an authority due to social pressures. Psychology has shown that people have a natural tendency toward obedience, whether this is socialized in them or somehow present in our biology, and the instinct is believed to have been necessary to make communal life among early humans possible. There is significant debate over the effect of obedience on the ethics of our behavior: that is, when one does something on the orders of a formal authority, how is the responsibility for that action distributed between the authority and the follower?

Object relations theory

One of the "four psychologies" constituting modern psychology, object relations theory is a model in psychoanalytic psychology according to which experiences with family and other caregivers as an infant shape the way the individual interacts with others as an adult. The theory builds on Sigmund Freud's concept of the object relation, the specific object that bodily drives seek in order to satisfy their needs.

Occupational health psychology

Occupational health psychology is the applied psychology field that focuses on the well-being and safety of workers, having emerged from organizational psychology in the late 20th century. Though areas of study include physical factors of occupational stress, especially those contributing to cardiovascular disease, much of OHP is concerned with psychological distress caused by the work environment or work-related economic factors, behavioral issues with health ramifications, psychosocial conflicts in the workplace from bullying to violence, and psychological factors in workplace accidents.

Occupy movement hand signals

Occupy Wall Street and the larger Occupy movement developed a system of hand signals, some of which have been used in Quaker meetings and by other protest movements, in order to silently express positions during consensus-building meetings. Twinkling fingers—both hands raised with wiggling fingers—indicate strong agreement, for instance, as does a thumbs-up gesture. Other hand gestures indicate having a question for the speaker, believing important information has been left out by the speaker, asking the speaker to return to the topic at hand, a break from consensus, or that the speaker needs to speak up.

Occupy Wall Street

Occupy Wall Street (OWS) is a protest movement that began in Zucotti Park on Wall Street in New York City on September 17, 2011. Beginning with the peaceful occupation of the park in order to bring attention to—among other things—economic inequality and the largely unpunished role of Wall Street's finance industry in the 2008 financial crisis, OWS inspired the Occupy movement in other parts of the country and of the world. The protest was initiated by the Canadian anti-consumerist magazine *Adbusters*, inspired by the Arab Spring, but was considered leaderless once set in motion. Its specific concerns or impact aside, OWS was notable for its anti-hierarchical structure and consensus-based approach to decision making. The OWS assembly draws on practices from the anti-nuclear movement, feminist protests, and Quaker practices, holding decision-making meetings in which all viewpoints are allowed time for expression, with facilitators calling on speakers waiting in line in a "stack," in which white men waited at the back of the line while marginalized groups like racial minorities were asked to cut to the front. Meetings attempted to reach consensus, with the bar lowered to a 90 percent majority vote if consensus proved impossible. Though formally leaderless, informal leaders emerged in the larger cities—in New York, more than 70 working groups were responsible for organizing and making decisions about Occupy Wall Street's activities at the height of its growth—as certain facilitators proved more or less adept at managing the crowd and encouraging participation in the most crowded or contentious assemblies.

Beginning on September 17, 2011, Zuccotti Park was occupied by hundreds of protestors during the Occupy Wall Street protest movement. (Wikimedia Commons/David Shankbone)

Offensive realism

Offensive realism is a variant of political realism, according to which because the main motive of states is survival, and because the world is in a constant state of aggression, the state rationally acts to maximize its ability to go to war. Arms races such as those of the Cold War are a natural result.

Office of the future

The "office of the future" is a concept dating from shortly after the construction of the first computers in the 1940s, which percolated through the popular imagination quickly and thoroughly enough to be satirized in comic strips and cartoons decades before most offices even phased out typewriters in favor of personal computers. The technological changes of the early Cold War years and the rise of the "organization man" painted a picture of what we now call a paperless office, with computers mediating most interactions among employees or between employees and management.

Ohio State Leadership Studies

The leadership studies conducted from 1945 through the 1950s at Ohio State University focused on identifying observable behaviors in successful leaders, in contrast with earlier studies that focused on trying to under personality traits common to effective leaders. The resulting Leaders Behavior Description Questionnaire in many ways constitutes the birth of modern leadership studies. Ohio State continues to run a strong leadership studies program, and in 1990 opened the OSU Leadership Center in the College of Food, Agricultural, and Environmental Sciences.

Old boys' club

The old boys' club or old boy network is a metaphor referring to social connections among members of male-only or traditionally male-dominated groups, and especially the way that these social connections ease the way to professional success. Common examples are fraternity membership or alumnus status with a private school or prestigious college. For instance, for many years, the bulk of the writing staff at *Saturday Night Live* was made up of former writers for the *Harvard Lampoon*, and the "white shoe" or prestigious and century-old law firms and banks of Boston and New York have a long tradition of hiring WASPs with Ivy League educations. The old boys' club also consists of family connections, as when someone gets a job interview with a company whose vice president went to the same school as one's father, or who summered at the same lake as one's grandfather. The old boys' club is for many reasons typically associated with not only maleness but whiteness and old money.

Old Testament

In the Old Testament (or Hebrew Tanakh), leadership is a trait bestowed by God to various individuals, and the relative worth of leaders is a frequent theme. While Moses is chosen to lead the children of Israel out of bondage in Egypt, for instance, and to receive the Ten Commandments, his brother Aaron speaks on his behalf and establishes the priesthood. Later, once the nations of Israel and Judah are established, Israel is without a monarch until the people demand one, leading to God's anointing of Saul, who is succeeded by the complex figure of David—guilty of some of the worst behavior of any Biblical protagonist but revered as one of the greatest kings. The Nevi'im, or books of the prophets, are characterized by their repeated warnings to Israel and other nations that their good fortunes are inextricably linked with their obedience to God and their reaffirmation that God is the source of worldly authority.

The One Minute Manager

The One Minute Manager is a best-selling business book published in 1982, and written by Ken Blanchard and Spencer Johnson. In keeping with the early 1980s climate of efficiency-obsession and competition with the management culture of Japan, *The One Minute Manager* prescribes three techniques for managers: one-minute goals, one-minute praisings, and one-minute reprimands, in order to maximize managerial effectiveness while minimizing time commitment. Blanchard later developed situational leadership theory with professor Paul Hersey, while Johnson wrote the best-selling book *Who Moved My Cheese?*

One-upmanship

One-upmanship is the practice of repeatedly outperforming a competitor, particular in response to his outperformance of you; arms races are one example, as is the idea of "keeping up with the Joneses." Dr. Seuss's work references one-upmanship several times, notably in the *Butter Battle Book* and *The Sneetches*.

Openness

Openness is one of the "Big Five" personality traits, and some studies of leadership personality traits have suggested that leaders should have a higher than average level of openness. It is sometimes called "openness to experience," and includes the following facets: active imagination, aesthetic sensitivity, attentiveness to inner feelings, preference for variety, and intellectual curiosity, traits that research indicates are strongly correlated with one another. Studies show that openness has a normal distribution in the population, with few people scoring very high or very low. Openness tends to correlate with creativity, general knowledge, the need for cognition, happiness, and positive affect, but has no correlation to life satisfaction. There is no significant difference between the scores of men and women.

Opinion leader

Opinion leaders exert a greater than average amount of influence when it comes to shaping the opinions of those around them. They may be perceived as experts or as possessing a cache that makes others want to be aligned with their tastes. Early adopters (cf.) tend to be opinion leaders, especially insofar as a sufficient number of them must adopt an innovation for it to thrive. Advertising and marketing researchers have done considerable work on opinion leadership in the quest to spend advertising dollars most effectively, and social media has offered a new wealth of data to be analyzed. Although opinion leaders can include professional reviewers and other members of the media, the importance of opinion leaders is principally that they have more influence on the formation of opinions than the professional media do.

Opportunity cost

In microeconomics, an opportunity cost is, in a decision-making situation, the value of the choice that is not selected: specifically, it is the value of the next-best possibility, not the sum or average of all rejected choices. In a simple example, a game show contestant choosing between the mystery prizes behind doors number one and two loses the value of door number two as an opportunity cost of selecting door number one. Every decision involves opportunity costs; inexperienced leaders or insecure decision-makers sometimes fixate on opportunity costs rather than weighing them against the gains of the choice selected. Similarly, pundits and politicians may discredit an opponent's choice by focusing not on the benefits gained but on the opportunity costs exacted.

The Organization Man

The Organization Man, published in 1956, is one of the most influential books published on management. Written by William H. Whyte—who later coined the term *groupthink*—it was based on in-depth interviews of the executives of the preeminent American corporations. Throughout the book, Whyte explored the idea that despite the overt idealization of individualism espoused in American rhetoric and entertainment, Americans were actually deeply collectivist, and more likely to trust organizations to make sound decisions than individuals. By extension, working for an organization made more sense than striking out on one's own. Whyte also discussed the commonality of risk-aversion among executives, and the ease of remaining an executive once attaining the position.

Organizational behavior

Organizational behavior is the study of the behavior of organizations and the individuals within those organizations, as well as the relationship between human behavior and the behavior, structure, and environment of the organization. Organizational behavior draws on the many tools of social science, including qualitative and quantitative research and statistical modeling. Where modern organizational behavior studies differ from earlier work in related fields is in their heavy reliance on computer simulation for both the macro- and micro-level of behavior in organizations. Studies often focus on specific behavioral problems like sexual harassment, workplace bullying and abuse by superiors, decision-making problems, and counterproductive work.

Organizational citizenship behavior

Organizational citizenship behavior (OCB) is individual behavior that helps to promote the well-being of the organization but occurs outside the set of behaviors that are explicitly rewarded by the organization, such as those that are rewarded by performance incentives or specifically requested by supervisors or policies. Since the 1960s, work on organizational citizenship behavior has illustrated how important this kind of employee behavior is to the effectiveness and well-being of an organization. The standard definition was articulated by Dennis Organ in the 1970s, but Organ's work has been challenged because of the difficulty of clearly identifying OCB in the workplace. Organ himself has noted that the definition was more useful when jobs had clearly defined tasks, and that the influence of management theory on the workplace, and the increase in ambiguously defined work roles, has blurred the lines between reward-motivated or rule-driven behavior and OCB. A similar, more recently articulated, concept is extra-role behavior.

Organizational culture

Organizational culture is the culture of an organization, both as a result of policies and practices adopted by management and as it emerges from the social interactions among workers. Google's organizational culture, for instance, includes its use of "Innovation Time Off" to motivate employees by allowing them to spend 20 percent of their time on their own projects, its internal slogans like "don't be evil" and "you can be serious without a suit," and the considerable amenities available to workers in the Mountain

View, California, "Googleplex." Like other types of culture, organizational culture includes both behaviors and values, and long-time employees may become attached to elements of corporate culture to a degree unexplained by those elements' practical value to them.

Organizational dissent

Organizational dissent is disagreement with the practices of an organization. Typically shown little tolerance by leadership, dissent may nevertheless be an important force, acting as a check against authority that oversteps, policies and practices that are unethical or immoral, or other problems.

Organizational identification

Organizational identification is the extent of an individual's identification with the organization, and the extent to which he shares its goals and values, participates in its culture, and engages emotionally with its work. Organizational identification is above all else the individual's perception of an "us" that includes the individual and an organization as contrasted with an external "them" that may include competitors, regulators, etc.

Organizational intelligence

Organizational intelligence is the ability of an organization to accumulate and use knowledge related to its goals, to learn from its experiences, and to make sense of complex situations in order to adequately make informed decisions.

Organizational justice

Organizational justice, injustice, or fairness is the treatment by an organization of its workers, and the workers' feelings about that treatment. While the law, industry regulations, and labor union agreements govern what an organization has the power to do, not everything in its power will be seen as fair by the workers; at the same time, not every action by leadership that is negatively received by employees will be negatively received because of perceived unfairness. Rather, organizational justice is the appropriate treatment of employees in their work roles, collectively and as individuals, and a commensurate response to changes or behavior. (cf. Perceived Psychological Contract Violation.)

Organizational psychology

Organizational psychology is the field of applied psychology focusing on human behavior in the workplace, as well as the behavior of organizations. It is one of the most widely recognized specialties in applied psychology, also known as industrial and organizational psychology, I/O psychology, occupational psychology, and work psychology. Organizational psychologists work to improve organizational health by improving the satisfaction and well-being of its employees and developing the organization's interpersonal relationships.

Organizational socialization

Organizational socialization or onboarding refers to the processes by which new employees become socialized to the organization, acquiring not only skills and knowledge but behaviors and organizational social norms. Some aspects of organizational socialization are formal, as with job training, new employee orientation, seminars for new members, and the freshman orientation activities of many American colleges. But many are informal, as new workers absorb "unwritten rules" of behavior and other norms, technical jargon and terms of art, informal slang endemic to the industry or the organization, and other elements. Studies have found that organizational socialization plays an important role in productivity and employee engagement, and employees may be more receptive to learning the preferred way to perform a task when they first begin a job than to being corrected later. Picking up the norms of a new workplace also helps with employee morale and feelings of acceptance and belongingness. However, at least one study (N. J. Allen and J. P. Meyer, 1990) found that organizational socialization increased employee commitment but actually reduced role clarity, presumably by delaying the new employee's engagement with his role-specific duties. There is also concern for the effects of what Soren Kierkegaard called leveling, which can result as the new employee's individuality is eclipsed by his adoption of organizational norms.

Organizational storytelling

An interdisciplinary field incorporating management and organization studies, organizational storytelling is an approach to understanding organizational culture and behavior. Organizational storytelling uses narrative in order to uncover the root and meaning of organizational behavior.

Organizational Studies

Organizational studies is the study of the structures, processes, and practices of organizations, their construction, and their social, cultural, and economic impacts. Organizational studies has usually been approached from a functionalist framework, which is interested in society as a complex system of interrelated parts, of which organizations are one kind. Functionalism studies the large social structures of society, their role in shaping society, and the way that parts of a large stable system work together. Functionalism is out of favor in the social sciences in favor of frameworks (like critical theory) that draw attention to contradictions, conflicts, and inequalities rather than assuming the premise of stability, but its methodology is still common in many disciplines.

Out of the Crisis

W. Edwards Deming's 1982 book *Out of the Crisis*, originally published as *Quality, Productivity, and Competitive Position* but reissued in 1986 to capitalize on Deming's fame as the consultant to Ford who inspired the development of the Taurus, was an influential work on management. Deming had introduced the Efficiency movement to postwar Japan and was credited with its economic miracle before returning to the United States as a management consultant. *Out of the Crisis* offered 14 efficiency-minded principles, inspiring a revival of the Efficiency movement called the Total Quality Management movement:

1. Constancy of purpose in improving products and services.
2. Recognize the need for change and commit to it.
3. Do the job right the first time, and minimize reliance on inspection.
4. Minimize total cost and seek a single long-term supplier for any one item.
5. Constantly improve the system of production.
6. On-the-job training.
7. Supervisors must be leaders.
8. Reduce fear that interferes with employee engagement.
9. Reduce interdepartmental barriers to teamwork.
10. Eliminate target goals and slogans that put the burden of productivity and quality on the employee, instead acknowledging

management's responsibility to lead employees to these goals.

11. Make supervisors responsible for quality, not numbers.
12. Eliminate management by objectives, which is contrary to good leadership practices.
13. Adopt a program of self-improvement.
14. Involve every employee in changing the organization.

Outgroup

A social group with which an individual does not identify. (cf. In-group).

Outside the box

The image of an idea originating from "outside the box" is a metaphor that has become popular in management to illustrate the idea of the paradigm. A paradigm is a conceptual framework, a pattern of reasoning about a given thing, which has developed over time. When information is incomplete, paradigms may be faulty, and work reaches a point where improvements can only be made by going "outside the box" and introducing ideas that contradict the accepted paradigm. This is an important phenomenon in Thomas Kuhn's *The Structure of Scientific Revolutions*, for instance, but has also been adopted as the way to improve management and business practices by challenging the presumption that the status quo represents the best solution. It is also used to support the usefulness of management consultants, who have not worked in the organizational culture of the businesses for whom they consult and have not absorbed the same assumptions. A typical example of "outside the box" thinking is the legend of the Gordian knot, in which Alexander the Great "solved" the problem of how to untie an impossibly tangled knot that had foiled others—by drawing his sword and slicing through it.

Overconfidence effect

The overconfidence effect is a cognitive bias whereby an individual's confidence in his skill or judgment is consistently higher than his accuracy or objective skill level. In many tests demonstrating the effects, for instance, people are asked a number of general knowledge questions in which they both provide an answer and rate the confidence they have in that answer. Subjects consistently rated their confidence much more highly than their performance warranted. This remains true in experiments in which the subject cannot possibly know the answer for certain, due to its obscure and trivial nature—in the Marc Alpert and Howard Raiffa study in 1982, one question asked how many eggs were produced by the American egg industry every year—and even in experiments in which subjects have the overconfidence effect explained to them ahead of time.

Overjustification effect

The overjustification effect causes intrinsic motivation for an activity to decrease in response to a reward being offered for the activity, which puts the focus on reward seeking and requires that rewards continue to be offered for the activity. This is a concern in parenting, for instance, when tying allowance directly to a chore can prevent the child from developing an intrinsic motivation to perform the chore (which may influence their attitudes toward housework, yard work, or other activities in young adulthood when allowance is no longer disbursed). Likewise, in the workplace, rewarding employees for specific tasks may help assure those tasks are performed but interferes with the employees' intrinsic motivations for performing them. When the reward is discontinued, no motivation exists to continue the activity. This runs counter to the school of thought prescribing positive reinforcement in order to encourage specific behaviors. The overjustification effect has been experimentally demonstrated since Edward Deci's first experiments in 1971.

Overplacement

Related to the Dunning-Kruger effect, the overconfidence effect, and narcissism is overplacement, the belief that one is better than one's peers. Overplacement is often less obvious than narcissism, and experimental evidence suggests it is more common. The most famous example is the 1981 study in which 93 percent of American drivers considered themselves better than the median.

Overton window

Joseph P. Overton of the Mackinac Center for Public Policy proposed the idea that there is a narrow range of possibilities—a "window"—that the public will accept in any given situation, and that the success or failure of any political proposition depends in part on fitting this window. The history of the Affordable Care Act, and its antecedents in the Clinton health care plan, makes an interesting study of an attempt to fit a wide-reaching reform into a narrow window.

Panda diplomacy

Panda diplomacy is a term for the long tradition in China of presenting other countries with gifts of giant pandas, beginning with the 7th century Empress Wu Zetian's gift of two pandas to the Emperor of Japan. The People's Republic of China has been especially active in panda diplomacy, making gifts of two dozen pandas from 1958 to 1982. So strongly were panda gifts associated with Chinese diplomacy that the offer of two pandas to Taiwan was debated for several years before it was accepted, in part due to concerns over the international trade of endangered species and in part because of Taiwanese fears about the implications of accepting a gift from China.

Papal conclave

The papal conclave is the method used by the Catholic Church for selecting a new bishop of Rome, more popularly known as the pope, the leader of the Church and successor to Peter. Since 1059, the College of Cardinals has served as the sole electoral body in papal conclaves, and since 1970 participating cardinals have been limited to those under 80 years old. A cardinal is a Catholic priest or bishop who has been selected to join the College of Cardinals, and usually has special duties beyond ordinary clergyman. The conclave holds a series of anonymous votes, typically interspersed with significant discussion both within conclave as a whole and in small groups (usually supporting one cause or another, such as liberal Catholics pooling their votes behind a common candidate). Proceedings are secret, and each day a fire is lit in St Peter's Basilica, with dark smoke indicating to the public that no pope has been elected or white smoke heralding the arrival of a new pope. (The color of the smoke is chemically manipulated; in the past, damp tinder was added to produce black smoke.)

Parental responsibility

The extent and effect of parents' responsibility for their minor childrens' action is a sometimes vague area of law. It is generally true that parents bear responsibility for their childrens' actions in civil cases, for instance, though this is often a moot point since children cannot consent to contracts without a parent co-signing and thus consenting to liability anyway. In criminal cases, parents are usually responsible for making restitution payments necessitated by crimes their children commit, but in most states, implicit in the criminal code as it bears on children is the assumption that most crimes they commit will not be of the most serious kind. The role and responsibility of parents whose children commit violent crimes is thus a largely unaddressed issue, and there is a movement to more strongly criminalize parental neglect in such cases as it leads to allowing these crimes to occur. As in many areas of law, California has led the way, with the 1988 Street Terrorism and Prevention Act, which allows parents to face prison sentences for "gross deviation from normal standards of supervision."

Parentification

Parentification is a role reversal phenomenon in which a child is forced to take the authoritarian, caregiving, or otherwise parent-like role in dealing with their own parent. This is distinct from children who "raise themselves" or self-parent, and is similarly not typically used to describe normal events of a parent–child relationship at the end of the parent's life, such as caregiving or financial assistance by a child to a sick or dying parent. More commonly it refers to the child providing emotional support, such as by mediating between the parent and other family members or friends, or by acting as a confidant or recipient of "venting." It can also refer to instrumental parentification, in which the child performs the practical tasks that would normally be considered the parent's purview, including bill paying and other household management, caring for sick family members, and taking care of siblings to an extent that clearly goes beyond the bounds of babysitting.

Parenting

Parenting is one of the most basic forms of leadership, as parents guide their children through their development, bear responsibility for their children's actions and behavior, and are required to adapt to changing circumstances as their children grow. As with business and political leadership, a significant amount of literature has been devoted to the promotion of different parenting styles. The leadership studies field has not ignored parenting either. Micha Popper and Ofra Mayseless have written about the lessons transformational leadership can take from parenting, while Franklin Kudo conducted a study in 2012 on the impact of authoritative parenting of adolescents on their development of transformational leadership skills.

Parenting style

A parenting style is an approach to or theory of parenting. Developmental psychologist Diana Baumrind has developed parenting styles into three general types: authoritative, in which the parent is both demanding and responsive, with a high expectation of the growing child's maturity and a focus on the child's feelings—not to indulge them but rather to teach the child emotional self-regulation and problem-solving skills; authoritarian, in which the parent is demanding but not responsive, with high expectations of the child's obedience to parental rules and a tendency to use punishment as a motivator; and indulgent, which is responsive but not demanding, with few specific expectations for the child and a dislike or outright rejection of punishment.

Pareto principle

The Pareto principle states that 80 percent of effects stem from 20 percent of causes. The term was coined and applied by management consultant Joseph Juran, and named for economist Vilfredo Pareto, who had written about 80 percent of Italian land being owned by 20 percent of the population, and that 80 percent of the peas in his garden came from 20 percent of the pods. Juran applied this formulation to quality control—80 percent of problems come from 20 percent of sources—but there have been numerous other management applications since, including the rule of thumb that 80 percent of sales come from 20 percent of customers, 80 percent of complaints come from 20 percent of customers, 80 percent of sales come from 20 percent of the product line, 80 percent of profits are made in 20 percent of the time spent, and 80 percent of workplace injuries come from 20 percent of potential hazards. The Pareto principle is an important one in setting priorities, illustrating that not every problem or activity is of equal concern or impact.

Participative system

One of Rensis Likert's management systems, the participative system is the one that most involves employees in decision-making processes, and was advocated by Likert as the most effective. Communication flows freely among all levels, rather than being directed mainly from the top of the hierarchy to lower levels, and managers are kept well-versed in events and problems at the lower levels. Employees as a group participate in setting policy and organizational goals.

Participatory management

In the 1920s, work in human relations theory led to recommendations by management researchers that organizations adopt a participatory management style: a management approach in which employees participate in some level of organizational decision making. Typically, upper management retains the final authority and responsibility for making decisions, but employees are engaged with the process and offer their input.

Passing the buck

"Passing the buck" is a phrase dating at least to the 19th century to refer to disavowing responsibility or explicitly assigning responsibility for one's own actions to someone else. Leaders are sometimes able to shield themselves from taking responsibility by letting subordinates fall on their swords; President Harry Truman explicitly distanced himself from such tactics with the sign on his desk in the Oval Office, reading "The buck stops here."

President Harry Truman famously had a sign on his desk that read "the buck stops here." (NARA)

Passive-aggressive behavior

Passive-aggressive behavior is the expression of hostility and negative emotions through passive methods rather than explicit aggression, such as through body language, tone of voice, deliberately poor or slow performance of work, insincerity or sarcasm, victim-playing, feigned helplessness in order to avoid performing a task, or other means. In the workplace, employee behavior like lateness or procrastination may be taken as passive aggressive, while managers may exhibit passive aggressive behavior through destructively negative attitudes or feigned helplessness that forces subordinates to perform menial tasks for them that they claim they cannot do themselves.

Pater familias

The oldest male in the household, the pater familias was the legal head of the family in ancient Rome, given legal power over his family's property and dependents (including his wife, children, adopted relatives, freedmen, and slaves), as well as legal responsibilities to see after their welfare, maintain his household's moral standing, and perform the duties of a good citizen, including political and civic engagement and honoring his ancestral gods. Legally, he had the power of life or death over any member of his family, though this right is invoked more often in historical fiction set in ancient Rome than it was actually seen in history, apart from the practice (widespread, legally mandated, but not universal) of putting to death infants with significant birth defects.

Paternalism

Paternalism is a style of leadership in which, just as parents limit the freedom of their children as part of their responsibility as parents, leaders limit the freedom and autonomy of those they lead. Paternalism is especially associated with governments, and with laws that limit individual choice in circumstances where those choices affect only the individual (the common examples being laws mandating seatbelt or motorcycle helmet usage), and the term tends to be used derogatorily. There is often disagreement about whether a requirement really is paternalistic: for instance, opponents of vaccination oppose vaccination requirements as paternalistic, while proponents point out that herd immunity and the existence of immunocompromised people means that whether an individual is vaccinated or not has a public health impact beyond the impact on the individual. In the workplace, a paternalistic approach to leadership might more frequently be styled micro-management.

Path-goal theory

The path-goal theory or model was developed by Robert House in 1971, and says that a leader's role is to guide followers to choose the paths that will meet their individual and organizational goals, which will require the leader to engage in different kinds of leadership behaviors as the situation demands. When followers are successful in meeting their goals, they will perceive this behavior positively. This model describes flexibility on the part of the leader, rather than adhering to a narrowly defined leadership style. Both environmental factors and the characteristics and needs of followers will impact leader behavior.

Patriarchy

Patriarchy is a social, political, or cultural system in which men occupy all or most of the leadership roles, especially one in which fathers are given authority over their households. In the modern world, few countries are legal patriarchies—the perpetuation of the patriarchy is rather a matter of tradition and norms, sometimes with laws supporting or informed by a patriarchal view without explicitly invoking it. For instance, in much of the world, marital rape—rape of a spouse by the other spouse—was not illegal, which is to say not legally recognized as rape, until the 19th or 20th century, and in jurisdictions where it is not explicitly criminalized, it is often impossible to prosecute. This legal fact does not make specific mention of a patriarchy, but it reflects the idea that the husband has a right to sex with his wife that exceeds his wife's right to say no. Outside of legal structures, patriarchy is perpetuated by unequal pay and unequal access to jobs, by unequal treatment due to gender, by the politicization of birth control and other women's health issues, by the perpetuation of the idea of women as homemakers and fathers as breadwinners, and other factors. In contrast with this, anthropologists generally believe that prehistoric human communities were egalitarian, leaving open the question of when patriarchal structures were developed.

PDCA

PDCA is a management method for continuous improvement, standing for Plan-Do-Check-Act: Plan, by establishing objectives, expectations, and the processes necessary to achieve them; Do, by implementing the plan; Check, by studying the differences between the plan and the results; Act, by correcting the plan. The method was popularized by management consultant W. Edwards Deming, who sometimes formulated it as PDSA, substituting Study for Check.

Peace through strength

Peace through strength is a phrase dating to at least as early as Emperor Hadrian of 1st-century Rome, and was likely old when he used it. It is a leadership strategy that seeks to avoid conflict by amassing such strength that one's opponents will not risk the losses they would face. This was also the strategy of both the Soviet Union and especially the United States during the Cold War, and was turned into virtually the defining feature of Ronald Reagan's campaigns and presidency.

Peak experience

A peak experience is an ecstatic state characterized by euphoria and feelings of interconnectedness. The term is particularly associated with psychologist Abraham Maslow, who may have used it in an attempt to find a term more neutral than religious or mystical experience. Though peak experiences do not appear on Maslow's hierarchy of needs, he considers them the next level, the goal of those who have satisfied and transcended the basic needs.

Pecking order

A term in both English and German for a stratified social hierarchy preserved by expressions of dominance, figuratively referring to the dominant pecking of hens, and the idea of each hen being pecked by the hen above it in the hierarchy and pecking the hen below it. This pecking need not actually occur to establish the hierarchy: the hierarchy represents each hen's relative ability to dominate, but that ability may be estimated based on size and the deference of other hens. Similarly, when pecking order refers to non-hen social systems, dominance may be maintained not through outright conflict but the mutually understood outcome of hypothetical conflict.

Pedagogy leaders

Pedagogy is the science of education. Most graduate programs in the humanities and social sciences, for instance, include a pedagogy course to impart skills to future professors. Pedagogy leaders are teachers and other educators who spread good teaching practices through a workforce. At Canons High School in the United Kingdom, for instance, pedagogy leaders were hired in 2012 in order to introduce top-down reforms to the teaching practices of the school. The best teachers in the school were selected to teach their methods to their colleagues in seminars.

Peer mentoring

Peer mentoring is mentoring among peers rather than between a mentor and a significantly younger mentee. Primarily associated with education, peer mentoring is sometimes found in the workplace with lateral colleagues rather than superiors who perform the mentoring, which has the potential to form bonds between the co-workers. Mentoring has been found to have a positive correlation with employee retention.

Peer pressure

The influence of a peer group on an individual's attitudes or behaviors. Generally, peer pressure exerts an influence that drives the individual's choices toward the group norm, although in some cases it may be a perceived group norm. Studies of undergraduate binge drinking, for instance, have found that discomfort with binge drinking is high even among participants, many of whom seem to believe they are alone in participating in a behavior that makes them uncomfortable and that the rest of the group finds normal. Peer pressure is a particularly valuable concept in sociology and psychology when it refers to pressures exerted accidentally or unconsciously, rather than acts of persuasion. The behaviors encouraged by peer pressure need not be negative, and some public health campaigns and leadership strategies have focused on using peer pressure to encourage good habits and behavior.

Penalty authority

Penalty authority is authority that a leader retains by creating an atmosphere of fear of punishment, such that he enjoys obedience because his followers fear they will suffer a loss of status, bonuses, or their jobs.

People's history

A "people's history" or "history from below" is an account of history from the perspective of "the people," rather than the from the perspective of the leaders, in contrast with the Great Man approach of the 19th and 20th centuries. Such histories tend to focus on class conflicts or conflicts between the oppressed and their oppressors, and share concerns with postcolonialism, Marxist history, feminist history, and new labor history.

People skills

The term *people skills* overlaps considerably with "soft skills," in consisting of skills concerned with interpersonal relationships, including not only communication skills, but empathy, emotional intelligence, and the ability to persuade and inculcate trust and respect. The difference is mainly in how they are talked about, "soft skills" being contrasted with the "hard skills" that bear directly on a person's job role.

Perceived psychological contract violation

The idea of the perceived psychological contract violation (PPCV) has been explored in organizational psychology since the 1990s, and refers to an employee's negative feelings about an employer's behavior when the employee believes the employer has betrayed a promise or agreement. The PPCV especially refers to breaches of implicit agreement rather than explicit breaches of contract, and usually refers to situations in which the employer has not overstepped their legal rights. Some studies have suggested that an employee's probability of feeling PPCV is inversely proportional to his identification with the organization.

Performance improvement

Performance improvement is a measurement of the improvement in a business process or procedure at the organizational, team, or employee level. It can be measured in a number of ways, including hard measurements like profits, costs, and output, and soft measurements like customer satisfaction surveys and other feedback. Quality control processes are responsible for measuring and improving performance.

Performance orientation

One of the global leadership cultural competencies identified by the GLOBE Project, performance orientation is the degree to which a group, organization, or society encourages excellence in its members by rewarding excellent or improved performance.

Pericles

A 5th-century B.C.E. general in ancient Greece, Pericles ruled Athens during its golden age, the internecine period between the Persian and Peloponnesian Wars. Historian Thucydides called him "the first citizen of Athens," and Herodotus based his political philosophy on the democratic system that the city-state enjoyed under Pericles. Among Pericles' initiatives were paying jurors for their time, so that poor Athenians could participate in jury service, and the promotion of the arts, education, and beautification of public spaces. He was celebrated both as a military leader and an inspiring orator.

Person culture

One of four types of corporate culture identified by Charles Handy and Roger Harrison. In a person culture, each member considers himself superior to the organization. This tends to be untenable for large organizations, but small partnerships can function from this perspective, especially when each partner has a distinct set of skills or resources that he contributes.

Person/situation debate

In psychology, the person/situation debate is the disagreement in the field over whether behavior is primarily the result of the individual's personality traits or the situation in which their behavior is enacted.

Personal branding

The term *personal branding* was first coined by business management writer Tom Peters in 1997, though as a practice it is much older and was a key part of self-improvement books like *Think and Grow Rich* as early as the 1930s. Personal branding is the marketing by the individual of himself and his professional identity, especially through techniques that distinguish his "brand identity" in the same way one would market that of a business.

Personal leadership

The study of leadership in terms of the characteristics of leaders, especially their skills, actions, decision-making strategies, and personality traits. Leadership gurus and the self-help industry traditionally focus on personal leadership, because this is a view of leadership that implies leadership can be taught.

Personality clash

A personality clash is a conflict that transpires not because of disagreement over a contested issue but because of an incompatibility in the personalities of the people involved. Personality conflicts have been the subject of psychological study since at least Carl Jung, who looked at the problems between opposed traits like thinking and feeling or extraversion and introversion and saw in them the root causes of many ostensibly intellectual disputes. Just as those intellectual disputes were not, in their time, acknowledged as personality clashes, so too today a conflict may develop between two people that is ostensibly waged over a particular issue or decision, but is really motivated by the personality difference between them and the different values or perceptions that they hold as a result. These underlying differences may not be expressed, which can make resolving the work at hand difficult.

Personality theories of leadership

Personality theories of leadership are those founded on the idea that someone can be a "natural" leader—that good leadership is a product of specific personality types, not specific skills (which is not the same as saying that skills are not important). The Great Man approach to history and leadership was the dominant view until the 20th century, and early leadership studies in the post–World War II years focused on personality traits possessed by leaders.

Peter Principle

The Peter Principle, named for Laurence J. Peter who introduced the concept in his 1969 humorous book of the same name, states that employees and managers are promoted based on their performance in their current role rather than demonstrated suitability for the new role, and that people are therefore promoted until they arrive in a job at which they are incompetent, while competent people are regularly shifted away from the roles at which they excel.

Philosopher

From the ancient Greek for "lover of wisdom," a philosopher is an intellectual engaged in developing and supporting claims of truth, especially with truth as an end in itself rather than, as in psychology, for the purpose of treatment of an individual. This does not mean philosophers are impractical, though; many branches of philosophy are engaged with specific practical issues, like political philosophy and ethics. Other branches like metaphysics and epistemology are admittedly more abstract.

Philosopher Kings

The ancient Greek philosopher Plato was a staunch critic of democracy as practiced in Athens (cf. Sortition and Craft analogy), and proposed instead that society should be ruled by "Philosopher Kings." Such leaders would be selected for their capacity to be trained for the role, and in being thoroughly trained—not only in leadership but in what we now call the liberal arts, with a thorough practical education as well—they would have the skills necessary to govern justly and effectively. In comparison, Plato found democracy to be little more than mob rule.

Piaget, Jean

The 20th century Swiss psychologist Jean Piaget contributed greatly to developmental psychology. Today he is best known for defining four developmental stages: the sensorimotor stage from birth to age 2, the preoperational stage from age 2 to 7, the concrete operational stage from age 7 to 11, and the formal operational stage as abstract reasoning develops. Even when psychologists disagree with some of the specifics of Piaget's theories, he was instrumental in introducing the idea that adult cognitive processes and abilities do not arrive in an instant.

Ping pong diplomacy

Ping pong diplomacy is a common term for the visits to China and the United States by ping pong players from the other country, at a time when few American citizens were permitted to enter China. The U.S. Table Tennis team, in fact, were the first Americans (along with the journalists accompanying them) to enter Beijing in 22 years, when they arrived in April 1971. The event led to the first real improvement in Chinese/U.S. relations in years, and was followed up by President Richard Nixon's visit to China in 1972, and that of a Chinese ping pong delegation to the U.S. several months later. China's attempt to invite similar delegations from other countries proved to have little success.

Planning fallacy

The term *planning fallacy* was introduced in 1979 by psychologists Daniel Kahneman and Amos Tversky, who also developed reference class forecasting. The fallacy refers to an observed pattern of individuals underestimating the time they will need to complete a task, even when they have previously had similar tasks run overtime. The effect is true for multiple kinds of tasks, both mental and physical, individual and group, but only when predicting one's own work.

Plato's Academy

The ancient Greek philosopher Plato, a generation after Pericles, founded his Academy in Athens in 387 B.C.E. Plato had studied with Socrates, Pericles's contemporary, who had argued for the good of teaching politics and ethics. Plato went one step further and argued that education, rather than aristocratic birth, could and should produce leaders. The complete curriculum is unknown, but mathematics and philosophy would have been included, and perhaps "natural philosophy," or what we now call the hard sciences. The academy attracted students from all over ancient Greece, and the traditional view of historians has been that it served as a leadership training center; it is difficult to say how much practical governance formed part of the curriculum, as opposed to more abstract political philosophy.

Pluralistic ignorance

Pluralistic ignorance is a phenomenon found in social groups, wherein the majority of members privately believe one thing but publicly espouse a conflicting thing, motivated by the belief that their real opinion is not shared by the others. The classic example is that of excessive drinking on college campuses. Numerous studies show that a large number of heavy drinkers in college drink more than they are comfortable with in the belief that they need to keep up with the others around them and that they are the only ones uncomfortable with it. "The Emperor's New Clothes" is often used as an illustration of the same effect.

Plutarch

The 1st-century Greek historian Plutarch is today best known for his work *Parallel Lives*. Like most historians of his era, he was concerned less with historical accuracy and context and more with the lessons that could be illustrated with reference to historical events or personages. *Parallel Lives* presents 50 short biographies, 46 of them arranged in pairs of one Greek life and one Roman life. The complete text has not survived, and some of the surviving text has been changed by a later editor, but the gist of it is clear. Plutarch was concerned with illustrating the moral character of his subjects, and the bulk of his energy was spent demonstrating the parallels between physical characteristics of his subjects and their moral and psychological characteristics—a tendency that persists in everything from phrenology to handwriting analysis to palm reading. He is a clear antecedent to the "Great Man" school of biography, which had been inspired in part by the revived interest in Plutarch during the Renaissance and subsequent strains of thought that developed throughout the Enlightenment.

Political frame

In L. Bolman and T. Deal's Four Frame model, the Political frame is one of the distinctive frames from which people approach the world. It perceives the world in terms of power, resources, and competition, highlighting differences in perspectives, needs, or lifestyles. It tends to approach things in terms of negotiation, coercion, or power alliances.

Political philosophy

The philosophical field devoted to the study of politics, law, justice, liberty, and authority.

Political science

A social science focused on the study of politics, the state and government, and political behavior. Political science has its roots in the work of Plato and Aristotle, and draws on numerous fields, overlapping with most of the social sciences.

Popular sovereignty

Popular sovereignty is the idea that the authority of the government originates with and is sustained by the consent of the people, which is the basis for social contract theories.

Populism

Populism is an approach to political thought that favors those things that will appeal to the people—it is not a specific ideology so much as it is a behavior. In the United States, it is a term rarely used reflexively, but this was not always the case. Up through the New Deal era, many politicians and activists referred to themselves as populist. Agrarian and farmers' movements of the 19th century were explicitly populist, and the Populist Party wielded some power in the presidential election of 1896. Since the 1930s, however, "populist" has more often become a pejorative term, one especially associated with preying on popular fears or misconceptions in order to garner votes. A number of candidates and officials have done their part to blacken the name. Populist governor and senator Huey P. Long was famous for his manipulation of public sentiment to amass power and wealth, and in the south after the civil rights movement, populism meant white peoples' populism: the Populist Party name was revived for the presidential campaigns of former

Ku Klux Klan leaders Willis Carto and David Duke. In the 21st century, several new populist parties have formed, while the Tea Party and the Occupy movement have been true populist phenomena.

Positive psychological capital

Positive psychological capital (PsyCap) is a state in which an individual experiences hope, optimism, resilience, and high self-efficacy. Helping employees achieve PsyCap in the workplace is one of the goals of positive psychology as implemented by organizational psychologists.

Positive Psychology

A school of psychology, developed in the late 1990s that emphasizes applications of psychological understanding to the improvement of normal life rather than simply the treatment of mental illness, crisis, or trauma. Like humanistic philosophy, positive psychology focuses on happiness. In the workplace, positive psychology focuses on employee engagement, emotional intelligence, and avoiding burnout.

Post, Jerrold

Psychologist Jerrold Post has theorized that collective or group narcissism emerges when a narcissistic charismatic leader is paired with individually narcissistic followers. The leader plays to their individual narcissism by praising the qualities of the group as a whole and its superiority to others; the leader–follower relationship that emerges is thus deeply narcissistic, with a leader who needs to be admired and followers dazzled by their leader's force of personality as a reflection on their own group identity. Hitler is the obvious example here, a charismatic leader who constantly invoked national and racial pride, contrasted with his condemnation of so-called weaker peoples.

Post-Fordism

Post-Fordism is a term often used to refer to the standard system of production in the industrialized world since the late 20th century, and the cultural, social, political, and economic institutions and phenomena associated with it. The name is coined in reference to Fordism, Henry Ford's approach to automobile manufacturing in the early 20th century. Post-Fordism is characterized by the increased participation of women in the workforce compared to previous eras, increasing specialization of businesses and jobs, and the rise of information technology, but beyond this there is considerable disagreement over what constitutes a post-Fordist business, and whether or not post-Fordism coexists alongside a changed Fordism or if it has supplanted Fordism entirely.

Power

In the social sciences, power is the ability to influence others. It may be exerted consciously or unconsciously. The term *agent of influence* is often used to refer to the person exerting power. The target—the person being influenced—may or may not be aware that they are being influenced, and even if they are aware that the agent of influence is responsible for the change, they may not think of the scenario in terms of a power dynamic. For instance, a history teacher may assign a textbook or give a lecture that changes a student's views of a political issue, but the student may not think of this as the history teacher having wielded power over him. In the 21st century, psychological experiments have suggested that those who have more power also have less empathy, and that this effect is causative: as they gain power, they become less interested in or less able to see circumstances from the viewpoints of other people. However, research also shows that those with greater power are more likely to be proactive; one study found that powerful people were three times more likely to offer to help a person in distress. The use of power in interpersonal or professional relationships is increasingly an area studied with game theory.

Power culture

One of four types of corporate culture identified by Charles Handy and Roger Harrison. In a power culture, culture is concentrated in a central figure or small group, with little bureaucracy.

Power distance

One of the cultural dimensions identified by Geert Hofstede, power distance is the difference in power between an executive and a given subordinate, or in a society, between the most and least powerful. The power distance index is the greatest difference in power between the most and least powerful that is acceptable to the least powerful.

Pragmatism

A philosophical school of thought originating in the United States, pragmatism began with the work of Charles Sanders Peirce, William James, and John Dewey in the late 19th century. It is best represented by the pragmatist maxim, which calls for examining a hypothesis in light of its practical consequences. Though pragmatism encompasses metaphysical, epistemological, and empiricist dimensions, in common usage it means a concern for practical ends. A pragmatic approach to management, for instance, is one that is less concerned with the implications of managerial practices and more concerned with their impact on meeting organizational goals. Similarly, pragmatic ethics focus less on the inherent moral value of a given action and more on the morality of its consequences. Classical pragmatism was actually not as ends-focused as it seems—John Dewey disparaged work and education being treated only as means to their respective ends, and thought each should be rewarding in itself—but has perhaps had its greatest impact on the public administration profession, in which administrators are principally concerned with evaluating potential programs and plans in terms of their practical consequences.

Pre-attentive processing

Pre-attentive processing is the gathering of information from an individual's surroundings by his unconscious mind, and the processing of that information by the unconscious before it is given over to conscious processing—before it is "noticed," in other words. Pre-attentive processing is the mechanism that is responsible for what an individual notices first about the stimuli in his environment, and which characteristics of a stimulus stand out. Does the model on the billboard stand out the most, the brand logo behind her, the tiger she is posed with, or the fact that a different billboard was there yesterday, thwarting his expectations? Poor sleep or lack of sleep slows down the process of pre-attentive processing, which is one of the specific phenomena making up the "grogginess" we feel when we first get up in the morning, or if we are suddenly wakened in the middle of the night. This is also one reason sleep is so important to mental or emotional work and decision making.

Precautionary principle

The precautionary principle is a concept in public policy, stating that in circumstances in which there is scientific uncertainty as to whether a given action poses a risk to the public or to the environment, the correct response is to avoid the action unless it can be shown that it is harmless. More a guiding principle of policy than an element thereof, it is in large part a reaction to the numerous practices of the past that were later learned to be harmful as science improved, including the public health impact of pesticides and the environmental impact of chlorofluorocarbons.

Prescriptive

There is a divide in philosophy and most of the social sciences between the descriptive and the prescriptive. While the descriptive simply models an aspect of the world as it is—descriptive linguistics describes how people use language, while descriptive leadership studies identify the things real-world leaders do or the traits they have—the prescriptive approach is concerned with identifying, defending, and advocating the best way to do something. Prescriptive grammar is the familiar rules-based grammar exemplified by William Strunk and E. B. White's *Elements of Style*; prescriptive leadership studies identifies the most successful model of leadership. Prescriptive works on leadership go back thousands of years, to ancient wisdom literature such as that of Ptah Hotep; descriptive works are essentially introduced by the social sciences and the study of management in the 20th century.

Presentism

Presentism is the depiction, construction, or response to the past that is inflected by anachronistic present-day perspectives. In discussing history and literature, this is problematic; as Pulitzer-winning historian John Lewis Gaddis wrote, "the times impose their values upon lives; there's no point in condemning individuals for the circumstances in which they find themselves." There is no way to usefully address the effectiveness of historical leaders without considering their actions in the context of their times. In philosophy, presentism also refers to a model of time that says that only events in the present are real.

Preventive diplomacy

Preventive diplomacy is practiced in order to prevent disputes from occurring or escalating, as opposed to diplomatic measures taken to control the damage of disputes already escalated.

Priming

In psychology, priming is a memory effect that influences the individual's response to a stimulus as a result of previous exposure to another stimulus. A simple experimental example is showing people strings of letters to see how quickly they can identify which strings are gibberish and which are real words. Words are identified more quickly when preceded by related words—yellow will be recognized more quickly after purple than after jalapeno, for instance.

The Prince

The most famous of the "mirrors for princes," Niccolo Machiavelli's *Il Principe* was first circulated in 1513 and officially published in 1532, after Machiavelli's death. Machiavelli had worked in the government of Florence from 1498 to 1512, while the Medici family was out of power, and wrote *The Prince* when they returned and the government was replaced. *The Prince* presents instructions for governance, and its apparent amorality is the inspiration for the term *Machiavellian*. Both the Catholic Church and the humanists of the Renaissance condemned *The Prince*, though Enlightenment philosopher Jean-Jacques Rousseau, in the 18th century,

interpreted the work as a satire of ruthlessness rather than a celebration thereof. Though this view has been echoed by more recent political philosophers, the questions of where Machiavelli stood and how exactly *The Prince* was meant to be received have not been satisfactorily resolved.

Private leadership

One of the Three Levels of Leadership, private leadership is James Scouller's term for the 14 behaviors (9 related to "maintenance," 5 related to the individual's task) that leaders use in one-on-one interactions with individuals. Private leadership is focused on increasing the confidence and performance of the individual with respect to the goal at hand.

Problem-solving courts

Problem-solving courts are those that seek a resolution to the issues brought before them other than simple punishment for crimes. In the United States, they began with the efforts of judges in the 1990s to divert drug addicts to treatment programs rather than sentence them to prison, in order to reduce recidivism, on the theory that their addiction had motivated their criminal behavior and would continue to do so until they had the means to overcome it. Drug courts have become increasingly common, in which judges have considerable leeway in the way they handle the cases brought before them.

Problem statement

A problem statement is a device used in problem solving, which concisely defines the problem, whose problem it is, the limitations (in resources like time or money) on possible solutions, and the form that the resolution can take. Problem statements are normally simply tools to get the problem-solving process going, but sometimes highlight issues that need to be addressed, such as an inability to clearly articulate what the problem is (which reduces the odds of finding a satisfactory solution) or the discovery that there are actually separate problems that can be dealt with independently.

Procedural justice

Procedural justice is fairness in the processes used by a group, organization, or government to distribute resources and address and resolve conflicts, a concept also known as due process when used in reference to U.S. law. Procedural justice implies some impartiality about what constitutes a fair outcome of a procedure, and perhaps some system of evaluating or contesting an outcome (such as the institution of the court of appeals, in the American legal system). High levels of procedural justice tend to be associated with group members feeling a high level of belongingness.

Process culture

One of four corporate cultures identified by T. E. Deal and A. A. Kennedy, characterized by slow feedback and low risk. Jobs in these cultures are generally low stress and secure, with the biggest sources of stress coming from interpersonal conflicts, incompetent co-workers or poorly designed work procedures, or in the case of public-facing roles, dealing with the public. Typical examples include the retail business, the hospitality industry, and banks.

Professional identification

Professional identification is the degree to which an individual defines himself as a member of his profession, as measured by a scale developed by Blake E. Ashforth and Fred Mael

in 1989. Work on the impact of professional identification has uncovered two clear phenomena: employees with a high degree of professional identification are more likely to perceive administrators as outsiders, restricting their degree of organizational identification; and professional identification is strongly associated with the perception that accords status to a high quality of work more than to a high salary or profit-making potential. (Much of the work on professional identification has been done on doctors, though, who have a high average salary.)

Professional network service

Professional network services are social networks that are intended for professional connections, interactions, and networking. LinkedIn is the most popular example, but there are numerous other networks, including some specific to industries or job types, and some focused more explicitly on connecting contractors with work.

Project engineer

A project engineer either works with or works as a project manager, depending on the needs of the company, in overseeing the planning, resource management, and execution of a technical project.

Project manager

A project manager is tasked with the planning, execution, and completion of a project. They are a specialized professional common in certain fields, notably the technology and construction industries. Professional certification exists, though it is not required by all firms, and although some graduate programs in project management are offered, the field's formalization is still young.

Promoting adversaries

When both sides in a conflict can benefit in some way from maintaining the conflict, this behavior or relationship is called "promoting adversaries." In the private sector, the "cola wars" of Pepsi and Coca-Cola in the 1980s led both companies to innovate and continue to develop their products. In international relations, a sustained conflict like the Cold War helps keep regimes in power and favors certain areas of government spending.

A button from the "cola wars" between Pepsi and Coca-Cola proclaims that the consumer picked Coke during a blind taste test. (Wikimedia Commons)

Proxemics

The term *proxemics* was coined by cultural anthropologist Edward T. Hall in 1963, to refer to an area in the study of nonverbal communication, specifically the use of space. While kinesics and haptics refer to nonverbal communication conducted by body language and touch, the way space is used for communication includes the distance people put between themselves and others, and the way people's posture and body positioning changes (along with changes in the pitch of their voice) as other people approach. The bounds of personal space and reactions to violations thereof are of particular concern.

Psychoanalysis

Psychoanalysis is a set of psychological theories and therapeutic mechanisms dealing with human behavior, the mind, human motivation, and the treatment of psychological problems. Popularized and largely formulated by Sigmund Freud, psychoanalysis was further developed by his colleagues Alfred Adler and Carl Jung, and later followers like Jacques Lacan. Psychoanalysis is one of the most influential theories on the layman's understanding of human behavior, and psychoanalytical concepts like free association, ego, Freudian slips, and the symbolism of dreams have trickled down into the popular imagining. As one of the first scientific approaches to understanding human behavior, psychoanalysis has provided numerous tools both to analyze leadership and to help leaders better understand their followers' needs.

Psychodynamic approaches to leadership

Psychodynamic approaches to leadership are theories or models of leadership that are influenced by psychodynamics, the area of psychology that systematizes and studies the motives, drives, and emotions underlying human behavior. Psychodynamic theories draw on Sigmund Freud, Carl Jung, and their successors, and are related to psychohistory, the branch of psychodynamics that explains the behavior of historical figures through reference to modern psychology. While many theories of leadership draw heavily on sociology or political science, psychodynamic approaches draw on concepts from psychology like individuation, regression, and the shadow self.

Psychology of reasoning

The psychology of reasoning incorporates psychology, cognitive science, linguistics, probability theory, and neuroscience to study the way people reason, solve problems, and make decisions. The relationship between emotion and reasoning, the development of reasoning, the impact of completeness or incompleteness of knowledge on reasoning, and the differences in individual versus group reasoning are all important areas of study. Psychology of reasoning studies both the processes of reasoning that occur internally—both consciously and otherwise—and the way people articulate their reasoning using natural language, which is especially important in decision making and attempts to persuade or influence others.

Psychological contract

The psychological contract is the set of perceptions, beliefs, and obligations held mutually by an employee and his employer. The term contrasts with an explicit written contract, and includes those elements of the relationship not included in the contract, whether implicit or explicit. For instance, an unspoken agreement between workers and a supervisor may say that employees will work productively, and in return the supervisor will not hover over them or micromanage, will safeguard the security of their jobs, and will be reasonable in responding to requests for vacation time. Psychological contracts became more important and arguably more detailed over the course of the 20th century, as the growing prosperity of the United States led Americans to develop a greater expectation of pleasure from their jobs and an adequate work–life balance.

Psychological immune system

The psychological immune system is a metaphor for the many mechanisms that protect an individual from negative emotions, and which work to reduce their intensity and duration. Because these mechanisms do not operate in view of the conscious mind, they are not accounted for in affective forecasting.

Psychological safety

Psychological safety is a condition in a group dynamic such that members of the team feel safe with one another—not simply physically safe, but rather, able to raise concerns or express honest opinions about the work at hand and other issues of concern to the group without fear of judgment or reprisals. Adept leadership inculcates psychological safety in the group, especially when group members are involved in the operations and decision-making procedures of the group and roles are clearly understood.

Psychometrics

Psychometrics is the area of psychology concerned with the creation of objective measurement tools for psychological qualities like skills, attitudes, moods, and personality traits, and with statistical research related to those tools. Like modern psychology itself, psychometrics arose in the 19th century and has been subject to numerous trends as well as changes brought on by technological advances. The foundational concepts to psychometrics are validity and reliability. Reliability is the easiest to test: the same measurement taken multiple times should have consistent results. Validity requires reliability, as well as statistical evidence that the test measures what it is intended to measure.

Ptah Hotep

The ancient Egyptian vizier Ptah Hotep lived in the 5th Dynasty period of Egypt, probably during the 25th century B.C.E., and is buried at Saqqara along with his descendents. Viziers were advisers to the pharaohs (Djedkare Isesi in this case) as well as overseeing much of the bureaucracy of the government. Ptah Hotep authored one of the oldest known books, *The Maxims of Ptah Hotep*, consisting of the wisdom he had accumulated in his lifetime and wished to pass on to the younger generation. Many of the maxims deal with leadership, including this simple one encouraging good works: "If you are a man who leads, who controls the affairs of the many, seek out every beneficent deed, that your conduct may be blameless."

Public administration

An interdisciplinary academic discipline, public administration studies the implementation of government policy and best practices for managing public programs. A somewhat older discipline than leadership studies, it followed a similar course in its development, originating as an area of common interest for academics in various fields (political science, economics, law, business administration, and sociology, primarily) a generation or so after the creation of New Deal programs contributed to the professionalization of civil service. Eventually it emerged as its own discipline, with dedicated studies and degree programs.

Public diplomacy

Public diplomacy is diplomacy conducted with the public of a foreign nation rather than with its leadership. Cultural diplomacy is sometimes discussed as a form of public diplomacy, but a different form of public diplomacy has been an important part of American foreign policy since the end of World War II, as the American government has sought to encourage foreign populaces to become disillusioned first with communist regimes and later with various regimes in the Middle East and North Africa. International broadcasting is a key element of public diplomacy efforts, and Radio Free Europe (RFE) has broadcast U.S.-sponsored news and propaganda since 1949. While European broadcasts cover a smaller range than they did during the Cold War, RFE (which formally merged with the similar Radio Liberty) now broadcasts in the Middle East as well.

Public interest

Public interest or the public good is the well-being of the general public. While government policy decisions need to take public interest into account, the private sector is not always required to do so, nor motivated to do so in such cases where working against the public interest will have no impact on profits nor on the private lives of the decision-makers (as in the case of outsourcing labor to a cheaper county). The regulatory framework of many industries is a compromise between bowing to the public interest and honoring the American ideal of a free market.

Public leadership

One of the Three Levels of Leadership, public leadership is James Scouller's term for the 34 leadership behaviors that leaders use when influencing a group of two or more people, such as in meetings. Scouller divides the 34 behaviors into groups: group building and maintenance (12 behaviors), ideation, problemsolving, and decisionmaking (10), executing the plan (6), setting the vision (4), and planning (2). Public leadership is concerned with driving collaborative and collective efforts and creating at atmosphere of trust that leads to high performance.

Public management

Public management is the administration of government and non-profit organizations, and especially the use of management tools borrowed from or analogous to those of the private sector in such administration. While the concerns and goals of the public sector differ from those of the private sector, many management approaches are goal-independent.

Public policy

As an academic discipline, public policy is the study of policies formulated and set by governments and their constituent parts, and of the decision-making processes behind such policies. It intersects with other social sciences, especially political science, economics, and sociology. Approaches to public policy vary considerably among the schools offering degree programs, with Indiana University focusing on multidisciplinary concentrations and non-profit management, the University of Illinois at Chicago focusing on decision-making processes, and the John F. Kennedy School of Government at Harvard taking a leadership-based approach grounded in political science.

Public–private partnership

A public–private partnership (PPP) is a venture conducted through a partnership of a government agency and one or more private businesses, often with the private business assuming all or most of the financial risk, in exchange for a high reward potential. PPPs are a way to shield taxpayers from the risks of certain ventures, while encouraging business opportunities. They range from public transit ventures to the privatization of emergency services in some jurisdictions.

Pygmalion effect

Named for the Greek myth of the statue given life, the Pygmalion effect results in individuals performing better as a result of higher expectations being set for them.

Quaker-based consensus

The Quaker model of consensus decision making is a method that has developed over time since about the 18th century, and that the Quakers introduced to anti-war protest movements in the 20th century. The process emphasizes allowing every interested party a chance to express their view, while a clerk or convenor acts as a facilitator. The facilitator prevents discussions from either spending too much time covering the areas where there is already general agreement or degenerating into arguments over trivialities; instead, they identify areas of disagreement, rephrase each side's viewpoint for clarification, and guide the discussion in order to attempt to resolve the conflict. The facilitator is not the decision maker, which is a key difference from decision-making processes in which the leader may attempt to facilitate discussion but nevertheless does not distance himself from his power. The facilitator has no more authority than anyone else. As the discussion develops, the facilitator continues to articulate the viewpoints as they come closer and closer to consensus. In the 21st century, large Quaker meetings are actually intentionally slowed down in order to moderate the tone of discussion. Volunteer runners bring wireless microphones to speakers waiting for their turn, and are asked to walk at a casual pace as an opportunity to slow the discussion.

Quality management

Quality management is the process of ensuring that an organization or the products and services it provides are consistent, and consists of both quality assurance and quality control, as well as planning elements and strategies for improvement.

Quality storyboard

A tool for quality management, a quality storyboard is a visual way to present a narrative about the quality control process.

Queen bee syndrome

Queen bee syndrome is a phenomenon wherein a female leader is more critical of her female subordinates than of males. Repeatedly found in the workplace since its coinage in 1973 by

Graham Staines, Toby Jayaratne, and Carol Tavris, queen bee syndrome has been observed and studied in high school and junior high in recent years, in response to an overall call in psychology and sociology to examine the problem of adolescent bullying. In the business world, queen bees tend to be older and politically conservative.

"Quest for causality"

James MacGregor Burns' evocative description of leadership studies. A Pulitzer Prize winner for his biography of Franklin Delano Roosevelt, Burns wrote one of the early major works in the field with his 1978 *Leadership*, which explored leadership from a historian's perspective, as the process of governance over social change. In investigating change, the work of the traditional historian is to determine cause. Burns thus saw leadership studies as a form of historical analysis.

Qui facet per alium facit per se

"He who acts through another does the act himself," says the Latin legal term, which assigns responsibility to an employer for the actions he hires an employee to do.

RAND Corporation

The RAND (Research ANd Development) Corporation is a non-profit policy think tank based in Santa Monica, California, and financed by a combination of private and public funding. Originally spun out of the Air Force in the early days of the Cold War to develop new weapons, it became famous for developing the doctrine of mutually assured destruction, and although about half of its work involved national security issues, it has expanded to include transportation policy, social welfare, and other areas. Its RAND Health Insurance Experiment was one of the largest health insurance studies. The RAND Corporation operates a small graduate school, the Frederick S. Pardee RAND Graduate School, for about 100 students seeking master's or doctorate degrees in policy analysis. Most classes are taught by RAND researchers, and include topics like economics, political science, arms control, criminology, and national security.

Random choice

A random choice is one that is arrived at without recourse to preference or reasons. Ideally, all possibilities are given an equal probability of selection. Random choice has sometimes been suggested as the best means to make certain decisions, including leader selection. The military draft, for instance, is considered most fair when it is random. Many augury techniques in the ancient world amount to random choice, and their popularity has been read by some anthropologists as indicating that, in the absence of the ability to determine the right choice based on evidence, a random choice may have a greater chance of being successful than a choice based on incomplete evidence or a faulty understanding. The random selection of public officials and other leaders is called sortition.

Ratchet effect

In sociology, the ratchet effect is the difficulty of reversing an activity or backtracking once a certain event has happened, thus "locking in place" a pattern or expectation. In business, this often refers to the effect on the expectations of higher-ups of a team achieving a performance benchmark; if the benchmark is exceeded, frequently this then becomes the minimum level expected for the next period's performance, which motivates managers to avoid exceeding target performance levels for fear of being "locked in" and committed to continually achieving that level.

Rational choice theory

Rational choice theory, sometimes just called choice theory, is used in the social sciences and economics as the framework for modeling human behavior. Originally used principally to model economic behavior, it has become much more widely used since the 1980s, in part due to Gary Becker's applications of rational choice theory to drug addiction, racial discrimination, crime, and family organization.

Rational-legal authority

Rational-legal authority is a concept from sociologist Max Weber's work on political leadership, and refers to political authority that is derived from and legitimized by a system of underlying laws. Further, the government has a monopoly on the enactment and enforcement of laws and on the use of physical force. The modern state as a rational-legal authority is almost universal now, but it emerged in the West from feudalism.

Reactivity

Reactivity is the change in behavior that an individual makes as the result of being observed. While important in psychological experiments, because the behavior of an individual knowingly participating in an experiment (as ethics regulations require) will not be exactly the same as in the real world, reactivity is important in management and leadership as well, in predicting and managing follower behavior.

Realism

In international relations, realism is a school of thought that developed in the early 20th century, building on the work of Niccolo Machiavelli and Thomas Hobbes. The realist view is predicated on four assumptions: the international system is anarchic, meaning that there is no entity above states that can govern them, and a state of constant antagonism prevails; states are the most important actors in the international system; all states are unitary and rational, meaning that they seek to attain resources and pursue self-interest; the primary concern of every state is survival. Realists, in contrast with earlier ideologies, see humans as inherently competitive and self-interested, and state behavior as growing from those influences.

Reference class forecasting

Reference class forecasting (RCF) plans for the future with reference to the outcome of past situations. It is a method developed by psychologists Daniel Kahneman and Amos Tversky, the former of whom was awarded the Nobel Prize in Economics in part for his contributions to the theory. RCF is intended to correct for the effects of cognitive biases like overconfidence, by forecasting the future of an outcome of an event through a three-part process consisting of identifying the reference class of the project and past projects included in that class; establishing a probability distribution for the reference class; and comparing the future project to the reference class distribution in order to forecast the outcome.

Referent authority

Referent authority is authority enjoyed by a leader as a result of charm, personality, and an ability to influence others and command respect.

Referent power

Referent power is one of John R. P. French and Bertram Raven's bases of power, and one of Patrick J. Montana and Bruce H. Charnov's varieties of organizational power. It originates as a result of the group or organizational affiliations of the individual. This power may be either positive or negative. For instance, there was a time in the 1920s when membership in the second incarnation of the Ku Klux Klan conferred greater social influence—power—within the community, whereas by the end of that century, David Duke's association with the Klan put a well-defined ceiling on his political aspirations.

Reinvent the wheel

To reinvent the wheel is to sink energy and resources into the development of something that simply duplicates the functionality of something that already exists, and especially something that is already optimized. The phrase is used in a number of contexts, the most important of which refer not to a company's product line but to their internal processes and procedures, and the danger of creating a new procedure simply for the novelty of it, when an optimized procedure already exists.

Relational leadership

In Wilfred Drath's coinage, relational leadership is a study of leadership that goes beyond consideration of the traits and characteristics of individual leaders in order to take into account the whole context in which leadership occurs, and the network of relationships leaders are surrounded by.

Relational transparency

One of the qualities of authentic leadership (cf.), relational transparency refers to the leader's openness about his thoughts, beliefs, and feelings, without overstepping into matters that would be inappropriate or unprofessional.

Relationship-oriented leadership

Relationship-oriented leadership is a leadership approach that focuses on team members, especially keeping them motivated, matching them to the best role, and keeping communication open. Relationship-oriented leaders support, mentor, and develop their workers, encourage collaboration, and may be proactive in seeking resolutions to conflicts among team members. The terms *employee-oriented leadership* (or employee-oriented management) and *people-oriented leadership* are also used. Relationship-oriented leadership is sometimes contrasted with task-oriented leadership, and studies of their relative effectiveness led to the formulation of situational leadership theory.

Relevance paradox

In a relevance paradox, an attempt to gather information for a decision-making process fails when the set of information that is eliminated because of its irrelevance actually includes critical information. This is a typical problem in identifying which information is necessary to a decision-making process or discussion, because the relevance of information is not always clear until the full circumstances of the situation are clear, and the full circumstances are revealed only by assembling all relevant information. The "Seattle way," the political procedure generally followed in Seattle and King County, Washington, is often criticized as being slow moving and circular, but one of the strengths of the tortoise-like pace of its deliberations is that it can avoid this pitfall. Discussions of the relevance paradox can often sound like a jumble of double-speak, as with Secretary of Defense Donald Rumsfeld's 2002 statement in a news briefing that there are "known unknowns; that is to say we know there are some things we do not know. But there are also unknown unknowns, the ones we don't know we don't know."

Terrorist attacks like those that took place in New York at the World Trade Center on September 11, 2001, have made organizational resilience increasingly more valued. (Flickr)

Reputation management

In public relations, reputation management is the conscious oversight of a person or organization's reputation, and the actions taken to influence that reputation. In the 21st century, this has become particularly associated with overseeing the online presence of search engine results associated with the subject, and attempts to manipulate those results. Reputation management is an extension of personal branding.

Resilience

Resilience in an organization is the ability to anticipate and adapt to disruption. Resilience is necessary to the organization's creation of long-term value. In the 21st century, organizational resilience has become increasingly valued, in part due to the threat of terrorist attacks made more palpable by the 9/11 attacks and the impact of several highly publicized natural disasters and the ongoing effects of climate change.

Respondeat superior

"Let the master answer," in legal Latin. A legal doctrine of responsibility, also called the master-servant rule and applicable not only in the Anglo-American common law tradition but encoded as civil law in many states. The doctrine assigns responsibility to an employer for the actions employees commit in the course of their employment, with a few exceptions.

Responsible autonomy

Responsible autonomy is one of the major ways to structure an organization, in which the units making up an organization—either individual members or small groups—are given autonomy in their choices and activities, while bearing responsibility for the outcome of those actions. This is the common form of organization in research institutes, for instance, as well as many think tanks, investment funds, and the Sudbury schools (as well as some alternative colleges).

Reward authority

Reward authority is authority enjoyed by a leader because of their use of positive reinforcement and the rewards they offer their followers for performance.

Reward dependence

Reward dependence is a personality trait, which tends to remain a constant throughout a person's life, characterized by having a strong response to signaled rewards such as compliments and social approval, and the tendency to adjust one's behavior in order to continue receiving those rewards. Reward dependence involves, but is not synonymous with, dependence on the approval of others, and is substantially correlated with extraversion. It is believed that reward dependence may be implicated in some addictive behaviors, in which the addictive substance is a substitute for the approval of family or peers.

Reward power

Reward power is one of John R. P. French and Bertram Raven's bases of power, and one of Patrick J. Montana and Bruce H. Charnov's varieties of organizational power. Reward, despite the name, includes both positive and negative incentives. A teenager given use of the car for a weekend trip as a reward for making the honor roll is a positive example of reward power, but grounding that teenager for crashing the car is still reward power, using negative incentive. Reward power uses the agent of influence's ability to give or take tangible or emotional rewards.

Right-wing authoritarianism

In personality psychology, right-wing authoritarianism (RWA) is willingness to submit to legitimate authority, whether in the form of individual authority figures issuing orders or adherence to social norms and conventions. People with a high degree of RWA are, furthermore, hostile to those who deviate from these norms or make trouble by resisting authority. People with a high degree of RWA may also have trouble accepting as legitimate the leadership of leaders who are not, themselves, sufficiently authoritarian, or may shift their allegiance to other elements in the leadership hierarchy—as with the attitude toward the Democratic President Barack Obama on the part of many right-wing authoritarians who treated him as a threat to social conventions and pledged their commitment to the Republican elements in Congress instead. That said, despite the use of "right-wing" in this term, RWA is not itself a politically partisan trait, nor one found either exclusively in political conservatives or universally in political conservatives, though the Canadian psychologist who first identified it believed it was more likely to be found in American Republicans and Canadian Conservatives.

Ringelmann effect

The Ringelmann effect is named for French agricultural engineer Maxmilien Ringelmann, who found that individual group members become less productive as the size of the group increases. There are two main causes of the Ringelmann effect: larger groups are harder to coordinate, and so the organization of the group and its division of labor becomes less efficient; and motivation decreases, often unconsciously. Because much of the Ringelmann effect is unconscious, group members do not always accurately self-report productivity and may not be aware of the effect.

Risk management

Risk management is the handling of risk, through the perception and assessment of risks in a situation and their prioritization, followed by the actions necessary to monitor such risks, mitigate their effects, or minimize their occurrence. Risks range from the possibility of a debtor not making good on their debt to a natural disaster, and everything in between. In business, risk management especially involves those related to any aspect of the business plan not playing out in the expected manner, from higher costs being incurred to profits not reaching their necessary threshold.

Risk perception

Risk perception is an individual's capacity to recognize the presence, nature, and severity of risk. Theories about how risk perception develops come from both psychology and sociology, with some focusing on the mechanics of the mind and others on the influence of culture on risk heuristics. Risk perception is key in understanding decision making, since so many decisions involve some amount of risk.

Robert's Rules of Order

A book of rules of order to be used by organizations following parliamentary procedures, Brigadier General Henry Martyn *Robert's Rules of Order* is the most commonly used such guide in the United States. First published in 1876, it has been reissued continuously, the most recent (11th) edition dating from 2011. Based on procedures used in Congress in the 19th century, it is nevertheless not intended for use by legislative assemblies but rather assemblies ranging from church meetings to town zoning committees to groups in the corporate world.

Role congruity theory

Role congruity theory says that the degree to which members of a group are perceived positively accords to the degree to which they fit the social roles associated with that group. The typical examples given in role congruity theory are gender roles—role congruity theory originated as a model explaining prejudicial treatment of female leaders, because traits associated with stereotypical female gender roles (helpfulness, empathy) are at odds with stereotypical leadership traits (competitiveness, assertiveness, authoritativeness). Work has also been done to demonstrate the relevance of role congruity theory to race.

Role culture

One of four types of corporate culture identified by Charles Handy and Roger Harrison. In a role culture, the bureaucracy is elaborate and individual roles and their relationships to each other are well-defined. Established procedures guide activity more than the personalities of leaders do.

Role engulfment

Role engulfment is a phenomenon whereby an individual's identity becomes subjugated by a specific role or trait that the individual has made preeminent in his self-image, such as "parent," "depressed," or "class clown." Role engulfment can impact work experiences in numerous ways, among them the possibility that an employee's self-image is too tied up in a specific work role, making them resist change.

Romance of leadership

Social constructionist leadership scholar James R. Meindl introduced the concept of the "romance of leadership" in 1995. The romance of leadership theory suggests that leadership is given too much credit for the outcome of group actions—that because we are, as a culture or a species, enamored of the phenomenon of leadership, we are too inclined to use leadership to explain both positive and negative outcomes. Similarly, this view finds that examinations of leaders are often too interested in personality traits, attributing "leaderness" to traits that have nothing to do with the role.

Roosevelt, Franklin D., as leader

Franklin Delano Roosevelt was elected president of the United Sates in 1932 after the failure of Herbert Hoover to adequately respond to the Great Depression of 1929, and was reelected three times, serving a total of 12 years until his death in 1945. One of the foremost leaders in world affairs in the middle of the century, he was as significant a president for his foreign policy—leading the nation into World War II and overseeing all but its final months—as for his domestic policy, which reshaped the structure of the federal government and its relationship to the people. FDR was best known for his "New Deal" programs, which not only provided relief for the Great Depression but sought to create a system that would lessen the effects of income inequality and break the boom-and-bust cycle that had dominated the American economy for over a century. His programs were successful, but his critics called him both a fascist and a communist. Further, his tactics in retaining power were questioned even by his allies. His own vice president, "Cactus Jack" Garner, opposed his efforts in 1937 to increase the size of the Supreme Court in order to add more Roosevelt allies to the bench, and many considered his pursuit of a third and fourth term—however successful—to be unseemly in light of George Washington's self-imposed two-term limit.

Root cause analysis
Root cause analysis is a problem-solving approach that seeks out the root causes of problems rather than focusing on causal factors that are implicated in but not necessary to the problem's occurrence.

Rost, Joseph
Joseph Rost was a professor of leadership studies at the University of San Diego from 1976 to 1996, a founder of its Institute for the Advancement of Leadership, and a posthumous recipient of the International Leadership Association's 2008 Lifetime Achievement Award. In his seminal 1991 work *Leadership for the 21st Century*, he was one of the first to emphasize the multidisciplinary nature of leadership studies. In that work he also proposed settling on a definition of "leader" that would be used by the whole of the community, arguing that this was necessary for the leadership studies field to progress.

Rotation method
The rotation method is a concept from philosopher Soren Kierkegaard's *Either/Or*, his debut book which focused on aesthetic and ethical thinking. Analogous to the crop rotation practice in agriculture, the rotation method is the constant change from one activity or interest to another, used by aesthetes to avoid boredom. The mental anguish of boredom in performing repetitive tasks is one of the themes of Kierkegaard's work.

Rutgers University School of Public Affairs and Administration
The Rutgers University School of Public Affairs and Administration is one of the top programs in the country in public management, and offers both bachelor's and graduate degrees. The school focuses on best practices in public management, accountability, and transparency, and was one of the first to offer an undergraduate minor in public service.

Sabotage
Sabotage is an action taken to disrupt or weaken an organization or its projects. Labor unions have used workplace sabotage as a means of taking direct action against intolerable working conditions, the most common forms of which are the labor strike and the slowdown, though the sick-out (essentially a one-day strike) is common as well. All these methods purposefully reduce productivity, and have been adopted by non-union groups of workers as well.

Sage kings
The sage kings, or five emperors, were mythological or semi-mythological leaders of ancient China in the 3rd millennium B.C.E. who were exemplars of moral leadership. Not every source agrees about which five emperors are included among the sage kings—often grouped with the "three sovereigns," rulers like the Yellow Emperor who possessed divine powers that

aided in their rule—but they were used as a reference point in Chinese philosophy, a standard against which later rulers were measured.

Salesman

The 1969 documentary *Salesman*, directed by Albert and David Maysles and Charlotte Zwerin, follows four salesmen in New England and Florida as they try to sell Bibles door-to-door in low-income neighborhoods. The film was inspired by Truman Capote's *In Cold Blood*—not its subject matter, but rather Capote's description of it as a nonfiction novel. *Salesman*, similarly, is a documentary constructed as a narrative. One of the most critically acclaimed movies of the year, and later released as part of the Criterion Collection, it was both an important social document and an intimate look at the mood, personality, and business of sales, the pursuit of which had become so important in American capitalism.

Sarbanes-Oxley Act of 2002

Sarbanes-Oxley is an American federal law named for Senator Paul Sarbanes and Representative Michael G. Oxley. In response to significant corporate and accounting scandals in the preceding years, sufficient to injure public confidence in the securities markets and cost investors billions of dollars, the act strengthened corporate board responsibilities, increased transparency and disclosure requirements, created the quasi-public Public Company Accounting Oversight Board, and created new criminal penalties for various actions associated with corporate fraud. The act passed with almost unanimous support in both houses, though it has since faced criticism by far-right Republicans, several of whom continued to oppose it after the 2008 financial crisis, arguing that Sarbanes-Oxley slowed recovery.

Satisficing

Political theorist and economist Herbert Simon introduced the term *satisficing* as a portmanteau of "satisfy" and "suffice." Satisficing is a decision-making approach that, instead of seeking the best possible outcome, explores options until the first reasonably acceptable outcome is found. This is best understood not as an alternative to seeking the best possible outcome but a description of behavior in circumstances where the choice leading to the best possible outcome cannot be determined. Simon was one of the first to describe the behavior of businesses in terms of the behavior of individuals, and in doing so, pointed out that that behavior is constrained by human limitations; individuals are not machines that sort through options and possibilities until the optimal route is determined. Satisficing is important both in understanding others' behavior and in evaluating decision-making processes when leading a group.

Savanna principle

Originally proposed by Satoshi Kanazawa, the savanna principle is a concept from evolutionary psychology that calls for understanding the development of the human brain, and the fundamentals of human psychology, in the context of its development as an optimal adaptation for a specific environment: the African savanna the human race once called home. The savanna principle presumes that there has been no significant evolutionary development of the brain in the last 10,000 years or more, which not all biologists accept.

Scenario planning

Scenario planning is a technique used in long-term planning, by developing possible future scenarios an organization may face and planning an appropriate response to them.

Originally part of the simulation games used by military intelligence and public policy makers, the private sector has adopted scenario planning as well. Royal Dutch Shell, for instance, engaged in scenario planning after the energy crisis of the 1970s.

Schema

In psychology and related fields, a schema is a mental framework organizing pieces or groups of information and the relationships between them. A given social role like "father" involves a schema, for instance, as does a stereotype about a given thing—neither is a single piece or list of information, but a structure consisting of multiple pieces of interrelated information.

Scientific management

Scientific management was developed in the late 19th century when Frederick Winslow Taylor studied the work being done in factories with the aim of improving their productivity by eliminating unnecessary elements of processes and allocating labor for maximum efficiency. Scientific management's heyday came in the 1910s as factory output increased, standardized parts became available in almost every industry, and Henry Ford began his assembly line. Scientific management was a response both to the new labor conditions of the Industrial Revolution and the birth of the social sciences, and was one of many instances in a larger turn of the century phenomenon of applying scientific thinking and methodologies to reorganizing various aspects of human life.

Scope creep

When a project is poorly defined, scope creep can result, as the scope of the project continually expands or changes.

Seagull management

A management style in which managers communicate with lower-level employees only in response to their perception that a problem has arisen, and especially one in which managers respond to problems hastily and impulsively, lacking the context to make an informed decision.

Secession

Secession is the act of withdrawing from a group entity, especially a political union (withdrawing from a treaty organization like the World Trade Organization is rarely expressed as a secession in English). Because secession involves repudiating the authority of the state, there has been debate over whether there is a right to secession, either inherent or in specific political circumstances. There remains disagreement, for instance, over whether the Confederate states had the right to secede from the United States—which is a question independent of the merits of their rationale for doing so. Certain formulations of the consent of the governed imply a right to secession, based on the idea that membership in the political union is voluntary and the product of continued consent. The pragmatics of secession raise other questions, when those who wish to secede do not own or otherwise control contiguous territory: though a right to secession would imply otherwise, in practical terms the secession of 5 percent of the voters in each state is less plausible and perhaps less defensible than the secession of all the residents of a single state.

Second-term curse

"Second-term curse" refers to a tendency of second presidential terms to be less successful than the first, and especially for them to suffer from failures that cannot simply be ascribed to the fact that the incumbent does not need to worry about reelection. Nate Silver, the statistician behind FiveThirtyEight.com, has confirmed that approval ratings are lower in second terms. Classic examples include presidents who faced scandals about their own conduct—Nixon, Reagan, and Clinton—as well as those who oversaw unpopular or failed wars, like Truman and Johnson. Franklin D. Roosevelt's second term began with his failed "court-packing plan," though he recovered and was reelected to third and fourth terms.

Second-wave feminism

While first-wave feminism, as it is now called, focused on obtaining basic rights for women, second-wave feminism, beginning in the 1960s in the United States, broadened its focus to include legal challenges like the laws surrounding spousal rape, cultural challenges with the treatment and portrayal of women, reproductive rights, and the same de facto inequalities faced by racial minorities. It ended in the early 1980s after the ratification deadline for the Equal Rights Amendment, making equal rights for women a Constitutional requirement,

A 1970 Women's Liberation March protest in Washington, D.C. Second-wave feminism continued until the passage of the Equal Rights Amendment in the early 1980s. (Wikimeida Commons/ Warren K. Leffler)

passed without successful ratification. Second-wave feminism was the first movement to address the role of women in the workplace, the fight for equal pay, and the need for women to have equal access to leadership roles as men do, a fight that continues in the 21st century.

Security dilemma

An important concept in international relations especially during the Cold War, the security dilemma is a phenomenon whereby one state takes actions intended to increase its security, resulting in other states taking similar measures. This is the basic foundation of defensive realism, and is a popular theory with scholars who see war as resulting from communication problems.

Self-awareness

Self-awareness is one of numerous concepts dealing with the self and personal identity, consisting of the capacity to identify one's consciousness with one's body (a capacity that may be lacking in some animals with no sense of self, for instance), distinct from other individuals: a being possessing one's thoughts, emotions, and memories, and directing one's actions. Self-awareness is a function or prerequisite of intelligence, at least as we usually conceive it, and while in biology it is treated largely as a binary (an animal is or is not self-aware), in psychology we may speak of degrees of self-awareness, such that one individual is more self-aware than another if he is possessed of an accurate sense of his abilities, competencies, and knowledge.

Self-concept

Self-concept is similar to the more familiar idea of self-image, but where self-image might be conceived of as a photograph (or "selfie"), self-concept is a portfolio, consisting of a system of beliefs about oneself, including identity traits like ethnic and sexual identity, social role information such as that related to gender, age, class, or employment, as well as knowledge, skills, and competencies.

Self-conscious emotions

Self-conscious emotions are those that are triggered by other people's reactions, or projections and fantasizing about those reactions, and include both positive emotions like pride and negative emotions like embarrassment, envy, shame, and guilt. The negative self-conscious emotions especially can play a restrictive role in people's participation in social settings and decision-making processes, discouraging them from showing dissent, contributing novel ideas, or sharing relevant information.

Self-consciousness

Self-consciousness is preoccupying self-awareness, especially in response to observation or a feeling of being observed. It is associated with unpleasant feelings arising in conjunction with a hyperawareness of one's appearance to others.

Self-determination theory

A theory of human personality and motivation, self-determination theory focuses on the individual's psychological needs and the extent to which the individual's behavior is driven by intrinsic or extrinsic motivations. Key to self-determination theory is the idea of the internalization of a motive: the attempt to take an extrinsic motivating factor like a reward or external pressures and internalize it, turning it into an internal motivation by adjusting personal values. Self-determination theory also categorizes goals according to whether they are intrinsic (furthering personal development) or extrinsic (attaining externally provided rewards like wealth or the attention of the opposite sex).

Self-efficacy

Self-efficacy is one's belief in one's skills, capacities, and ability to achieve goals.

Self-esteem

Self-esteem is similar to self-concept or self-image but consists of the evaluation of the self rather than specific information about the perceived self. While a self-evaluation involves the individual's feelings about their traits, behavior, performance, or abilities in specifically defined areas, self-esteem is the individual's overall feelings about themselves, including basic statements ("I am a good person"; "I am weak-willed") and positive or negative emotions like pride or shame. Self-esteem is important in psychology and management due to its implication in well-being and emotional health, its impact on things like employee engagement and assertiveness, and its presence on Maslow's hierarchy of needs. Many leadership studies scholars believe that effective leaders have strong self-esteem.

Self-evaluation maintenance theory

Self-evaluation maintenance theory is a psychological theory of interpersonal relationships. It posits that two people who know each other will each attempt to make themselves feel good through comparison to the other person. Some people, as a result, deliberately surround themselves with less intelligent, attractive, or successful people, which keeps their self-evaluation positive. Others seek out people who approximate their own capabilities in order to constantly challenge themselves to improve. One of the suppositions of self-evaluation maintenance theory is that people are more threatened by the success of friends than that of strangers.

Self-image

Self-image is an individual's mental picture of himself. Though not limited to a single picture, it represents more limited information than the self-concept, and includes information both about how the individual sees himself and how he believes he is perceived by others.

Self-management

Self-management or labor management is the management of an organization by its workers, which has been advocated by many socialists. This may take the form of direct democracy via meetings of workers to make decisions, or the election of managers in a form of representative democracy. In either case, workers retain a high degree of autonomy in the performance of their job roles. The goal is to eliminate the exploitation of labor. For instance, self-managed farms flourished during the Great Depression to the point that half of American farmers worked for a self-managed farm (often now called a "co-op"). The rise of industrial agriculture after World War II changed this, though self-managed farms did not entirely disappear.

Self-monitoring

In psychology, self-monitoring is a behavior related to impression management and dramaturgy, consisting of paying close attention to one's self-presentation in terms of how others are likely to perceive it and making adjustments as appropriate. People with low self-monitoring activity tend to dislike the idea of playing a role or of presenting an outward self that contrasts with their self-image, while people with high self-monitoring activity tend to be more concerned with manners, etiquette, social conventions, and other artificial constructs governing social interactions. Low self-monitors may also have difficulty compromising or experiencing empathy for others. Self-monitoring is important in organizational psychology and the sociology of work, because of the necessity in many workplaces to adapt to social circumstances and modulate one's expression of inward feelings.

Self-perception theory

Psychologist Daryl Bem's self-perception theory is a model of attitude formation in which, in cases where there is no relevant previous experience leading to the development of an attitude, people develop attitudes by monitoring their own behaviors and deriving the attitudes they believe to be the cause of those behaviors.

Semmelweis effect

The Semmelweis effect is the phenomenon in which new evidence is rejected because it contradicts an established paradigm or way of doing things. It was coined in the 20th century in reference to Ignaz Semmelweis, the doctor who discovered that childbed fever mortality rates could be decimated if doctors would wash their hands with an antiseptic solution but who was unable to convince his colleagues to follow his recommendations (often because the suggestion that a doctor's hands could be the source of contamination was seen as crass).

Sensation seeking

The personality trait of sensation seeking leads the individual to seek out experiences and sensations and to be open to risk-taking behaviors in search thereof, though risk-taking is not necessary for satisfying the itch. Sensation seekers may gravitate toward thrill-seeking like skydiving and scuba diving may seek new sensory experiences through drug use, meditation or mysticism, or various arts, or may be drawn to disinhibiting environments where heavy drinking or unrestricted sex are the norm. Sensation seekers tend to be easily bored and restless.

Serious games

Serious games are simply those that are designed and played for a purpose other than play, or which incorporate play as a learning tool. Many simulation games are employed as serious games, and the military has a long history of using war games to teach strategy.

Servant leadership

Servant leadership is an approach to leadership that puts the needs of others first and shares power rather than wielding it from the top of a hierarchy. The term was coined by management theorist Robert Greenleaf in his 1970 essay "The Servant as Leader," having founded the Center for Applied Ethics in 1964 (since renamed the Greenleaf Center for Servant Leadership) to develop his leadership theories. Servant leadership has ancient roots, especially in the *Tao te Ching*, and Greenleaf's articulation of the theory was inspired in part by his reading Herman Hesse's 1932 novel *Journey to the East*, in which the servant of a religious sect that includes a range of figures from Pythagoras and Mozart to Tristram Shandy and Puss in Boots is revealed to be the sect's leader. Greenleaf's prescription is for leaders to similarly view themselves as servants first, working to realize the goals of their followers, which involves participation by followers in goal-setting and decision-making processes, as well as open communication. Greenleaf's work lists 10 characteristics of servant leaders: listening, empathy, healing, awareness, persuasion, conceptualization, foresight, stewardship, commitment to the growth of others, and building community. The idea of servant leadership has since been further explored by others, including Kent Keith, James Sipe, and Don Frick.

Service learning

A presentational mode of liberal arts education in which students are engaged in community service as part of their learning experience. Service learning prioritizes both personal reflection and community investment, and may be part of a program or course within a college curriculum or built into the institution's approach and expectations. Hampshire College, for instance, has a service learning component in the form of its Third World Expectation, which requires students to engage in a substantial project or program benefiting the third world, whether abroad or in the United States (traditionally through direct action, not simply fund-raising or raising awareness).

The Seven Habits of Highly Effective People

One of the most successful management or self-help books, Stephen Covey's *Seven Habits of Highly Effective People* was published in 1989. The seven habits Covey explores are proactivity, beginning with the end in mind, putting first things first, thinking "win-win," empathic listening, synergy, and spiritual renewal. The book also contrasts "abundance mentality," the belief that there is enough success to go around, with "scarcity mentality," which leads to competition for perceived scarce resources.

Shared information bias

Shared information bias is a cognitive bias that affects group decision making. It is the tendency of groups to spend most of their time, or a disproportionate amount of time, reviewing and discussing the information that every member of the group is already familiar with, rather than bringing members up to speed on information known to only some members. This does not have to result from the desire to actually hide that information from the other members, it simply has that effect. When the unshared information would lead the group to making a different, and more optimal, decision, the phenomenon is also known as hidden profiles. One of the reasons information remains unshared is because groups are often more motivated to reach a consensus than to make the best decision, and this can simply be more easily accomplished by focusing on information known to all. Further, because unnecessary time is spent reviewing shared information, a member with information that is new to the others may feel that sharing it would be a time burden, or would make them uncomfortable by putting them in the position of disagreeing, or seeming to disagree, with the proto-consensus.

Shunning
Shunning is an act of social rejection by a group, consisting of the group members avoiding contact or association with the shunned individual. Used as a formal punishment in some legal systems and religious groups, it is used by informal social groups to inflict shame on the subject, especially for transgressing some social norm.

Shyness
Shyness is characterized by mildly unpleasant feelings like fidgetiness, awkwardness, or nervousness when interacting with, in proximity to, or being observed by other people; in some shy people, this is more pronounced when the other people are strangers. Shyness is often associated with low self-esteem or social inexperience, and is not the same as introversion: while some introverts may be shy, preferring limited social activity does not always mean being uncomfortable with social activity. Stronger forms of shyness constitute social anxiety. While on the surface, shyness seems like a hurdle for a leader to overcome, some people feel shy only in regard to one-on-one or unstructured social interaction and are more adept at impersonal contexts like public speaking or addressing a group from the comfort of a defined social role. Such shy leaders, however, would have difficulty being authentic leaders (cf.).

Simon, Herbert A.
Twentieth-century economist and political scientist Herbert A. Simon was a major contributor to the behavioral theory of the firm in the 1950s. Simon's work examined the behavior of decision makers within companies in uncertain situations, in which bounded rationality resulted in their "satisficing": aiming for realistic goals rather than maximized profit or utility. Prior to the behavioral theory of the firm, the theory of the firm treated companies as monoliths, without considering the behaviors of individual employees and leaders, or their conflicts and incomplete information access.

Simulation theory of empathy
The simulation theory of empathy is a theory in the philosophy of mind, stating that empathy works through the mirror neuron system by setting up mental processes that mirror the behavior of others to make sense of that behavior.

Situated cognition
In psychology, the theory of situated cognition says that knowing exists in situ—"in position" or "locally"—with doing, and that all knowledge has a context that includes activity, culture, language, and social elements.

Situational leadership theory

Situational leadership theory (SLT), originally called the Life Cycle Theory of Leadership, was developed by professor Paul Hersey and leadership guru Ken Blanchard in the 1970s. SLT is based on the idea that there is no one-size-fits-all approach to leadership, but rather that successful leaders are flexible and adapt their style to suit the situation. By the 1990s, SLT was wildly successful in the leadership training world, and had been adopted by most Fortune 500 companies. Little research affirmed the specific claims made in SLT literature, however, which sorted leadership styles into four types of behavior (telling, selling, participating, and delegating) and follower groups into four levels of maturity (representing their experience, skill level, and willingness to take responsibility).

Smith, Adam

Scottish philosopher Adam Smith was one of the central figures of the Enlightenment period, and his 1776 work *An Inquiry Into the Nature and Causes of the Wealth of Nations* is the first modern study of economics, introducing ideas of free market capitalism still influential today. One of Smith's key concepts was that of rational self-interest—the idea that well-informed economic actors in an unregulated market will take actions that, though motivated by self-interest, will benefit the economy as a whole. His view of management was simple and taken up by the Industrial Revolution: management should maximize productivity.

Social anxiety

Social anxiety is a very common state of discomfort felt by individuals during social interactions or at the prospect of social interactions, especially when encountering circumstances that are emotionally charged or unfamiliar.

These feelings may be motivated or exacerbated by uncertainty about norms or how one's behavior will be received, or may be felt as a sense of being overwhelmed by social inputs. Social anxiety is a normal phenomenon in childhood and adolescence as part of social and emotional development, and is felt by most adults at some point in their lives. Very specific social anxiety, revolving around formal presentations or performances in front of others, is typically referred to as stage fright, while low-level social anxiety focused on interaction with strangers is often considered mere shyness, but about one-sixth of American adults suffer from an anxiety disorder, in which anxiety is chronic and impacts quality of life, as well as social skills and abilities. Anxiety is also one of the disorders most frequently treated with medication, which has become increasingly common and complex since the heyday of Quaaludes in the 1970s.

Social cognition

In psychology and cognitive science, social cognition refers to a group of social abilities involving cognition processes—the storage, retrieval, and processing of information by the brain. Such processes involve the use of schemas to organize information, and as a result, new information is handled in light of how easily it is integrated into existing schemas (it is generally thought that the more detailed a schema is, the harder it is to process information that contrasts with it). Someone who has unexamined biases about race or ethnicity may have mild difficulty absorbing information conflicting with the stereotypical views they hold; someone who is an active member of a racist organization, who devotes time and thought to propagating racist views, will face much greater difficulty. Culture, social environment, and personal experiences all impact the schema we develop. For instance, staying on the theme of stereotypes, Americans tend to have fewer schema dealing with members of Eastern religions than they do with members of Abrahamic religions, due in part to lack of frequent contact and in part due to lack of representation in the media.

Social cognitive theory

In psychology and education, social cognitive theory is the theory that some amount of a person's knowledge acquisition occurs during social interactions and the observation of others (including via media), and that a key element of knowledge acquisition has always involved replicating observed actions and behaviors rather than simple trial and error. This idea is important not simply in studying how people learn but how social norms are formed, how behaviors can be "contagious," how morality develops, and the influence of culture on the individual.

Social compensation

Social compensation is the tendency of individuals working in a group to work harder than they would if they were working alone.

Social competence

Social competence represents an individual's collection of skills and motivations that contribute to success in the social sphere. These include social and communication skills, as well as self-efficacy, cognitive skills, emotional intelligence and empathy, and many others.

Social desirability bias

Social desirability bias is the tendency of individuals in a survey or other setting to offer answers that they believe will be viewed favorably, even in circumstances where there is "no wrong answer," or responses are anonymous and the individual will be shielded from the consequences of their answers. This is especially a concern in social psychology studies of embarrassing, criminal, or unethical behavior, from sexual infidelity to drug use, and the manner in which the bias affects reporting is not always consistent: for instance, some people may underreport their past recreational drug use, while others who have not experimented with drugs may report having done so for fear of seeming prudish. Further, in the workplace, the bias can make it difficult for management or third parties to obtain an accurate picture of employee attitudes.

Social emotions

Social emotions are an area of study in behavioral neuroscience, the rise of functional imaging allowing a greater neurological investigation into the role of emotions in decision making. Social emotions are those that require the presence or imagined representation of other people. While sadness requires only a knowledge of one's own state, for instance, pride, embarrassment, guilt, and envy all require the knowledge of another person's state of mind. Social emotions develop later than the more basic emotions, with young children having difficulty understanding (and perhaps feeling) them. Social emotions develop as our social skills and awareness of other people do; our ability to feel embarrassed is in a sense an unfortunate side effect of our ability to empathize.

Social engineering

Social engineering is the attempt to influence social behaviors on a large scale, through scientific methods. Advertising and marketing are essentially profit-motivated social engineering, and when the term is used derogatorily, it is often in that context. However, the term also refers to the processes behind many public service announcements (PSAs) and public health campaigns, including campaigns against suicide, domestic violence, and rape. True social engineering involves more than just a public service announcement against littering; its techniques are backed by statistical analyses, and its aims focused on the areas where the most good can be done. In the 21st century, grassroots campaigns have engaged in social engineering via social media, in the form of propagated memes and Twitter hashtags.

Social entrepreneurship

Social entrepreneurship is entrepreneurship over a venture that seeks to solve some social problem or provide value to society. While this often transpires in the non-profit sector, it need not be limited to that, and there has been a rise of socially conscious businesses, from microfinance lending institutions to fair trade coffee microroasters.

Social exchange theory

Social exchange theory is a theory in sociology and psychology that views social behavior as resulting from an exchange process developed out of a cost-benefit analysis that individuals conduct in order to determine the risks and benefits of any given social relationship. Although the theory presupposes that most of this analysis is conducted unconsciously, it is also implicitly acknowledged in pop culture, from magazine quizzes on knowing when to break up with a romantic partner to sitcom characters who make pros-and-cons lists about potential girlfriends. Social exchange theory posits that this calculus occurs not just for romantic relationships, but friendships and professional relationships as well as the ephemeral

relationships that exist between people making small talk at a bus stop, exchanging words with a customer at the cash register, and so on. Any exchange of activity or conversation, between two or more people, involving some amount or kind of reward or cost, constitutes social exchange, as first discussed by sociologist George Homans in 1958. Homans focused specifically on dyadic exchanges—those between two people—and on mechanisms that reinforce behavior, while later theorists expanded the focus of social exchange theory to other social groups and mechanisms. "Rewards" in social exchanges can be seemingly trivial—a nod of acknowledgment, a smile, anything that contributes to positive feelings like a sense of acceptance or belongingness—while costs may be nothing more than the time it takes to interact with the other person, or the diversion of concentration from some other matter. The rules governing social exchanges, beyond reciprocity and negotiated agreements, have not yet received much attention from researchers, as Russell Cropanzano and Marie S. Mitchell pointed out in their 2005 *Journal of*

"Rewards" in social exchange in the business place include smiles, nods of acknowledgment, or anything that makes the employee feel that they are accepted and belong. (Photos.com)

Management article "Social Exchange Theory: An Interdisciplinary Review."

Social exclusion

Social exclusion is the exclusion of individuals or communities from resources accessible by most of society, resulting in alienation and de facto disenfranchisement. While many forms of such exclusion are illegal if they prevent a person from, for instance, obtaining a job or buying a house, not every social category is protected, and discrimination against even explicitly protected groups can transpire in contexts the law does not regulate, such as when members of such groups are excluded from socialization at or after work.

Social facilitation

Social facilitation is the theory that individuals perform tasks differently when in view of others: specifically, the sense of evaluation leads simple tasks to be performed more easily, familiar tasks to be performed better and faster, and unfamiliar tasks to be performed worse because of the imagined pressures the individual feels. Social facilitation is one of the oldest theories in social psychology, dating to the late 19th century. The phrase itself was coined in 1924 by Floyd Allport, the founder of social psychology, and various theories have explained the phenomenon through reference to social pressures or the impact of perceived observation on attention to the task.

Social inhibition

Social inhibition is the avoidance of social interactions or group social situations, whether conscious or unconscious. Consistently high levels of social inhibition are associated with disorders like social anxiety, but moderate levels of social inhibition can also affect work performance and the fit between a workplace culture and an individual worker.

Social integration

Social integration is the process by which an individual is integrated into a social group. Social integration in the workplace can be important in order to make workers feel like part of the organization, and to keep up employee engagement, though by the same token attempts to encourage social integration can easily seem artificial and forced.

Social intelligence

Social intelligence is similar in some respects to social skills or emotional intelligence, but represents competence in social environments and relationships, including politics and interpersonal conflicts, collaboration, reciprocity, and personal relationships (family, friendly, or romantic). Some scientists, notably archaeologist Steve Mithen and psychologist Nicholas Humphrey, hypothesize that social intelligence is the form of intelligence that differentiated humans from their ancestors and the rest of the animal kingdom. Daniel Goleman has described social intelligence as consisting of two major dimensions: social awareness (which includes empathy, emotional intelligence, and social cognition) and social facility ("people skills," as well as social influence and self-presentation).

Social intuitionism

The theory of social intuitionism says that moral judgments are derived from intuition rather than reason, in contrast with the traditional rationalist models of morality and moral judgment, which have largely prevailed. In social intuitionism, reason is still implicated, but its primary role is in its use to generate a justification for a decision dictated unconsciously by intuition. In a sense, intuition points to a destination, and reason draws the map. As an explanatory framework, one of the strengths of social intuitionism is its ability to explain how an action can feel "inherently wrong." Its drawback, though unavoidable if it holds true, is that reasoning presents an easier model by which to convince others of one's moral conclusions.

Social justice

Social justice is the equitable distribution of resources and opportunities within society, and the capacity of members of that society to achieve their potential as individuals and to contribute to the society. Member enjoy such privileges regardless of background membership, such as gender or sexuality, religious or political affiliation, disability, race or ethnicity, or socioeconomic background. The term was coined in the 19th century to refer to a concept present in philosophy in some form or another since the classical era, but has especially gained traction since John Rawls' 1971 *Theory of Justice*, which integrated social justice into the idea of the social contract. "Justice denies that the loss of freedom for some is made right by a greater good shared by others," he argued. With this and other work, Rawls reinvigorated the field of political philosophy. Social justice has since become associated with various human rights movements, from liberation theology to the young socially progressive subculture of Tumblr, which has been influential in speaking out against transphobia and cultural appropriation.

Social loafing

One half of the Ringelmann effect, social loafing is the phenomenon of group members spending less effort on their work than they would as individuals, and reducing their effort as the size of the group grows.

Social norm

A social norm is a belief held by a social group about appropriate behaviors in a given context. While social groups may have explicit rules, norms are less formal, and in fact may even contradict explicit rules adopted by and binding the same group. Consider local speed limits, and the fact that a driver staying strictly within a posted 35-mile-per-hour speed limit will, if driving on a main thoroughfare, not only inevitably be passed by other drivers but may be treated as if they are holding up traffic. Norms within social groups may also contradict laws or rules of a larger group or culture to which the social group belongs, as in teen groups in which underage drinking is the norm. Norms may also be more subtle; speaking without affect or avoiding eye contact violates a common American social norm, for instance, but neither is a behavior many Americans would actually condemn. Norms are learned from one's social groups and arise from social interactions. Tolerance of deviance varies from group to group, and not all members within a group are accorded the same leeway.

Social proof

Social proof is the phenomenon of people checking and emulating the actions of the people around them in an attempt to exhibit the correct behavior for a given situation.

Social psychology

Social psychology is an interdisciplinary branch of psychology and sociology concerned with the way the behaviors and mental states of people are influenced by other people. Social psychology research is highly experiment-driven, with American research tending to focus on the effects felt on the individual, while European work tends to deal with group dynamics. The forms of social influence studied include not only those manifest in direct social interaction but those involving the presence of imagined people or implied people, such as watching movies or reading books, or represented by internalized social norms. Persuasion, influence, conformity, attraction, communication, self-concept, and social exchange theory are among the popular areas of study. Some of the best-known experiments in the social sciences come from social psychology, including the Milgram study, the Stanford prison study, and Asch's conformity experiments.

Social sciences

The social sciences are a group of academic disciplines that were formalized in the 19th century (to which many aspects of modern education can be dated), all of which concern society and the human condition. The social sciences include anthropology, economics, political science, psychology, and sociology, as well as interdisciplinary fields like area studies, environmental studies, and international studies. History is sometimes considered a social science (and certainly draws on all the social sciences), sometimes one of the humanities, just as management straddles the span between the social sciences and business.

Social skills

Social skills are those skills dealing with interaction with other people, whether one-on-one or in groups, and are often referred to as interpersonal skills in management literature. Social skills include the ability to empathize and to listen, to persuade or entertain others, to glean information from others' behavior, communication skills, and of course leadership. Social skill ability is curtailed by various disorders, most commonly including attention deficit, mood, personality, and autism spectrum disorders.

Social undermining

Social undermining is the activity of preventing a person from achieving a goal by directing negative emotions and statements toward them, whether to discourage them and undercut their motivation or to discredit them with peers and co-workers. It can be a problem in competitive workplaces in which employees evaluate their own success, performance, and potential to advance in comparison to that of those around them.

Socially distributed cognition

In psychology, the theory of socially distributed cognition as formulated in the 1980s by Edwin Hutchins says that an individual's knowledge exists not simply within him but in the social and physical environments surrounding him. In this framework, cognition is not a process simply performed by an individual but in conjunction with other individuals interacting with the environment. Hutchins built on work by John Milton Roberts, who argued that social organization could be seen as cognition performed by a community, and later sociologists who proposed models by which beliefs were distributed across a society. The importance of this theoretical framework is the way it underscores learning as a social phenomenon.

Sociotropy

Sociotropy is the personality trait of being overly invested in interpersonal relationships, both with individuals and with social groups, especially characterized by a need for acceptance and to maintain numerous close relationships. Sociotropy can lead to depression in the wake of a rift in these relationships, and has been linked experimentally both to low self-esteem and to identification with traditionally feminine gender roles.

Soft power

Soft power is a term coined by Joseph Nye to refer to certain approaches to diplomacy and persuasion, in contrast with the "hard power" represented by military threat and economic reward, or more broadly, by overt displays of reward or punishment. "Soft power" was first used in Nye's 1990 *Bound to Lead: The Changing Nature of American Power* and related journal articles, and expanded in the course of his work and others'. Soft power is now regularly acknowledged and discussed in foreign policy discussions. Pope John Paul II's work against the communist regimes of eastern Europe, especially his 1979 visit to his native Poland, is considered a key example of a successful use of soft power, though this is easier to say in hindsight than it would have been in the intervening decade in which the eommunists retained their position of power.

Pope John Paul II in Poland in June 1979. The trip sparked the formation of the Solidarity movement. (U.S. White House/Eric Draper)

Soft skills

Soft skills are those associated with feelings, insights, emotions, and relationships with other people, as opposed to the "hard skills" drawn upon to perform tasks in one's job role. Soft skills include communication, friendliness, empathy, and persuasion. Some jobs are noteworthy for the role soft skills play in an individual's overall success, more significantly than do hard skills, such as the law or social work; in some leadership theories this is true for leadership as well.

Soldiering

Soldiering was Frederick Winslow Taylor's term for the habit of workers performing at the slowest rate they could manage without being disciplined for it, also called malingering, loafing, goldbricking, or dogging. While many management approaches are discipline oriented, Taylor and Lillian Gilbreth recognized that the problem here was motivation and employees who were not sufficiently engaged or interested in their work, and that better motivating employees would both increase productivity and reduce the workload of supervisors.

Somebody Else's Problem

Originally named by humorist Douglas Adams, Somebody Else's Problem is a phenomenon that has been studied by psychologists and philosophers, in which individuals and groups distance themselves from the need to solve a problem or address an emergency. Climate change, especially as caused by controllable human behaviors, is sometimes used as an example.

Sortition

Sortition is the random selection of political decision makers. In ancient Athens, which pioneered democratic institutions, sortition as the method for appointing most public officials was considered a cornerstone of democracy. It is today used to select jurors, and in some cases to select a jury foreman from among a group of jurors. Sortition has been proposed by several political thinkers as a method for appointing legislators; it is less commonly recommended as a method for determining the executive official (for example, a president, governor, or mayor, among other positions).

Sound style

One of the leadership styles plotted on the managerial grid model, the sound style was originally called the team style. Sound managers have a high concern for both people and production, and have the same leadership style as Theory Y (cf.).

Spreadthink

Spreadthink is a measurable phenomenon in which a group is persistently unable to agree on a complex issue, typified by an inability to even agree on the prioritization of sub-issues or perhaps the relevant facts, and marked by the fact that this inability is not the result of faulty decision-making processes or a lack of organization.

Stability-instability paradox

The stability-instability paradox is a theory about nuclear weapons in international relations, stating that when two countries both possess nuclear weapons, although the probability of war between them decreases (cf. Mutually assured destruction), the probability of indirect conflicts between them increases, as seen in the many proxy wars and other conflicts of the Cold War, and between India and Pakistan today.

Stakeholder

Historically, a stakeholder was a neutral third party without an interest in the financial matter at stake, such as a person who holds gamblers' stakes and is responsible for distributing them to the winner. This original literal meaning was then broadened to encompass escrow agents and other figures who hold money or property while a transaction between other parties is conducted. As so often happens, the term was repurposed by the business world, and since the late 20th century it has become common to discuss "stakeholders" in the sense of "all those who have a stake in the issue at hand." In some

decision-making processes it can be important to include all stakeholders in the discussion, not just those who have the authority to make the decision.

Standing on the shoulders of giants

A metaphor dating back at least as far as the 12th century and popularized by Isaac Newton in the 17th century, "standing on the shoulders of giants" illustrates the idea of one's work depending on the past work of others, and of achieving greatness by building on those earlier foundations. It is sometimes phrased in an accusatory sense, particularly if the subject standing on the shoulders is perceived as taking credit for the height of the giants.

Stanford prison experiment

The Stanford prison experiment was conducted in 1971 by Philip Zimbardo, and was funded by the U.S. Office of Naval Research, which sought a better understanding of the conflicts between military prisoners and their guards. The experiment has become one of the most famous psychological experiments, in which participants were randomly assigned roles of prisoners and guards. Prisoners were brought to their cells in a Stanford University basement, where guards worked in teams for eight-hour shifts. Over the course of the experiment, guards enacted authoritarian behaviors on their own initiative, treated prisoners cruelly, and pitted them against each other, while the prisoners passively accepted it, except for two who quit early. (The experiment as a whole was also ended early.) The experiment supported a model of behavior dictated by situation rather than personality traits, and Zimbardo himself was surprised by the extent to which participants became absorbed in their roles. The experiments received the publicity they did in part because of high-profile prison riots at San Quentin and especially Attica shortly after the study's conclusion, and was back in headlines in 2004 when Zimbardo testified as an expert witness in the trial of one of the guards accused of prisoner torture at Abu Ghraib.

State within a state

The idea of a "state within a state" or imperium in imperio (the original state motto of Ohio, reflecting its influence on the early nation) is that of a faction within a country that acts outside the legitimate civilian government. Historically, the United Fruit Company in the Caribbean was one such example, operating independently of the Caribbean nations in which it operated and setting up "banana republics" in several countries. The American intelligence community is sometimes accused of being a modern example.

Statesmanship

A statesman is simply a politician or other public official, but the word usually refers to one with the benefit of a long career, and by extension statesmanship is governance or diplomacy that is conducted with wisdom and finesse. John Stuart Mill used the term in a fairly neutral sense—requiring the adjective preceding it—when he said "a great statesman is one who knows when to depart from traditions," while a century later on the Bicentennial of the United States, Britain's Queen Elizabeth II declared, "We lost the American colonies because we lacked that statesmanship to know the right time, and the manner of yielding, what is impossible to keep."

Status group

In Max Weber's sociology, status groups are social groups that are differentiated on non-economic bases, such as prestige or religion, in contrast with political groups or social class. Modern status groups are an analogue to the social importance of concepts like honor in earlier Western societies.

Status quo style

One of the leadership styles plotted on the managerial grid model, the status quo style was originally called the middle-of-the-road style. Status quo managers try to balance workers' needs with the company's goals, often with the result of doing an incomplete job of both.

Stereotype threat

One of the most intensely researched phenomena in social psychology, stereotype threat is the feeling an individual has that he faces the risk of confirming one or more negative stereotypes about a group of which he is a member. Performance-related stereotypes can result in poor performance precisely because the individual is undermined by the worry that his performance will not be good enough to overcome the stereotype.

Stewardship

Stewardship is an ethical concept named for the domestic steward, a household servant whose duties involved running the household of a noble or wealthy family: distributing labor among household staff, overseeing their work, administering disciplinary actions, and managing finances related to the staff and their expenses. As an ethical framework, stewardship implies a form of leadership or administration that entails responsible resource management and the idea that ownership resides elsewhere. In Christian theology, for instance, stewardship is the idea that humankind are the stewards of the Earth, with a moral duty to preserve and respect natural resources, which are only given to them to manage, not to own or deplete. In management, stewardship similarly calls for managers to responsibly manage the resources over which they are given control.

Stogdill, Ralph M.

Ralph M. Stogdill was an influential leadership studies scholar, whose 1948 article "Personal Factors Associated with Leadership: A Survey of the Literature" summed up many of the findings of trait-based leadership studies to that point. A member of the Ohio State University leadership studies, Stogdill initially did not believe that there were specific traits associated with leadership, but changed his views by the time he published his *Handbook of Leadership* in 1974, several years before his death. Stogdill's handbook presented his articulation of trait theory, identifying adaptability, alertness to the social environment, ambition, assertiveness, decisiveness, dependability, dominance, energy, persistence, self-confidence, and a willingness to take responsibility as critical for leaders, as well as social and communication skills, administrative ability, creativity, and knowledge specific to the group's work.

Strategic contingencies theory

One of the Aston Group of organizational researchers, David Hickson developed the strategic contingencies theory in 1971. The theory underscores the importance of social interaction and communications in order to maintain leadership, and positions power as, in part, the ability to deal with uncertainty and control contingencies. In this framework, leaders are principally problem solvers; personality traits and personal charisma are less important to their leadership effectiveness than their ability to solve the problem at hand.

Strategic management

Strategic management is the oversight, development, and implementation of a company's major goals, and is key to forming and preserving the company's core identity.

Strategic planning

Strategic planning is the process of formulating and elaborating an organization's strategy, and identifying the ways this strategy impacts priorities and other decision-making processes, as well as ensuring that the organization's strategy is appropriate for the resources it has access to.

Straw man

The straw man argument is an informal fallacy that misrepresents the opposing side, and so is structured to refute a point other than the one

This editorial cartoon from a 1990s issue of Harper's Weekly *shows President William McKinley shooting a cannon at a straw man and its constructors. The caption reads "SMASHED!"*
A straw man argument is structured to refute a point that one's opponent is making. (Public Domain)

the opponent is actually making. This is a common tactic used to score a metaphorical point with the audience, because it allows the arguer to present an argument the audience will agree with. Experienced rhetoricians, while certainly aware of the fallacy, are able to use it to great effect, depending on the audience to react emotionally rather than to examine the logical underpinnings of the debate.

Strong versus weak governors

In the United States, while the executive of every state's government has the same title—governor—the powers of those executive offices vary greatly from state to state. Despite producing many nationally famous governors, Texas has been the classic example of a weak governor state. The governor of Texas has no cabinet, for instance, and limited influence on the boards and commissions of the executive branch, members of which cannot be fired, and two-thirds of whom serve terms of more than two years. This not only empowers the legislative branch, which is better able to exert influence on executive branch agencies through funding measures, but decentralizes the power of the executive branch, such that many agencies are basically self-run (and headed by elected officials). While the Texas governor has the power to veto legislation—a power all governors have, since North Carolina amended its constitution in the 1990s to allow it—he is not allowed a "pocket veto," and legislation he neither signs nor vetoes becomes law.

Structural frame

In Lee G. Bolman and Terrence E. Deal's Four Frame model, the Structural frame is one of the distinctive frames affecting the way people view the world. The structural frame is invested in rules, procedures, policies, hierarchies, specificity, and well-defined roles. It tends to see organizations as bureaucracies.

Structure

In history and the social sciences, "structure" refers to institutions and cultural elements that form the context in which people act. The social relationships in society, both formal and informal, both emerging from individual actions and determining those actions, constitute the social structure, from the micro scale of individual behavior in the context of social norms and etiquette to the macro scale of the socioeconomic class system and the roles played by attitudes toward gender, race, ethnicity, religion, sexuality, and language use. Different approaches model these structures differently. Marxist sociology, for instance, focuses on the economic effect of social structures, treating cultural effects as side effects.

Substantive representation

Substantive representation is a measure in political science, representing the effect that elected or appointed members of a government body who are members of a particular group have on its activity. This is a contrast with descriptive representation, which represents their simple mathematical proportion in that body. For instance, women may make up a particular proportion of the membership of a state legislature, but if they are not members or heads of the important committees within that legislature, or otherwise represented in the leadership of the legislature, their impact on legislation passed will not be proportional to their raw numbers.

Substitutes

In substitutes for leadership theory, substitutes are workplace factors that reduce the necessity of leadership. This includes subordinate skill and professional orientation; routine and unambiguous tasks, such as menial labor; satisfying tasks; clear job goals; and self-managed teams.

Substitutes for leadership theory

A leadership theory developed by Steven Kerr and John Jermier in 1978, substitutes for leadership theory deals with elements in the workplace that impact leader effectiveness: substitutes, neutralizers, and enhancers. Substitutes increase subordinate performance without the need for leadership; neutralizers reduce leader effectiveness; enhancers increase leader effectiveness. The theory received a lot of attention in the 1980s until the rise of transformational leadership.

Succession planning

Succession planning is the process of preparing individuals within an organization to take over leadership positions at some point in the future. While the emphasis is often on identifying "backups" for senior management positions in order to ensure a smooth transition in the event of a senior executive departing, succession planning also includes identifying and preparing viable candidates for middle-management and team leader positions. Succession planning can be assisted by internal leadership development. In smaller businesses, succession planning is key to the business's survival of the retirement, or even reduced participation, of the founders.

Sudbury school

A Sudbury school, named for the Sudbury Valley School founded in 1968 in Framingham, Massachusetts, is a school run by direct democracy in which both students and staff are enfranchised. The core principle of Sudbury schools is that the only trait children lack that adults possess is experience, and so the role of teachers is to guide students to and through experiences. Students decide how to spend their time, and school governance and policy decisions are made through meetings modeled after New England town meetings. This includes even aspects of governance that town meetings usually delegate to an elected body or professional administrators, like hiring and firing decisions. The school day is only lightly structured, with no separation into age-based groups nor required courses. In some ways the Sudbury schools resemble the experimental and alternative liberal arts colleges founded in the same era, like Hampshire College in nearby Amherst, Massachusetts, but for younger students (Sudbury Valley is attended by students ages 4 to 19).

Superior orders

Superior orders or lawful orders is a defense used in the Nuremberg war crimes trials in the aftermath of World War II. The plea, based on the precedent of command responsibility established 20 years earlier, argues that an individual is not guilty when the actions he committed were ordered by a superior officer. The defense was not sufficient to avoid punishment, but did succeed in lessening it in many cases. Since Nuremberg, courts have been inconsistent in their opinions on the superior orders defense.

Supermajority

In voting systems, a supermajority is the requirement that a proposal pass only with a proportion of votes that is some specific amount fewer than a mere majority of the votes—such as the two-thirds supermajority vote required for Congress to override a veto, or the three-quarters supermajority required for states to ratify a Constitutional amendment.

Suppression of dissent

The act of suppressing disagreement with those in power, whether through punishment or silencing. Indirect suppression may take the form of social and economic pressures that make an individual unwilling to express dissent, or to continue expressing it, because of consequences either in the workplace or in his chances of being retained or promoted in the future.

Symbolic Frame

The Symbolic Frame is one of the distinctive frames affecting the way people see the world, and is based on Lee G. Bolman and Terrence E. Deal's Four Frame model. The Symbolic Frame echoes the viewpoint of Erving Goffman's *Presentation of Self in Everyday Life*, focusing on the dramaturgy of human interactions, the roles people assume, and the rituals and stories of human cultures.

Systems thinking

Systems thinking is concerned with the understanding of systems and their components and processes, such as the people, procedures, structures, and norms that make up an organization, with special regard for their linkages and interactions. Systems thinking involves a more holistic or "big picture" view of phenomena, which can help prevent unintended consequences. Developing a thorough understanding of an organization through systems thinking improves organizational communication and identifies problems before they become critical.

Tao te Ching

The *Tao te Ching* is the foundational text of the philosophical and religious system of Taoism, having been written in China by the sage Lao Tzu around the 6th century B.C.E. In it, several passages advocate what is now called servant

A Taoist priest (daoshi) in Macau, China, in 2006. The religious and philisophical system of Taoism is based on the Tao te Ching. (Wikimedia Commons)

leadership, including "When [the sage's] task is accomplished and things have been completed, all the people say, 'We ourselves have achieved it!'" and "The highest type of ruler is one of whose existence the people are barely aware."

Task culture

One of four types of corporate culture identified by Charles Handy and Roger Harrison. In a task culture, every group is formed to address a specific problem or decision and organization tends to be according to expertise, with highly skilled roles.

Task-oriented leadership

Task-oriented leadership is leadership that is focused on specific tasks necessary to the meeting of team goals, with an emphasis on process and procedure, structure, well-defined roles, and time management. Task-oriented leadership is sometimes contrasted with relationship-oriented leadership, and early work in leadership studies addressed the issue of whether task- or relationship-orientation was more effective. Situational leadership theory developed out of that work.

Taylor, Frederick Winslow

The father of scientific management, Frederick Winslow Taylor was a mechanical engineer who became one of the first management consultants during the Industrial Revolution. Before the word *productivity* even entered usage in its labor-output meaning, Taylor had devoted himself to increasing productivity in factories by increasing the efficiency of both machines and work processes. He helped to develop high-speed steel at Bethlehem Steel, but left his position in 1901 and promoted himself as a management consultant, writer, and lecturer. "Taylorism" consisted of four related principles: rule of thumb or traditional procedures were replaced with those derived from a scientific study of the task being performed; employees were trained rather than teaching themselves; each individual task to be performed by any employee was defined through detailed instruction; and managers were developed in order to better distribute the operations of the company into planning and supervision (managers) and the actual task performance (workers). One of the areas where he has faced the most criticism is in this fourth principle, since he had no interest in worker autonomy, and preferred as much control as possible to be in the hands of management. Adopting scientific management occasionally led to strikes as a result.

Team

Leadership studies, as well as psychology and management literature, use the terms *team*, *group*, *work team*, and *work group* interchangeably, to refer to formal or informal groups of workers engaged collaboratively in a task, project, or area of an organization's activities.

Team-based leadership

Leadership in team-based organizations is distributed more broadly than in hierarchical organizations, and is similar to horizontal or collective leadership. The defining factor is that leadership is performed by individuals other than (in addition to) the appointed leader, sometimes described (as in the work of Jay B. Carson, Paul E. Tesluck, and Jennifer A. Marrone) as an emergent property of the team as a result of the distribution of influence throughout team members. Team leadership and teamwork are increasingly vital areas of study in the 21st century, but the research is fairly young. Areas of study include the use of social network analysis to reveal team leadership behaviors, factors and behaviors that facilitate team leadership, the role of external support or leadership, and the stages and life cycles of team-led groups.

Team composition

Team composition is the aspect of a team consisting of the collection of attributes of its members, which is a strong determining factor on other aspects of the team and its functions. There are conflicting schools of thought about what kind of team composition is most effective for a healthy and productive dynamic, as well as which member attributes are important. Being an outlier in a team—differing from the rest of the team in some attribute like type or quantity of experience, race, gender, age, or previous work background—can place a team member at a disadvantage, but many schools of thought suggest that neither should a team be too homogenous. A sufficiently large heterogenous team can be thought of as possessing a faultline dividing it into homogenous sub-teams as a result of the social roles team members adopt.

Terror Management Theory

Terror Management Theory stipulates that humans are uniquely predisposed toward existential terror, because they possess both the same self-preservation instinct as other animals as well as a unique capacity for abstract thinking and advanced cognition that makes them aware of their mortality. Many social and cultural institutions are thus developed to cope with this fear of death, including a belief in an afterlife, resurrection, reincarnation, and systems of morality and behavior that increase our happiness or feeling of self-worth, in order to offset that terror. Leaders naturally arise as individuals who affirm our terror-dampening social constructs are elevated.

Theory of constraints

In management, the theory of constraints says that a small number of constraints stand in the way of an organization's goals and that the organization should be restructured around them.

Theory of the firm

The theory of the firm is a system of economic theories describing the nature and behavior of the firm (a company or corporation) and its relationship to the market. In the 1960s, managerial and behavioral theories of the firm began to focus on the role of individuals (especially leaders and managers within the hierarchy) in determining traits and behavior of firms.

Theory Theory

Theory Theory is a psychological theory about people's psychological theories, in a sense. Theory Theory says that an individual's ability to empathize with other people and understand their behavior is connected to an internalized "folk psychology" that they have developed based on their experiences, observations, and the ideas to which they have been exposed. This internalized psychological theory begins developing when the individual is a young child, and so at first consists of very basic observations, many of which are undoubtedly false (the child has little sense of his parents' lives outside of childrearing). According to the Child Scientist theory, many child behaviors are explained as children testing out psychological theories in the world.

Theory X and Theory Y

Theory X and Theory Y are theories of management developed by MIT Sloan School of Management professor Douglas McGregor and presented in his 1960 book *The Human Side of Enterprise*. Each theory is based on a different attitude managers take toward their employees. In Theory X, management acts from the assumption that employees have an inherent dislike of work, which they will indulge if so allowed, and therefore prevent this by adopting a hierarchical system of management in order to closely supervise all levels of production and work within the organization. Because of the negative view of workers, negative incentives tend to be used to guide behavior instead of offering rewards for positive results. Similarly, job roles are highly structured because of the assumption that a dislike of work will prevent employees from taking initiative. Theory Y, on the other hand, assumes work is a natural pursuit that employees can enjoy, and that the conditions can be created in which employees will actively seek out tasks and responsibility. This is more likely than Theory X to lead to a climate of trust and open communication. Theory Y is an application to the workplace of much of the work of psychologist Abraham Maslow.

Theory Z

Theory Z is a term coined in reference to Theory X and Theory Y. Various "Theories Z" have been coined representing an approach to management that is neither Theory X nor Theory Y. Abraham Maslow, for instance, used it to refer to an even more positive view than Theory Y, one adopted by those who had transcended self-actualization, whom he alternately calls mystics or transcenders. Transcenders are those for whom "peak experiences and plateau experiences become the most important things in their lives," and who comfortably speak the language of poets and the profoundly religious. Everything is potentially sacred to them, and they perceive in everyone the potential for greatness. Maslow offered little guidance for the management applications of Theory Z, however. Hawaiian business professor William Ouchi offered a more pragmatically minded Theory Z, as part of his "Japanese management" style that he taught during the 1980s in response to the Asian economic boom and the often explicitly xenophobic American paranoia over Japanese economic competition. Ouchi's Theory Z focuses on the well-being of employees as Theory Y does, but ensures loyalty by providing a life-long job, so that the employee associates the organization's well-being with his own. Theory Z management prizes stability in the organization as well as high employee morale, and treats these as necessary preconditions to meeting organizational goals.

Think tank

A think tank is an organization devoted to research, whether in the sciences or related to public policy. Policy think tanks, often called policy institutes, are often but not always partisan in their design: for instance, the Cato Institute, Heritage Foundation, and Center for American Progress are American policy institutes promoting libertarianism, conservatism, and progressivism, respectively. Functionally, think tanks have some similarities with the role monasteries played in the intellectual development of medieval Europe, but in their modern form they date to the 19th century. Think tanks enjoyed two major periods of growth: the 1940s and early 1950s, due to the Cold War and rapid technological growth; and the 1980s through the early 21st century, when globalization motivated the creation of more than

half of today's think tanks. The oldest American think tanks—the Carnegie Endowment for International Peace, the Brookings Institution, the Hoover Institution, the National Bureau of Economic Research, and the Council on Foreign Relations—are devoted to public policy or economic policy. In 1946, the RAND Corporation was established by the Air Force, and its initial focus on weapons development broadened quickly, with RAND contributing to the space program and artificial intelligence, the technologies leading to the Internet, wargaming and game theory, and social choice theory.

Thomas, Kenneth

Kenneth Thomas identified five styles of negotiation in his work on conflict management in the mid-2000s: accommodating (in which the negotiator acts to solve the other party's problems, pays attention to the emotional and nonverbal signals from the other party, and may feel taken advantage of); avoiding (individuals who avoid negotiating if they can, and tend to be reserved and tactful, avoiding confrontations); collaborating (negotiatiors who enjoy problem solving and try to address all concerns, with the risk of overcomplicating an issue by introducing too many factors); competing (highly strategic negotiators who treat the process like a game and risk harming their relationship with the other party); and compromising (negotiators who want to reach a fair outcome but do not like to dally and spend too much time on the details).

Three Levels of Leadership

The Three Levels of Leadership model was presented in James Scouller's 2011 book by the same name, and is sometimes called the 3P model or Integrated Psychological model. Scouller's goal was to adapt the strengths of previous leadership theories while escaping their limitations. The

"3 Ps" of the model are public, private, and personal leadership. The first two refer to outward behaviors, of which Scouller enumerates 34 public leadership behaviors and 14 private (one-on-one) leadership behaviors. The third and innermost level is personal leadership, consisting of the leader's skills, emotions, competencies, and leadership presence. Effective leadership means harmony among these three levels and developing one's personal leadership traits while practicing effective outward leadership behaviors.

Time and motion study

Time and motion studies were introduced by the Efficiency movement that developed around scientific management. Time studies were originally developed to establish standard performance times for the tasks constituting a business's operations. Frank and Lillian Gilbreth later conducted motion studies that established the best series of motions for such tasks, by improving posture and eliminating unnecessary or inefficient movement. The purpose of each was the same: to standardize the work done in a company (originally in factories, with later scholars extending the idea to other types of businesses) in order to maximize efficiency.

Tombstone mentality

A term in the aviation industry that is useful in general discussions of organizations, "tombstone mentality" refers to the idea that aviation safety is improved only in response to a death, as a result of the insufficient economic motive of safety in the absence of specific market pressures.

Total Quality Management

Not to be confused with quality management (cf.), Total Quality Management (TQM) was a specific movement in the 1980s, inspired by W. Edwards Deming's *Out of the Crisis*, and was in many ways a revival of the Efficiency movement in American industry. In response to manufacturing competition from newly competitive countries like Japan, TQM sought to improve American competition by improving management practices and work processes. Beyond the manufacturing industry, it was adopted by many elements of the U.S. military.

Totalitarianism

Totalitarianism is an approach to governance in which the state is given the greatest possible control over society and its institutions. In Weimar Germany, totalitarianism was first developed as a positive possibility, one in which the state and society were ideologically unified. As practiced, totalitarianism in, for instance, Nazi Germany, fascist Italy, the Soviet Union, and North Korea, is a dictatorship in which the ruling group extends its influence beyond merely the political and economic, monopolizing cultural and social power as well, controlling art, education, and private life.

Paintings of dictators Kim Jong-il, Supreme Leader of the Democratic People's Republic of Korea (North Korea), and his predecessor and father, Kim Il-sung. Kim Jong-un succeeded his father, Kim Jong-il, in 2011. (Wikimedia Commons)

Tough-guy macho culture

One of four corporate cultures identified by Terence Deal and Allan Kennedy, characterized by rapid feedback and high risk. Jobs in these cultures are high stress as a result of the risk, the stakes, and the difficulty of the work, as in police work, professional sports, and jobs where the cost of failure is high, such as surgery.

Town meeting

The town meeting is a mechanism of direct democracy in which all adult members of the town are welcome in a discussion of a local policy issue, and to participate in the vote determining the course of action on that policy issue. Although the term is also sometimes used to refer to discussion-only sessions, in which the decision is made by some elected or appointed body after taking input from voters, the first meaning has special significance as a form of government rarely practiced anymore outside of New England. The town meeting and its participants essentially assume the legislative duties for the town, and in many cases the powers of the executive branch are significantly curtailed, beyond what is authorized or ordered by the ballot issues resolved at town meeting. Less common in cities, town meetings remain common in towns, suburbs, and unincorporated areas in Maine, New Hampshire, and Vermont, while slightly modified in Massachusetts and Connecticut. In most cases, day-to-day administrative duties are delegated to a body such as a board of selectmen, and at a minimum, an annual town meeting begins the business of the government for the year, discussing and voting on budget issues, changes to the law, regulations, or the tax rate, progress on long-term projects, the results of promises or concerns expressed the previous year, etc. Further meetings may be called in response to specific issues, and town meetings may also be held separately to determine courses of action for a school district, water district, or other special administrative district.

Toxic leader

A toxic leader is one whose management of a group worsens their work, group affective mood, employee engagement, or some other element of their situation as a direct consequence of their management style. There is no one style of toxic leadership; like being a "good leader," there are behaviors and styles associated with it, some combination of which aggregates to toxicity. Arrogance and condescension are commonly identified problems, but toxic leaders may go even further, competing with their followers, bullying them, exploiting them, playing mind games with them, or actively deceiving them.

Toxic workplace

Similar to a toxic leader, a toxic workplace is one whose social and procedural environment actively makes things worse for its workers, whether because of one or more toxic employees (a problem solved by their removal or rehabilitation) or because of corporate culture factors that harm employee engagement, productivity, satisfaction, or other measures, or which encourage an unsafe level of workplace stress. Even when policies and procedures are reasonable and no one individual is toxic, for instance, a workplace that is consistently understaffed or unprepared for some emergency circumstance may become toxic. Toxicity of this sort also leads to frictions among employees that can encourage bullying, distrust, and antisocial behavior.

Toynbee, Arnold J.

Arnold Toynbee was a 20th century British historian who is best known for his monumental

12-volume *A Study of History*, published from 1934 to 1961. The work combined the modern historical approach pioneered by Leopold von Ranke in the previous century and applied it to the early 20th century's fascination with "universal history" (which took as its subject the whole of human civilization, not just a single nation-state), tracing the development and decay of Toynbee's 19 major civilizations, four abortive civilizations, and five arrested civilizations, focusing in each case on the leaders who guided their civilizations through change to varying degrees of success.

Toyota Production System

The Toyota Production System (TPS) is a production system developed by Toyota, the Japanese automotive manufacturer, from the 1940s through the 1970s. TPS is designed to eliminate unnecessary waste and inefficiency in production, while at the same time encouraging teamwork, respect for others, and the ongoing improvement of business operations and organizational knowledge. TPS continues to be influential today, and is one of the influences on Lean.

Traditional domination

Traditional domination is one of Max Weber's three ideal types of leadership, and refers to leadership that is derived from tradition or custom. The traditional authority of a father/husband over the other members of his family for much of Western history is one such example, and on a larger scale, feudalism was based on leadership that is inherited or distributed according to traditional rules.

Trained incapacity

American economist and sociologist Thorstein Veblen coined the term *trained incapacity* in 1933, to refer to the phenomenon in which a trained, skilled individual's abilities are detrimental to their accurate view of the world.

Trait ascription bias

Trait ascription bias is a cognitive bias resulting in people seeing themselves as capable of a significant range of moods, behaviors, and personality, while other people are less complex and capable of a narrower, more predictable range of the same. As a result, the behavior of others is viewed as representative of their personality, while behaviors of oneself may be described as situational and not something one should fairly be judged by.

Trait-based theories of leadership

Personality and trait-based theories of leadership are among the oldest leadership theories, growing out of the Great Man approach to history. Such theories focus on the personality traits associated with effective leaders, rather than on behaviors or methodologies of leadership. Studies suggest leaders have above-average intelligence, for instance, though typically they are not too significantly more intelligent than their followers. Leaders also tend to be sociable, confident, and determined. However, not all people who possess the traits associated with leadership become leaders, and critics of trait-based theories say that they focus too much on what leaders are like rather than on what they do.

Transactional leadership

Transactional leadership is a leadership style that uses rewards and punishment to motivate followers. Typically, transactional leaders look for faults in followers' work in order to be corrected, and the style is generally reactive rather than proactive. It is characterized by dealing with followers in terms of appeals to their self-interest and by working within the organizational culture to maintain the status quo.

Transatlantic Policy Consortium

The Transatlantic Policy Consortium is a network of higher education institutions in the public policy and public administration fields, devoted to promoting dialogue and joint research on transatlantic public policy issues.

Transformational leadership

Transformational leadership is a leadership style that seeks to increase followers' motivation and performance through various means. The name alludes to the role of the leader in shaping—transforming—his followers, and was coined in part to differentiate from transactional leadership. The means by which transformational leaders mold their followers include intellectual stimulation, the individualized consideration they give each one, the leader's ability to inspire their followers, and the ability of the leader to act as a role model who influences their followers' choices and behavior.

Transpersonal business studies

Transpersonal business studies is the application of transpersonal psychology to the world of business and management: the study of the spiritual side of business, management, and work, as well as the application of transpersonal psychology to the act of management. Transpersonal management prioritizes the importance of emotional intelligence and transformational leadership, as well as creativity, innovation, and self-actualization.

Transpersonal psychology

Transpersonal psychology is an approach to modern psychology that has a special concern for the spiritual or transcendent spheres of the human condition, including peak experiences, religious practices, and spiritual self-development. It developed in the 1960s amid the backdrop of increased academic interest in altered states of consciousness and the mystical, the Fourth Great Awakening, and the human potential movement, though Abraham Maslow also pioneered the focus in psychology on peak experiences. Transpersonal psychology should not be confused with parapsychology, but is interested in understanding some of the same phenomena, notably near-death experiences and mystical experiences. Critics argue that the school sometimes offers a cloak of legitimacy to ideas or thinkers who are merely rehashing New Age philosophy without scholarly rigor, and some transpersonal psychologists have themselves chastised their colleagues for not being better at policing the fringe.

Triarchy theory

Triarchy theory suggests that there are three fundamental ways to structure an organization: hierarchy, the most familiar form; heterarchy, in which different elements of the organization are unranked; and responsible autonomy, in which individuals or groups act autonomously and bear the responsibility for the outcome of their actions.

Tridimensional personality questionnaire

The tridimensional personality questionnaire (TPQ) was developed by C. Robert Cloninger and measures three dimensions of personality: reward dependence, novelty seeking, and harm avoidance. The test consists of 100 questions the respondent answers with true/false. Cloninger has used the test as the basis for personality genetics research, correlating the three dimensions with low noradrenergic activity, low dopaminergic activity, and high serotonergic activity, respectively.

Trompenaars' model of national cultural differences

In the 1990s, management theorists Fons Trompenaars and Charles Hampden-Turner developed a model of seven cultural dimensions representing values and behaviors of a culture. The model is intended to assist with cross-cultural communication, especially in the world of international business. The seven dimensions are universalism (favoring broad general rules and using the best fit for a given situation) versus particularism (which considers each case on its own merits); individualism versus collectivism; neutral (or stoic) versus outwardly emotional; specific versus diffuse (the degree to which work and personal life are kept separate); achievement versus ascription (is the source of status personal achievement or something granted externally, such as according to seniority?); sequential (doing tasks one at a time) versus synchronic (juggling several tasks at once); and internal versus external control.

True self and false self

Mid-century psychoanalysis began to work with the concepts of the "true self" and "false self," building on the work of Donald W. Winnicott. The false self is a facade the individual constructs (initially as a child) and presents to the world, overlapping with but not identical to Carl Jung's concept of the persona. The true self is the real self beneath. James Masterson has argued that personality disorders have in common their conflict between the true and false self, while Alexander Lowen has emphasized the importance of the false self in analyses of narcissism and narcissistic personality disorder.

Trust management

In management sciences, trust management is the creation and maintenance of systems that allow parties to assess reliability, both of other parties and of potentially risky transactions, in the interest of developing trusting professional relationships.

Truthiness

Truthiness is the characteristic of an assertion or argument that "feels right," especially one that is made authoritatively, without considering the evidence or engaging with opposing views. The concept was introduced in the October 17, 2005, premiere episode of Stephen Colbert's *Colbert Report*, a satirical news show that especially focuses on the rhetoric of conservatives in the Bush and Tea Party eras. It became *Merriam-Webster*'s *Dictionary*'s Word of the Year the following year, and appears in the *Oxford English Dictionary*. The concept resonated as much as it did because it attaches a vivid

First Lady Michelle Obama during an appearance on Stephen Colbert's The Colbert Report *in 2012. Cobert introduced the concept of "truthiness" in 2005. (Wikimedia Commons)*

descriptive name to an important phenomenon in rhetoric and leadership: the appeal to emotion, especially one framed in a way to cast aspersions on recourse to conflicting facts.

Turf war

A turf war is a struggle for control over territory, whether physical, cultural, in the market, or in some other sense. The term is originally associated with frontier livestock herders and later used in reference to struggles between criminal groups in the early 20th century, but today often refers to factions or individuals within companies or political entities.

Turnover

Turnover is the rate at which an organization loses and gains employees, the duration an average employee tends to remain. High turnover is associated with instability and inefficiency because it prevents the accumulation of job-specific knowledge by employees, although some businesses (particularly those relying on large amounts of unskilled low-paid labor) assume high turnover as a given in their business model (for this reason, when the Bureau of Labor Statistics reports turnover rates, farm labor is typically excluded). While the average turnover rate is about 3 or 4 percent over a year, businesses in some industries like hospitality can have normal turnover rates as high as 80 percent.

Twinkling fingers

A method of expressing agreement with a speaker during a discussion, without the interruption caused by clapping. Hands are raised with the fingers wiggling. If hands are pointed down, it indicates disagreement. Also known as spirit fingers. Associated mainly with consensus-based decision making.

Two-step flow of communication

According to the two-step flow of communication model, individuals' opinions are more influenced by the opinion leaders they come in contact with than by the media, though the opinion leaders themselves are influenced by the media. For some, this model illustrates the importance of opinion leaders, while for others, it simply points out opinion leaders' role as the means by which the media's influence is disseminated.

Typical intellectual engagement

Typical intellectual engagement is a personality factor that deals with an individual's enjoyment of or engagement with activities that are intellectually stimulating and challenging. Unlike intelligence quotient (IQ) tests, it is concerned not with an individual's maximum performance level, but their typical performance in intellectual domains. It has a moderate correlation to general knowledge and is significantly predictive of academic performance.

Tyranny of the majority

The "tyranny of the majority" is a problem in democratic systems in which a minority group suffers oppression at the hands of the ruling majority. The most common solution is that of the American federal government: constitutional limits on the power of the government over its people, including the Bill of Rights, which recognizes specific rights that a mere vote is insufficient to supersede. The danger of the tyranny of the majority is one reasons that the process of altering this foundational document of the government is more difficult than that of electing officials or passing laws in the legislature.

Uncertainty avoidance

One of the cultural dimensions identified by Geert Hofstede, uncertainty avoidance consists of an organization's activities, both rational and irrational, that help it cope with the uncertainty of the future, including recordkeeping, aspects of accounting, and the organization's planning activities.

Unconscious cognition

Unconscious cognition consists of the mental processes of which the conscious mind is unaware, including learning, perception, memory, and thought. The role of the unconscious mind in various cognitive processes is not fully understood, but its presence in those processes is undeniable and has been at the center of psychological thought and research since Sigmund Freud and Carl Jung. One area where there seems to be the most agreement on the role of the unconscious is in data gathering; phenomena from optical illusions and hallucinations to subliminal messages have shown this. Unconscious attitudes about race, gender, and other traits have an impact on decision making, from the weight we give someone's input to hiring and firing decisions.

Unconscious thought theory

Unconscious thought theory (UTT) is the theory that the unconscious mind not only continues to work on problems and tasks initiated by the conscious mind but outperforms conscious effort in complex tasks with many variables, while underperforming in simpler tasks with few variables. The term was coined in 2006 but goes back at least to Sigmund Freud, who recommended that the most important decisions be made by the unconscious. The experimental data is, to be fair, unclear: until Ap Dijksterhuis's experiments in the 2000s, the bulk of experiments in the 1980s and 1990s suggested that the unconscious was suited only to simple problem solving. Among the points in UTT's

favor, however, are the unconscious mind's lack of certain cognitive biases that interfere with the utility of conscious thought: especially the problem of weighting, in which deliberation over a decision can warp one's reasoning, and the rule-based pattern of conscious decision making which sometimes results in poorer choices than the associative thinking of the unconscious.

Un-everyday-ness

German political scientist Max Weber coined the term *un-everyday-ness* to refer to the exceptional nature claimed by charismatic leaders. In religious contexts, this un-everydayness would be a divine calling, having been selected by God, perhaps even proven through the performance of miracles. Political candidates sometimes similarly position themselves as specially chosen subjects of destiny, especially if they have a parent or ancestor who was a beloved statesman. Specifics vary, but this un-everday-ness is a quality or characteristic other than mere skill that sets the leader apart from his followers.

University of Pittsburgh Graduate School of Public and International Affairs

A University of Pittsburgh school offering graduate programs in public administration, international development, and public and international affairs. The school is also home to the Johnson Institute for Responsible Leadership, which develops course material on accountability and ethics for the school's core curriculum.

Unschooling

Unschooling is an educational method that focuses on experiential learning over the trappings of compulsory education, and usually eschews standardized curricula or tests, traditional grading methods, and performance metrics like multiple-choice or short-answer tests. Unschooling is particularly associated with home schooling, but enjoys overlap with other educational approaches like those of some alternative schools and the Sudbury schools.

Up or out

"Up or out" is an approach to employee management, whereby any employee who is not promoted within a certain period of time (usually excepting those above a certain level) is fired. The U.S. military, for instance, discharges any officer twice passed over for promotion, while the Cravath system of law firm management gives associate lawyers 10 years to reach partner.

Valence

In Victor Vroom's expectancy theory, valence is the value of a specific reward for performing a task, as perceived by the individual who would receive it. It is affected by the individual's wants and needs and familiarity with the reward.

Varieties of Power (Montana and Charnov)

In their 2008 book *Management*, Patrick J. Montana and Bruce H. Charnov build on John R. P. French and Bertram Raven's *Bases of Social Power*, classifying seven types of organizational power available to a leader: legitimate power, reward power, coercive power, expert power, charisma power, referent power, and information power.

Veblen, Thorstein

Thorstein Veblen was an American sociologist and economist who developed institutional economics and coined the term *conspicuous consumption*, referring to the spending of money as a method of demonstrating wealth and especially social status. His less commonly known contribution was the phrase *conspicuous leisure*, referring to the display and use of leisure time to similarly denote social status and importance—one explanation for the vacations and golf days traditionally associated with doctors, for instance.

Vicarious liability

In common law, vicarious liability is a form of secondary liability carried by a third party who has the right, ability, or duty to control the actions of the violator who is primarily liable. The typical example is that of a superior who bears some responsibility for the actions of his subordinate, and it is part of the legal framework that makes a business liable for some of the actions of its employees when those actions are committed in the course of their employment (there are many exceptions, notably in the case of assaults committed by employees). Parents are generally held to bear vicarious liability for the actions of their minor children, though this is its own unique area of common law.

Victim playing

To play the victim is to play out the role of victim as a strategy for seeking attention, manipulating others, or calling attention from one's own abuse of others. It may be found in the workplace when the work environment is emotionally unhealthy, especially when the atmosphere is not a trusting one.

Villard, Henry

Henry Villard was a 19th century financier who made his fortune in the transportation industry. German sociologist Max Weber used him as an example of the power of charisma, as at one point Villard raised money from investors without telling them the nature of the investment—requiring them to evaluate their desire to invest based purely on their faith in his judgment, rather than on their own judgment of the specifics.

Vitality curve

A vitality curve is a method in which a workforce is evaluated according to the productivity of its individual workers. For instance, former General Electric CEO Jack Welch advocated the "rank and yank" method, in which a workforce is divided into its most productive 20 percent, the "vital 70 percent" in the middle, and the least productive 10 percent, who are fired. Similar systems have been used by IBM and Dow Chemical since the mid-2000s, by Motorola in the 1990s, and throughout the accounting and management consulting industries.

Voluntariness

Voluntariness is an important philosophical and legal concept, the state of making a choice according to one's free will, without coercion. Contracts in most legal systems require voluntary agreement by both parties at the time of signing, as does a guilty plea in a criminal court.

von Ranke, Leopold

The 19th century German historian Leopold von Ranke is one of the most important historians in the development of the field, and instituted the standards followed by modern historians today, notably its use of primary sources and attempt at objectivity. He favored narrative histories—history told as a story, especially chronologically—and was instrumental in the rise of diplomatic history and the continued dominance of Great Man histories, treating history largely as the product of the actions of significant leaders. It is because of von Ranke that nearly all historical analyses, especially those grounded in the methodologies of traditional history, are also studies of leadership.

Vroom-Yetton contingency model

Yale School of Management professor Victor Vroom and Phillip Yetton developed a contingency model of situational leadership in their 1973 work *Leadership and Decision-Making*, which Vroom later expanded in his 1988 collaboration with Arthur Yago, *The New Leadership*. The model identifies five types of leadership for different situations: Autocratic Type I, Autocratic Type II (with followers providing information for the decision-making process), Consultative Type I (leader meets with specific followers individually to seek their input), Consultative Type II (leader meets with specific followers for a group discussion to provide input), and Group-Based (in which the leader and followers work together to make a decision). Seven yes/no questions determine the best leadership style for the situation:

1. Is there a quality requirement or technical or rational grounds for selecting one solution above others?
2. Does the leader have sufficient information to make a quality decision?
3. Is the problem structured? Are there alternative courses of action?
4. Does implementing the solution require acceptance or cooperation by subordinates?
5. If the leader makes the decision himself, is it likely to be accepted by followers?
6. Do subordinates share the organizational goals relevant to the decision?
7. Are subordinates likely to conflict over choosing the right solution?

War as a metaphor

In American political discourse, "war" has often been used as the term for "a serious campaign by the government to eradicate a given thing." Federal Bureau of Investigation head

J. Edgar Hoover waged a "war on crime" in the 1930s, and since the 1960s, many presidents have defined a large part of their presidency by their metaphorical war of choice—even those who were also engaged in actual wars. Lyndon B. Johnson's (LBJ) "War on Poverty" set the precedent, followed by Richard Nixon's "War on Drugs," and Jimmy Carter did not explicitly adopt a "War on Overseas Oil Dependence" but did use the war metaphor in his discussions of the 1974 energy crisis. In the 21st century, the war metaphor has seen increased usage as an accusation rather than policy signaling; conservative Republicans have accused their opponents of waging a "War on Christmas," while Democrats have defended against the "War on Women." What this derogatory usage seems to lack, in contrast with the LBJ strain, is the implication that where there is a war, there are generals and heroes.

War's inefficiency puzzle
The question of why states that are otherwise rational actors would choose to fight wars is one that has long puzzled scholars. The costs of war vastly outweigh the benefits; only an invaded country given no choice can really claim that going to war is a better choice than not going to war, in terms of costs. This is in part because war is famously unpredictable; only in the most drastic power imbalances do wars proceed predictably. Most international relations scholars agree that there are three likely answers for war: an abundance of optimism leading decision makers to drastically overestimate the benefits of war and underestimate its costs; problems of commitment, which includes the decision to go to war by one side when the other side is slowly increasing power, because it means that a war now is less costly than a war later; and issue indivisibility, when the war is

fought over something that cannot be distributed among multiple parties, as with the Crusades' fight for control of Jerusalem or the disputes in a civil war.

Warren Harding Effect
Warren G. Harding was elected president of the United States in 1920 on the promise of a "return to normalcy" after World War I and a rise in American radicalism, his campaign being one of the first to rely heavily on advertising professionals. Though he won by the largest popular vote margins in presidential history, his presidency is widely considered the worst in history, including a staggering number of scandals (most of them events of genuine substance, not merely manufactured by political opponents), instances of corruption, and numerous extramarital affairs. The tendency to be blinded by a leader's attractiveness despite their lack of merit has been called the Warren Harding Effect.

Weber, Max
German philosopher Max Weber was, with Emile Durkheim and Karl Marx, one of the founders of sociology in the 19th and early 20th centuries, and was notable for his examination of the roles of religion and culture in the invention and rise of capitalism. In his political theory, he extensively studied styles of political leadership, and much of the early work on public administration was influenced by him.

Weber's ideal types of political leadership
Sociologist Max Weber defined three ideal types of political leadership or authority: charismatic domination, traditional domination, and legal domination, the last of which included the modern bureaucracy. Weber was the first to study bureaucracy, and considered it the most efficient form of governance.

Typically, controversial wedge issues that divide a social or political group have a populist theme, relating to matters such as national security, race, or gay marriage. (Wikimedia Commons/Max Halberstadt)

Wedge issue

A controversial social issue that divides a social or political group. In the 21st century, gay marriage and marijuana legalization have been wedge issues among American conservatives, with vastly different opinions held by the two increasingly powerful segments among conservatives: the libertarians and the Religious Right. Earlier in the century, the wars in Afghanistan and Iraq were similarly divisive among Democrats. Pushing a wedge issue can damage one's own party—though failing to resolve the conflict can similarly cause damage—and more commonly, members of one party are accused of leveraging the wedge to hurt the other.

Wharton School

The Wharton School of the University of Pennsylvania is an Ivy League business school within the University of Pennsylvania, and was the first university business school. Founded in 1881 by Philadelphia industrialist Joseph Wharton, it was intended to offer a means of attaining business knowledge other than the apprenticeship system, and to prepare corporate and public leaders for the rapid changes of the Industrial Revolution.

Whig history

A British term in origin, a Whig history is an approach to history that presents a narrative in which the past took an inevitable and inexorable path toward progress and enlightenment, especially one resulting in the development of modern-day Anglo-American political institutions. The term *Whiggish history* is sometimes preferred when not specifically referring to a political history of the United Kingdom; a Whiggish history of science, for instance, assumes modern scientific understanding in its specific formulation to be an inevitability and the history of science to be one of ever greater acquisition of knowledge, an accusation often leveled against historians of science.

Whistleblower

Someone who reports wrongdoing in an organization, especially an employee of that organization reporting the wrongdoing to a government or regulatory agency in the name of the public interest, is called a whistleblower. Whistleblower protection laws in the United States date to 1778, initially protecting whistleblowers from libel; more recent laws have attempted to protect whistleblowers from other reprisals.

White Collar: The American Middle Classes

Sociologist C. Wright Mills's 1951 *White Collar: The American Middle Classes* popularized the notion of the white-collar worker, a term coined 20 years earlier by Upton Sinclair, and chronicled the growth of this new class in growing American cities. Like other major works on corporate America in the 1950s—*The Man in the*

Gray Flannel Suit and The Organization Man—it focused on the alienation felt by the individual in the capitalist world of Cold War America.

Who Moved My Cheese?

Who Moved My Cheese? by Spencer Johnson is one of the most popular business fables, published in 1998. The story about mice and "little-people" hunting for cheese portrays responses to change, and gained popularity in an age of widespread corporate structural change in the form of mergers, downsizing, the dotcom boom and bust, and globalization, resulting in numerous cases of supervisors purchasing and distributing copies of the book to their employees. Johnson had previous success co-authoring The One Minute Manager.

Whuffie

In Cory Doctorow's science fiction novel Down and Out in the Magic Kingdom, set in a post-scarcity society in which most resources are free for everyone, Whuffie is a reputation-based currency transacted online. Popular or unpopular behavior leads to gaining or losing Whuffie, and certain social access is restricted to those with sufficient Whuffie scores. Though referred to as a currency, Whuffie does not transfer between individuals—giving someone Whuffie in response to one's approval of their actions does not deplete one's own Whuffie, just as "liking" a Facebook status does not expend a like from one's own status.

The Wire

One of the most critically acclaimed television dramas of all time, The Wire aired on HBO from 2002 to 2008, and was created by former police reporter David Simon. Though ostensibly focused on the efforts of city police to rein in the Baltimore drug trade, the scope of the series encompassed the labor unions of the seaport, the city government and its relationship to key civilian leadership groups, the school system, and the local newspaper. Several key themes emerged: the dysfunction of American institutions, and especially the similarities in their dysfunction despite drastic differences in their functions; phenomena, especially negative ones, resulting from poor communication between different levels in an organization's hierarchy, including but not limited to the top level's active disinterest in listening to the bottom level; the struggle of the individual against the inertia of the institution or organization with which he is affiliated; and the different styles and motivations of leaders of these institutions. One notable behavior shown in most of these institutions is "juking the stats": selectively classifying performance data for the sake of achieving specific benchmarks, even though the ability to do so thus renders those benchmarks meaningless.

Wisdom of the crowd

The wisdom of the crowd is a process of consulting a large group for answers to a question. For certain kinds of questions, this process, through averaging, cancels out individual biases and tendencies toward error. Studies have found that the collective opinion yielded by this process is as accurate or more accurate than the opinion of any one member of the group in several areas, including general world knowledge.

Woodward, Joan

An important scholar in leadership studies and contingency theory in the 1950s and 1960s, British sociologist Joan Woodward identified six types of contingency that impact an organization's decision making in any given scenario: technology, suppliers and distributors, consumer interest groups, customers and competitors, government factors, and union factors.

Workers' council

A workers' council is a governing body of a workplace, farm, school, or other enterprise that is self-managed by workers. While some self-managed organizations are run by meetings where decisions are made by vote, others hold elections to appoint delegates to a workers' council, usually with the requirement of a high turnover rate to avoid the creation of a managerial class.

Work-hard, play-hard culture

One of four corporate cultures identified by T. E. Deal and A. A. Kennedy, characterized by fast feedback and low risk. Typical of software companies and restaurants, jobs in these cultures involve large workloads with rapid follow-through required, but involve little uncertainty.

Workplace bullying

Bullying in the workplace is recurring mistreatment of an employee, whether by a superior or a co-worker. Bullying need not be physical, and can transpire within the rules of the workplace, taking forms like the belittling of an employee's opinions (work-related or otherwise), jokes at the employee's expense, teasing and insults, social isolation, belittling the employee's work or pointedly ignoring their work or its positive aspects, or in the case of bullying supervisors, assigning unfair or impossible workloads, deadlines, or other work conditions, or purposely setting the employee up to fail. It is easy for workplace bullying to change the culture of the workplace, and a personal conflict between two employees may lead to a culture of bullying within the organization. Several states have passed laws on abusive work environments, but none have focused specifically on bullying.

Workplace democracy

Workplace democracy is the adoption of democratic principles of leadership and decision making in the workplace, including voting, due process, and some form of power sharing. Some trade unions are committed to democratic structures in their function, for instance, and management science has investigated the use of democratic structuring in businesses.

Workplace friendship

Workplace friendship is simply a friendly relationship between co-workers, but studies have found that both job satisfaction and career success are related to the quality of workplace relationships, and that not all workplaces are equally conducive to such friendships.

Workplace gossip

Workplace gossip is rumor, innuendo, or confidences about third parties exchanged by co-workers. While generally unavoidable, when gossip pervades the workplace, it can have an unhealthy disinhibiting effect on conversation and composure, as well as undermining trust.

Workplace harassment

Workplace harassment is the offensive or aggressive behavior of a worker directed at one or more other workers. Workplace harassment causes significant work stress, even for those other than the workers targeted, and when the harasser is a manager or other superior, the effect on employee engagement, absenteeism, and turnover can be profound.

Workplace listening

The workplace requires active listening skills and an awareness of the importance of nonverbal communication in order to avoid misunderstandings and conflicts. This is particularly true for leaders, whose followers may feel ignored or unvalued if they do not feel they are being listened to.

Workplace politics

Workplace or office politics refers to the networks of power, influence, alliance, and social connections that exist in the workplace, and in some cases the ways in which individuals accrue intangible status that is not entirely derived from their rank or job role. Workplace politics may center around issues related to the work at hand or may be driven primarily by social factors.

Workplace wellness

Workplace wellness is the promotion of healthy behavior in the workplace and by employees, including health and wellness fairs, on-site fitness facilities, and any form of health or fitness education, weight mangement program, or medical screening offered to employees.

WYSE International

WYSE (World Youth Service and Enterprise) International is a charitable organization providing education and leadership development for young people in conjunction with the United Nations Department of Public Information. Established in 1989, it has offered courses to participants in 100 countries.

Xeer

Xeer is the legal system of Somalia, which for years provided the only stable governance of the essentially stateless society as a result of the civil war preventing the formation of an effective government. (Somalia has maintained a largely informal economy in the same period.) Xeer developed in the Horn of Africa in the 7th century, under no known outside influences, and was the only legal system in the region until Europeans arrived in the late 19th century. Under xeer, elder Somalis consult the precedent of previous cases in mediating disputes and criminal matters, and the law emerges from their collective decisions. Each head of an extended family, selected by its elder members after lengthy deliberation, is the judge for that family. A decentralized legal system, xeer is one reason Somalis have resisted ascribing legitimacy to any centralized government formed since its independence from colonial powers.

Zedong, Mao

Mao Zedong, transliterated as Mao Tsu-tung in older texts, was the founding father of the People's Republic of China, and served as the Chairman of the Communist Party of China from 1945 to his death in 1976. A young man during the Chinese revolutions of the early 20th century, Mao was exposed to Marxism and Leninism in college and founded the Communist Party of China (CPC) in 1921. The CPC based its ideology on that of Soviet premier Vladimir Lenin, who had been instrumental in the October Revolution that brought communists to power in Russia in 1917. Leninism focused on democratic decision making and discussion followed by total unity in commitment to the results of the decision-making process. When Mao came to power after the CPC overthrew the Chinese government following a 10-year civil war, he made China a single-party state, launched several initiatives against his "counter-revolutionary" enemies, and attempted to transform the Chinese economy into an industrial one, diverting resources away from agriculture and contributing to the deadliest famine in history. A cult of personality developed around him during the Great Leap Forward, his industrialization program, and there continues to be widespread disagreement over his legacy. The

Chinese Communist Party has rejected many of Mao's economic principles while officially considering him a national hero. Outside China, scholars point both to the terrible atrocities he ordered in the name of stamping out resistance to the revolution and to the possibility that his leadership created a communist state better able to survive than those of eastern Europe.

Zero Defects

Zero Defects was an approach to management in manufacturing in the 1960s and 1970s, which sought to eliminate defects from manufactured products as a means of eliminating waste and reducing cost. Zero Defects originated in the vastly expanding defense industry, in which defective products posed a concern even more significant than those in other industries. However, because of its reliance on costly inspections and quality management systems, Zero Defects was criticized as inefficient by later schools of thought, including that introduced in W. Deming's *Out of the Crisis*.

Further Readings

Adler, Nancy J., and Allison Gundersen. *International Dimensions of Organizational Behavior.* Boston: Cengage, 2007.

Aguayo, Rafael. *Dr Deming: The American Who Taught the Japanese About Quality.* New York: Simon & Schuster, 1991.

Amin, A., ed. *Post-Fordism: A Reader.* Oxford: Blackwell, 1994.

Anyon, Jean. *Radical Possibilities: Public Policy, Urban Education, and a New Social Movement.* New York: Routledge, 2014.

Autry, James A. *The Servant Leader.* New York: Crown Business, 2004.

Barber, James D., and Barbara Kellerman. *Women Leaders in American Politics.* Englewood Cliffs, NJ: Prentice-Hall, 1986.

Bass, B. M. *Bass & Stogdill's Handbook of Leadership: Theory, Research, and Managerial Applications.* New York: Free Press, 1990.

Beatty, Jack, and Peter F. Drucker. *The World According to Peter Drucker.* New York: Free Press, 1998.

Bennis, Warren G. *Why Leaders Can't Lead: The Unconscious Conspiracy Continues.* San Francisco: Jossey-Bass, 1989.

Bennis, Warren G., and Patricia W. Biederman. *Still Surprised: A Memoir of a Life in Leadership.* San Francisco: Jossey-Bass, 2010.

Berridge, Geoff. *Diplomacy: Theory and Practice.* New York: Palgrave Macmillan, 2005.

Black, Jeremy. *A History of Diplomacy.* London: Reaktion, 2010.

Blake, R., and J. Mouton. *The Managerial Grid: The Key to Leadership Excellence.* Houston: Gulf Publishing, 1964.

Blanchard, Ken. *Servant Leader.* New York: Thomas Nelson, 2003.

Block, Peter. *Community: The Structure of Belonging.* San Francisco: Berrett-Koehler, 2009.

Bolman, Lee, and Terrence Deal. *Reframing Organizations: Artistry, Choice, and Leadership.* San Francisco: Jossey-Bass, 2008.

Bolman, Lee G., and Joan Gallos. *Reframing Academic Leadership.* San Francisco: Jossey-Bass, 2011.

Box, Richard C. *Citizen Governance: Leading American Communities Into the 21st Century.* Thousand Oaks, CA: Sage, 1997.

Burns, James M. *The Crosswinds of Freedom.* New York: Knopf Distributed by Random House, 1989.

Burns, James M. *Leadership.* New York: Harper & Row, 1978.

Burns, James M. *Packing the Court: The Rise of Judicial Power and the Coming Crisis of the Supreme Court.* New York: Penguin Press, 2009.

Burns, James M. *Transforming Leadership: A New Pursuit of Happiness.* New York: Atlantic Monthly Press, 2003.

Burns, James M. *The Vineyard of Liberty.* New York: Knopf Distributed by Random House, 1982.

Burns, James M., and Susan Dunn. *The Three Roosevelts: Patrician Leaders who*

Transformed America. New York: Grove Press, 2001.

Carlyle, Thomas. *On Heroes, Hero-Worship, and the Heroic History.* Boston: Houghton Mifflin, 1998.

Caves, Richard E. *Creative Industries: Contracts Between Art and Commerce.* Cambridge, MA: Harvard University Press, 2000.

Chandler, Alfred. *Strategy And Structure: Chapters in the History of Industrial Enterprise.* New York: Doubleday, 1962.

Chickering, Arthur W., and Linda Reisser. *Education and Identity.* San Francisco: Jossey-Bass, 1993.

Cohen, William A., and Peter F. Drucker. *A Class with Drucker: The Lost Lessons of the World's Greatest Management Teacher.* New York: AMACOM, 2008.

Cooper, Robert K., and Ayman Sawaf. *Executive EQ: Emotional Intelligence in Business.* London: Orion Business, 1998.

Daft, Richard. *Organization Theory and Design.* Boston: Cengage, 2012.

DeDreu, Carsten K. W., and Michele Gelfand, eds. *The Psychology of Conflict and Conflict Management in Organizations.* New York: Psychology Press, 2013.

Deming, W. Edwards. *Out of the Crisis.* Cambridge, MA: MIT Press, 1986.

Drucker, Peter. *The Practice of Management.* New York: Harper & Row, 1954.

Dugatkin, Lee A., and Hudson K. Reeve. *Game Theory and Animal Behavior.* New York: Oxford University Press, 2000.

Edersheim, Elizabeth H., and Peter F. Drucker. *The Definitive Drucker.* New York: McGraw-Hill, 2007.

Farnsworth, Kent. *Leadership as Service.* Lanhan, MD: Rowman and Littlefield, 2006.

Fiedler, Fred E. *A Theory Of Leadership Effectiveness.* New York: Harper & Row, 1967.

Fiske, S. T. *Social Beings: Core Motives Approach to Social Psychology.* Hoboken, NJ: Wiley, 2004.

Flaherty, John E. *Peter Drucker: Shaping the Managerial Mind.* San Francisco: Jossey-Bass, 1999.

Florida, Richard. *The Rise of the Creative Class and How It's Transforming Work, Leisure and Everyday Life.* New York: Basic Books, 2002.

Gabor, Andrea. *The Man Who Discovered Quality.* New York: Penguin, 1992.

Gardner, Howard. *Leading Minds: An Anatomy of Leadership.* New York: Basic Books, 2011.

Gmelch, Walter, and Val Miskin. *Chairing an Academic Department.* New York: Atwood Publishing, 2004.

Greenleaf, Robert K. *The Servant as Leader.* Westfield, IN: Greenleaf Center for Servant Leadership, 2008.

Greenleaf, Robert K. *Servant Leadership.* New York: Paulist Press, 2002.

Harvard Business Review (HBR). *HBR's 10 Must Reads On Change Management.* Cambridge, MA: Harvard Business Review, 2011.

Harvard Business Review (HBR). *HBR's 10 Must Reads On Leadership.* Cambridge, MA: Harvard Business Review, 2011.

Harvard Business Review (HBR). *HBR's 10 Must Reads On Managing People.* Cambridge, MA: Harvard Business Review, 2011.

Harvard Business Review (HBR). *HBR's 10 Must Reads On Managing Yourself.* Cambridge, MA: Harvard Business Review, 2011.

Heifetz, Ronald. *Leadership Without Easy Answers*. Cambridge, MA: Harvard University Press, 1994.

Heifetz, Ronald A., Alexander Grashow, and Marty Linsky. *The Practice of Adaptive Leadership: Tools and Tactics for Changing Your Organization and the World*. Harvard Business Review Press, 2009.

Heifetz, Ronald A., and Marty Linsky. *Leadership on the Line: Staying Alive Through the Dangers of Leading*. Cambridge, MA: Harvard Business School Press, 2002.

Hemphill, John K. *Situational Factors in Leadership*. Columbus: Ohio State University Bureau of Educational Research, 1949.

Henry, Jane. *Creative Management*. Thousand Oaks, CA: Sage, 2001.

Heron, John. *The Complete Facilitator's Handbook*. London: Kogan Page, 1999.

Hersey, Paul, Ken Blanchard, and D. Johnson. *Management of Organizational Behavior: Leading Human Resources*. Upper Saddle River, NJ: Pearson Education, 2008.

Hesmondhalgh, David. *The Cultural Industries*. Thousand Oaks, CA: SAGE, 2002.

Hesse, Herman. *The Journey to The East*. New York: Picador, 2003.

Hickman, Gill R. *Leading Organizations: Perspectives for a New Era*. Thousand Oaks, CA: SAGE, 2009.

Hughes, Richard, Robert Ginnett, and Gordon Curphy. *Leadership: Enhancing the Lessons of Experience*. New York: McGraw-Hill, 2014.

Janis, Irving. *Victims of Groupthink: A Psychological Study of Foreign Policy Decisions and Fiascoes*. Boston: Houghton Mifflin, 1972.

Johnson, Craig E. *Meeting the Ethical Challenges of Leadership: Casting Light or Shadow*. Thousand Oaks, CA: SAGE, 2013.

Kaltman, Al. *Cigars, Whiskey, and Winning: Leadership Lessons from General Ulysses S. Grant*. Upper Saddle River, NJ: Prentice Hall Press, 2000.

Kellerman, Barbara. *Bad Leadership: What it Is, How it Happens, Why it Matters*. Boston: Harvard Business School Press, 2004.

Kellerman, Barbara. *The End of Leadership*. New York: Harper Business, 2012.

Kellerman, Barbara. *Followership: How Followers Are Creating Change and Changing Leaders*. New York: Harper, 2008.

Kellerman, Barbara. *Reinventing Leadership: Making the Connection Between Politics and Business*. Albany: State University of New York Press, 1999.

Kohn, Alfie. *Punished by Rewards: The Trouble With Gold Stars, Incentive Plans, A's, Praise, and Other Bribes*. Boston: Houghton Mifflin, 1999.

Kohn, Alfie. *No Contest: The Case Against Competition*. Boston: Houghton Mifflin, 1992.

Kotter, John P. *Leading Change*. Cambridge, MA: Harvard Business Review, 2012.

Kouzes, James M., and Barry Z. Posner. *Encouraging the Heart: A Leader's Guide to Rewarding and Recognizing Others*. San Francisco: Jossey-Bass, 2003.

Kouzes, James M., and Barry Z. Posner. *A Leader's Legacy*. San Francisco: Jossey-Bass, 2006.

Kouzes, James M., and Barry Z. Posner. *The Leadership Challenge: How to Make Extraordinary Things Happen in Organizations*. San Francisco: Jossey-Bass, 2012.

Kouzes, James M., Barry Z. Posner, and Steven J. DeKrey. *Making Extraordinary Things Happen in Asia: Applying the Five Practices* of Exemplary Leadership. San Francisco: Jossey-Bass, 2013.

Lawler, Edward E., III. *Management Reset: Organizing for Sustainable Effectiveness.* San Francisco: Jossey-Bass, 2011.

Lennard, Diane. *Coaching Models: A Cultural Perspective.* New York: Routledge, 2010.

Lewis, Carol, and Stuart C. Gilman. *The Ethics Challenge in Public Service: A Problem-Solving Guide.* San Francisco: Jossey-Bass, 2012.

Lipsky, David, Ronald Seeber, and Richard Fincher. *Emerging Systems for Managing Workplace Conflict: Lessons from American Corporations for Managers and Dispute Resolution Professionals.* San Francisco: Jossey-Bass, 2003.

McMillen, William. *From Campus to Capitol: The Role of Government Relations in Higher Education.* Baltimore, MD: Johns Hopkins University Press, 2010.

Mezirow, Jack. *Fostering Critical Reflection in Adulthood: A Guide to Transformative and Emancipatory Learning.* San Francisco: Jossey-Bass, 1990.

Miner, J. B. *Organizational Behavior: Behavior 1: Essential Theories of Motivation and Leadership.* Armonk, NY: M. E. Sharpe, 2005.

Morgan, Patrick. *Deterrence Now.* New York: Cambridge University Press, 2003.

Mortimer, Kenneth, and Colleen O'Brien Sathre. *The Art and Politics of Academic Governance.* Lanham, MD: Rowman and Littlefield, 2010.

Norman-Major, Kristen A., and Susan Gooden, eds. *Cultural Competency for Public Administrators.* Armonk, NY: M.E. Sharpe, 2012.

Northouse, Peter G. *Leadership: Theory and Practice.* Thousand Oaks, CA: SAGE, 2012.

Peltier, Bruce. *The Psychology of Executive Coaching.* New York: Routledge, 2009.

Rath, Tom, and Barry Conchie. *Strengths Base Leadership: Great Leaders, Teams, and Why People Follow.* Washington, DC: Gallup Press, 2009.

Rima, Samuel D. *Leading from the Inside Out: The Art of Self-Leadership.* New York: Baker Books, 2000.

Rodin, Robert, and Curtis Hartman. *Free, Perfect, and Now: Connecting to the Three Insatiable Customer Demands.* New York: Simon & Schuster, 1999.

Rost, J. C. *Leadership for the Twenty-First Century.* Westport, CT: Praeger Press, 1991.

Salsburg, David. *The Lady Tasting Tea: How Statistics Revolutionized Science in the Twentieth Century.* New York: W. H. Freeman, 2001.

Schultz, Duane P., and Sydney Ellen Schultz. *Psychology and Work Today: An Introduction to Industrial and Organizational Psychology.* Upper Saddle River, NJ: Prentice Hall, 2010.

Schuman, Sandy. *Creating a Culture of Collaboration: The International Association of Facilitators Handbook.* San Francisco: Jossey-Bass, 2006.

Schuman, Sandy. *The IAF Handbook of Group Facilitation: Best Practices from the Leading Organization in Facilitation.* San Francisco: Jossey-Bass, 2005.

Schwarz, Roger M. *The Skilled Facilitator: A Comprehensive Resource for Consultants, Facilitators, Managers, Trainers, and Coaches.* San Francisco: Jossey-Bass, 2002.

Smith, John. *Evolution and the Theory Of Games.* New York: Cambridge University Press, 1982.

Spencer, Laura J. *Winning Through Participation: Meeting the Challenge of*

Corporate Change with the Technology of Participation. Dubuque, IA: Kendall/Hunt, 1989.

Stein, Guido. *Managing People and Organizations: Peter Drucker's Legacy.* Bingley, UK: Emerald, 2010.

Synan, Vinson. *The Holiness-Pentecostal Tradition: Charismatic Movements in the Twentieth Century.* New York: Eerdmans, 1997.

Tarrant, John J. *Drucker: The Man Who Invented the Corporate Society.* Boston: Cahners Books, 1976.

Tittemore, James A. *Leadership at All Levels.* Toronto: Boskwa Publishing, 2003.

van Vugt, M., and A. Ahuja. *Naturally Selected: The Evolutionary Science of Leadership.* New York: Harper, 2012.

Van Wormer, Katherine S., Fred H. Besthorn, and Thomas Keefe. *Human Behavior and the Social Environment: Macro Level, Groups, Communities, and Organizations.* New York: Oxford University Press, 2007.

Vroom, Victor H., and Arthur G. Jago. *The New Leadership: Managing Participation in Organizations.* Upper Saddle River, NJ: Prentice-Hall, 1988.

Vroom, Victor H., and Phillip W. Yetton. *Leadership and Decision-Making.* Pittsburgh, PA: University of Pittsburgh Press, 1973.

Weber, Winfried W., and Dirk Baecker. *Peter F. Drucker's Next Management: New Institutions, New Theories and Practices.* Göttingen, Germany: Sordon, 2010.

Wheatley, Margaret J. *Leadership and the New Science: Discovering Order in a Chaotic World.* San Francisco: Berrett-Koehler, 2006.

Wheeler, Daniel W. *Servant Leadership for Higher Education: Principles and Practices.* San Francisco: Jossey-Bass, 2012.

Wheeler, Donald J. *Understanding Variation: The Key to Managing Chaos.* Knoxville, TN: SPC Press, 2000.

Whyte, William H. *The Organization Man.* New York: Simon & Schuster, 1956.

Wren, Daniel A. *The Evolution of Management Thought.* Hoboken, NJ: Wiley, 2008.

Wren, Thomas. *The Leader's Companion: Insights on Leadership Through the Ages.* New York: Free Press, 1995.

Zull, James. *The Art of Changing the Brain: Enriching the Practice of Teaching by Exploring the Biology of Learning.* New York: Stylus Publishing, 2002.